FIRST, I BELIEVE YOU

FIRST, I BELIEVE YOU

A Memoir

Carol C. Boyce

Jane Publishing

San Francisco

JANE Publishing

Copyright @ 2022 by Carol C. Boyce

All Rights Reserved.
Published in the United States by Jane Publishing Corp
ISBN 979-8-9861946-0-8 (Paperback)
ISBN 979-8-9861946-1-5 (Hardcover)
ISBN 979-8-9861946-2-2 (ePub)

Printed in the United States of America

Cover Design by Nick Castle

DISCLAIMER

This book is a memoir, reflecting the author's present recollections of experiences. Many events were happening concurrently, and the book represents over sixty years of emotions, memories, and experiences condensed into one cohesive narrative. Names, locations, and identifying characteristics have been changed to protect the privacy of those depicted. Some events have been compressed, and dialogue has been recreated.

The book is intended to help others recover and may be difficult for some readers. It is designed for adults only. I regret any unintentional harm resulting from the publishing and marketing of my story. Any perceived slight of any individual or organization is unintentional.

The resources in this book are provided for informational purposes only. They should not be used to replace the specialized training and professional judgment of a health care or mental health professional. Neither the author nor the publisher can be held responsible for the information provided within this book. Always consult a trained professional before making any decision regarding the treatment of yourself or others. The reference section lists many helpful references, including the Suicide Prevention Hotline--800-273-8255.

DEDICATION

This book is dedicated to my husband and children for their unwavering love and support throughout my recovery and the writing of this book. My love for you has no end. In my darkest days, you gave me the reason to live and keep fighting.

To my therapist, Paul, for his steadfast patience, inspired guidance, and belief that I could and would recover. I will always be thankful for the miracles you worked in my life, marriage, and children's upbringing.

To all survivors of traumatic amnesia, sexual abuse, and Complex PTSD. I hope you face your challenges with undaunting courage, strength, and truth, no matter the price. I also join in the #MeToo campaign and dedicate this book to all survivors for having the courage to put their face on this vast, worldwide epidemic of sexual assaults.

I am not anxious to be the loudest voice or the most popular. But I would like to think that at a crucial moment, I was an effective voice of the voiceless, an effective hope of the hopeless."

Whitney M. Young Jr.

Table of Contents

Author's Notes

L ost in PTSD, anxiety, strange fears, and an eating disorder, I sank into depression and panic. I had no idea what was wrong, and I was terrified. From my experience, I knew general knowledge and understanding of this type of trauma remained in its infancy. It would have helped me enormously to see a written account of a path out of my suffering had one been written. I could find none. I knew I had to write about my experience to bring light to this issue and move the conversation forward to help all those suffering from this life-threatening mental condition.

Reducing the secretive nature and shame that isolates survivors, this book is an unflinching look at the damage from abusers in the frequent guise of family and primary caregivers. I hope to help other trauma survivors and their families identify the cause of their symptoms, find a quicker path to recovery, reduce the severe consequences to their life, and place all blame on the perpetrators. It is critical to show victims and their loved ones the connections between traumatic amnesia, Complex PTSD, suicide, and addiction.

I hope my experiences can provide a roadmap and direction for the extraordinary life survivors deserve, free from terror. With love and hope, recovery and empowerment will be yours.

Out of the huts of history's shame, I rise. Up from a past that's rooted in pain, I rise. Leaving behind nights of terror and fear, I rise into a daybreak that's wondrously clear.

I rise.

Maya Angelou, 1978

Carol C.Boyce

Chapter 1

Don't Go to Sleep

My picture window creates a safe, bright world in my large pink bedroom during the daytime. I love how it shines on the dolls my nana made just for me and the floral wallpaper Mommy let me pick out last year when I was seven. Licorice purrs when the warm sun hits her. I love to lay next to her and stroke her long black fur.

My room is dark and scary at night, though. My window only brings darkness and shadows around me. The crickets chirping outside break the eerie silence as I lay down for bed. I blame the moon for not being like the sun and leaving me in darkness. Why does the night always return? I wish it would never come again.

Closing my tired eyes, the men appear outside my window. I don't know them because they have no faces. They say nothing but glance at me sometimes—to see if I'm awake. They silently and ever so slowly play catch with a big, blow-up ball—back...and forth...back...and forth...back...and forth. My body curls tightly as I shiver under the scratchy wool blanket.

The men, dressed alike, are always outside my window, and I know why. They patiently—endlessly--wait for me to fall asleep. They will slip through the glass, without a sound, to hurt me when I finally do. No one will hear them come in—not Mommy, Daddy, or even our watchdog, Brutus—they're so quiet. No one will ever hear, but I'll know they came in. I whisper to myself: *Don't go to sleep, don't go to sleep. The men will hurt you...badly...if you do.*

I pray they'll go away, but they never leave. I know the men must hurt me first and will wait as long as necessary. Back...and forth...back...and forth...the men throw the big ball. The endless rhythm finally puts me to sleep.

Carol C.Boyce

Chapter 2

Really Splendid

*"There was once a Velveteen Rabbit, and in the
beginning, he was really splendid."*
Margery Williams, "The Velveteen Rabbit" 1922

I was an Eisenhower baby, a Baby Boomer, born in the after-
math of World War II. My family moved into a new subdivi-
sion in the San Fernando Valley, northwest of downtown Los
Angeles, soon after I arrived in 1954. Dad and Mom had been
married in Chicago while he finished medical school, and they
wanted the warm, sunny weather of California. The new housing
for thousands of young families slowly replaced the vast orange
and walnut orchards, and the new aerospace, television, and
movie industries employed most people in the valley. Several sec-
ond-tier stars of the latest popular sitcoms of the day were
amongst us.

A finned station wagon was in many driveways, and our
long block of thirty homes overflowed with fifty kids. We never
lacked playmates. My best friend lived two doors down from my
house, and by the time we were three, Susie and I were insepara-
ble.

One warm, sunny afternoon smelling the crisp air and fresh-cut lawns, I petted my black Persian cat as she purred against my leg. Susie's big brother, Bob, nine, and mine, Mark, now seven, shot baskets noisily on our steep driveway. My younger sister, Debbie, three years old and always in full cowboy attire, and tow-headed baby brother, Timmy, had to stay inside. They were too little.

Susie and I bounded to the sidewalk, squealing delightfully at being five and old enough to be outside alone. I pulled some messy chalk out of my shorts pocket, and both of us, with my blonde and her mahogany ponytail swinging, marked the gray concrete sidewalk with ten squares. Carefully numbering them, we hopped our way through early childhood, oblivious to the world around us.

On special days, my three siblings and I would sit in the living room surrounding Mommy, seated in her plush chair. We noisily wrestled with being closest to the well-loved family book of *Winnie the Pooh*. With her favorite opera, *La Boheme*, playing softly in the background, she put Timmy in her lap as I pushed Debbie out of my way. She admonished us, "Settle down, kids so that we can begin."

With a different voice for each character, Mommy began. "Here is Edward Bear, coming downstairs now, bump, bump, bump, on the back of his head, behind Christopher Robin..." My eyes twinkled, relishing the warmth of those special moments.

However, my favorite story was Mom's beloved childhood book, *Jiji Lou*, which she only read to me. I loved these rare moments. Jiji Lou, a cast-off doll, built a pumpkin house in a pumpkin village. With my smile sparkling as Mom shared this family treasure, I dreamed of living there. Maybe it was always warm and loving there.

Because of Mom, I could count on Christmas being the best time of the year. She'd announce, "Kids, gather round. It's time for our annual Christmas craft." At seven, I squealed with excitement. Two-inch-high white ceramic angels, paintbrushes, and sparkly gold paint on the kitchen table made my eyes brighten. Jumping up and down, I forgot I was holding my full paintbrush and sprayed some on the table and floor. "Oops," I whispered under my breath, scared Mom would notice. I frantically grabbed a dishrag and cleaned up the mess.

I brushed the shimmery color onto my angel and giggled. "Look how pretty it is, Mommy! Look, Mark!" He rolled his eyes and tried to ignore his pest of a sister, even though I thought he secretly liked my angel. When the other kids finished and the angels dried, Mom set them out on the top of our new dial, black and white console television. I beamed with pride, thinking mine was the prettiest.

Afterward, she shooed us out of the room and finished placing gleaming ornaments on our beautiful, large Christmas tree to prepare for their glamorous parties this holiday season.

Later, Dad would turn on the sparkling tree lights, and Mom would play "Silent Night" on the guitar. We'd all sing, with us children wiggling and jumping with joy, as we eagerly anticipated Christmas's arrival.

I loved Mom when she was calm and kind--but it wasn't often.

Mom and Dad attended posh dinner dances and balls the hospitals and local charities hosted for physicians and their spouses. My eyes glowed brightly when Mom came out of their bedroom in a glorious, sequined gown and Dad in a black tuxedo. Her dramatic blue eyeshadow, red lipstick, and heavily hair-sprayed updo left me dreaming of being Cinderella at the ball. I couldn't wait until I was old enough to dress up, too.

One night before an elegant event when I was eight, Dad played a Strauss record on our phonograph. "Come here—I'll show you how to waltz."

"Ok." I was excited to get his undivided attention.

Dad stretched out his arm to hold my right hand, putting his left arm on my back. "Put your arm out like this. Slide, touch, touch. One, two, three…one, two, three. Don't move your shoulders." I put my small feet on Dad's shoes and my hand in his as he led me around our large living room. "That's right. And then I'll twirl you. You're getting it. One, two, three, slide, touch, touch." He smiled broadly at my twinkling eyes. Twirling under Dad's raised arm and pretending I had on a billowing satin gown, this distant, untainted world that felt so safe and beautiful engulfed me.

It should have been a glorious childhood

Chapter 3

A Silhouette

I jumped up and down with my ponytail bouncing. "May I please sleep over at Susie's tonight, Mom?" My blue-eyed, freckled eight-year-old face smiled broadly.

She furiously typed a short story about our new pet squirrel on her manual typewriter. She loved to write. "I guess so, but get your chores done before you go."

I stood on the stool and hurriedly rinsed the dishes, putting them carefully in the dishwasher, and cleaned the bathrooms. I raced to my room, so excited to pack for this special night. I'd never slept over at anyone's house without my family before. I decided my Barbie doll and my giant purple snake would be the most fun toys to bring. I couldn't wait.

As I entered Susie's house, I knew to walk fast past her brother Bob's room. He kept leathery lizards and real snakes in his room, which creeped me out.

I went straight to Susie's bedroom and shut the door. "You have to be Ken this time. I had to be him last time." I begged her as I combed Barbie's blonde hair. Neither of us ever wanted to be Ken, but Susie played him better than I did, and it was her turn. Fair was fair.

She rolled her eyes, accepting her fate. "Okay, you can be Barbie, but just for a while. Then we'll switch." We happily played house until it was time to go to bed.

Laying in her separate twin beds, Susie's sweet mom, Holly, kissed her goodnight. "Goodnight, Carol. It's so nice to have you sleepover." She gave me a warm smile and turned off the lights.

I didn't like the darkness. I didn't like it at all. Susie's father walked into the room, and I could see his silhouette as he kissed Susie and then walked to my twin bed to say goodnight. A large man, his shadowy figure, loomed over me in the dim light. My eyes widened and my heart raced as I slid deeper under the covers.

"Goodnight girls. Sleep tight." He left the room and shut the door, leaving us in the dark.

Fear tinged my reddening skin. *I can't do this.*

"I hafta go home, now. I need my dad to come to get me." My voice trembled as the tears spilled onto my cheeks.

Susie, half asleep, rubbed her eyes. "What's wrong? I thought you were having fun."

"I—I don't know, but…I'm gonna be sick. I must go home. Now!" I looked down, ashamed and confused by my fear. I didn't know what was wrong.

My father arrived with a scowl on his face and said to me. "I have no time for this nonsense. Why can't you sleep over?" To Susie's parents, he muttered, "Well, thanks anyway. I can't imagine what's wrong with her." He grabbed my arm and, in a huff, pulled me home.

I stopped trembling, so relieved to be safe in my house though Mom was also disappointed in me. "What's wrong with you. Why are you so afraid?"

It was ironic. I always felt safe in a place where I never was.

In 1962, my family arrived home on a rainy evening from a camping trip to Yosemite. Dad loved to hike the spectacular National Parks, teaching us about their geology. We untied our wet suitcases from the top carrier on the car while Dad stowed the damp camping gear in the garage. After the long drive, it was good to be in our warm house, greeted by Licorice rubbing against my legs while Brutus slurped my face.

"It's bedtime—all of you. I mean now. I've had enough." Mom bellowed from the living room as she snapped open the Sunday paper. "No dawdling." She slowly drank a martini from her crystal glass.

Mom got mad if we didn't obey her first command. Her temper always scared me, so I hurried as fast as I could. Debbie, now five, and I, eight, darted to the living room and kissed Mom and Dad's cheeks as they read. I heard a clap of thunder in the distance.

It was now dark and shadowy as I switched off the light and pulled my blanket tight under my chin. With a clap of lightning breaking the shadows in my room, I caught my breath.

A gray, tightly curled, and gnarled wired surface filled my vision as I shut my eyes. The strange and sinister picture filled my young eyes with a dark and scary image. My body tensed with its peculiar shadows, and I shivered as I twisted into a protective ball.

Within minutes, the vision flipped. A pristine, perfect white surface now appeared. It calmed me with its purity, its simpleness—my body, relaxed. I was relieved for the moment, but I knew the comforting image would disappear quickly. Night after night, the eerie and dark vision returned along with the white one, adding to my alternating emotions: safe, unsafe, safe, unsafe. Eventually, I'd fall into a sound sleep.

Despite my confusion and terror, I never told anyone about my visions, not my parents or even Susie. I already knew not to speak up or question them, and I never thought of them during the day or tried to figure out what they meant.

I would have had to know the truth if I did.

Chapter 4

Who I Admire Most

One Saturday, as a nine-year-old, I sauntered down our long hallway that displayed my father's impressive lineage. One dour face after another scowled at me in their heavily decorated uniforms, with five generations of Annapolis-educated Navy admirals. Two presidents and our membership seal from the General Society of Mayflower Descendants stood out on the wall. No one from Mom's side made the display—farmers didn't make the cut. I sighed a long breath, absorbing my extraordinary pedigree. I wondered if I would ever meet the implied achievement expectations of the family.

I heard Dad casually singing in his rich baritone voice as I entered the family room. "Somewhere, over the rainbow, bluebirds fly..." I'd never heard anyone who could sing more beautifully than Dad. His voice was spectacular to my mind—and I could listen to him all day.

I went into the kitchen to empty the dishwasher. Mom was making turkey sandwiches for lunch. "Dad has such a pretty voice. It's beautiful, don't you think?"

"I dunno. I guess so—never thought about it. Hurry up there." She went back to putting lettuce on the sandwiches.

I didn't understand why no one else could hear what I heard, but singing wasn't valued like the piano in our home.

I went into the living room to play with my dolls, and Dad followed. Holding a place of honor at the end of the large living room stood our mahogany baby grand. After seating himself, he closed his eyes and paused for a moment of reverence for the instrument before him. He placed his hands on the ivory keys and began to play a masterpiece, Debussy's *Arabesques*. His playing swelled and ebbed like a frolicking sea under a moonless sky, exposing his incredible talent. I never wanted to forget his music, a true gift to my soul.

I put my doll down and thought about how much I loved Dad and how proud and lucky I was to have such a talented, gentle, and kind father.

By December of 1963, it had been a rough year already. My fourth-grade teacher, Mrs. Boda, cried openly, telling us about President Kennedy's assassination last month. I'd never seen a teacher cry before, and it shook me. I couldn't figure out why someone would shoot a president, though I knew he was a Democrat. My parents and grandparents never had a good word to say about them. I didn't understand, but I felt sad and confused.

After the shock of the assassination, Mrs. Boda talked about the Cold War we were in with Russia. Because of it, she explained the need for our monthly "duck and cover" exercise. I learned that my wood and metal-legged desk could perform miracles. We'd be secure from a Russian nuclear bomb dropped on it if we covered our heads while under it.

As instructed, when the alarm bell rang that afternoon, I dove onto the dirty floor and covered my head under my desk. Since girls couldn't wear pants to school, I worried more about my underwear showing than the impending nuclear bomb. Plus, my gross classmate, Harry, had stuck gum under my desk and I was scared I'd get my long hair in it. I'd have to hit him if it did. After what seemed like a long time, the all-clear bell finally rang. I got up and hurriedly straightened my gray jumper and retied one of my scuffed saddle shoes.

Stern and uncompromising, Mrs. Boda always wore a starched fitted dress with a full skirt. Her heels clapped sharply on the Formica floor. "I have a new homework assignment for you. You are to write about who you admire most. Choose someone you look up to, someone you'd like to know more about. The report is due Friday." She clip-clopped back to her carefully organized desk.

I thought the assignment would be easy. I chose to write about my father. Everyone loved Mom too, but our community revered Dad. Something was different about him. He was the best person I knew, and everyone seemed to agree. I loved everything about him and looked up to him like everyone else. Last week when the family went to church, Mrs. Pride. Mom's friend said, "Your father is the greatest doctor. Our family just loves him!" Mrs. Clark, a skinny, beaked-nosed lady, also gushed, "Your dad's a fine man and wonderful physician. You kids must be so proud." I glowed, and my freckles reddened.

I wondered what I should write. Besides Dad's voice and piano-playing, I couldn't pinpoint one or two specific things that genuinely made him great. Writing had never been my strength, as I'd usually panic at the sight of a blank sheet of paper, but I thought Dad would know what to say.

After dinner, I went to his chair, where he was reading the LA Times. "Excuse me. I must write about someone I admire." I fidgeted, playing with my hair. "Uh...I've decided to write about you." I smiled shyly, hoping he'd be happy with my choice.

He cleared his throat as he closed the paper. "Oh? That's nice of you."

My eyebrows lifted. "But...uh...what should I write?"

Dad spoke with a strong voice. "Well, I'm an avid sailor, and if I say so myself, I'm excellent at it. I worked hard and went to college for ten years. I paid for it myself—I'm a self-made man, if you want to know the truth." He paused and stared in space a moment." I became a doctor, a healer that helps sick people get better. That's what I am, a healer." He went back to his paper.

I guessed he had nothing more to add. I ran to my room and finished my report in my most careful cursive.

My report came back the next week with an "A" in the top corner. " Your dad would be pleased to know you have written a paper that shows so much love and appreciation for him," Mrs. Boda said with a rare smile. "You must be so proud of him."

I was.

One day after school, Susie and I took a break from learning the latest thing—the hula hoop. It kept falling to our feet when it was supposed to be at our waist. Frustrated, we sat under our large walnut tree in front of my house. Licking fruit popsicles on this sultry, languid day, we tried to catch the drips but were only partially successful.

Carol C.Boyce

Susie unscrewed her roller skates with her key and became lost in deep thought. "Would you rather live with your family or mine?" As ten-year-olds, we often compared our families.

After some thought, I replied, "Well, I don't know. Your mom talks and watches old movies with us. I like that. Remember when she put nail polish on our nails and curled our hair? It was so much fun. My mom never does stuff like that. She just yells or is too busy."

Susie looked down and picked at the grass. "Yeah, but your family does important things. Your parents travel all over the world. You get to dress up and go to church and the theater. My family never does those things." She stared out in space.

I could see where the conversation was going. Christmas again--somehow, everything came down to that one time of year for Susie." My family barely celebrates Christmas, and you always have fun—even getting a real Christmas tree. I'd give anything to have a real tree." Susie's voice trailed off as she straightened her pants leg.

It was true. We always had a real tree with lots of presents on Christmas morning. Doing fun things like seeing musicals, riding horses, going to church, and taking piano lessons was great, and I was sad Susie didn't get to do them. I had thought everyone got to do these things. In quiet moments, Susie whispered secrets to me. She'd tell me her dad whipped her and her brother and called Susie bad names, like stupid and slut, which I knew wasn't right. My parents didn't call me names or whip me at all.

I could understand why Susie was jealous of my family and I wanted to help her. I'd invite her to our home whenever my mother let me, and she came over at Christmastime. I helped her put up her family's fake tree and gave her a present to have at least one under it.

With our limited perspective, Christmas remained our most relatable childhood measuring stick. Nothing else seemed as important at our young ages. It made me proud to realize that I had the best family on the block, the best family of anyone I knew. I was so lucky.

Little did I know what was to come.

Chapter 5

Nourishment

Just before Christmas, when I was ten, Licorice purred in my lap as I stroked her long black fur. All mine, I loved holding and petting her as she snuggled against me. She would wander the house, quietly watching the goings-on without comment, just like me, and I could tell her anything.

Mom yelled from the kitchen, "Carol, it's time to set the table and empty the dishwasher, and I mean now."

"I'll do it in a minute, Mom. I'm busy." I scratched Licorice's ears and smiled at her.

"What did you say, young lady?" She became enraged. I regretted my response immediately and sprinted to the kitchen-- but it was too late. Coming close, she towered over me with a blank, cold look in her eyes. She grabbed my wrist, yanked my arm, and dragged me down the hallway to the bathroom sink. I whimpered and tried to fight her hold on me but lost the battle. Before I had time to escape, she jammed a wet bar of soap into my mouth. "Don't you ever, ever talk back to me. Do you hear me?"

I tried to gurgle a response, but nothing came out.

Her face looked contorted, and a vein popped out of her forehead. "I said, do you hear me?"

Gagging and choking, I nodded my head. My silence infuriated her more and the punishment continued. I looked up at her with imploring eyes. *Stop. What are you doing, Mom? It's me, Carol. Why are you hurting me like this?*

When she had finished, I slowly spit out the bitter remnants of my punishment, cleaned my over-stretched lips, and wiped away the tears of shame bubbling down my red face. I couldn't understand why she'd humiliate and choke me with a bar of soap. Was I as bad as Mom believed?

I stumbled into the kitchen with my head and eyes down and unloaded the dishwasher in a shattered silence.

Mom's continual hostile moods dominated my homelife. She could twist from a quiet homemaker into an ugly rage in a heartbeat. To cope, I'd usually hide in my room after school, staying safe and avoiding her wrath.

One day, I snuck out of my room to get a glass of skim milk. I clumsily dropped the glass on the floor, and it shattered. Mom, two rooms away, came out with her eyes ablaze and stormed into the kitchen. "What is wrong with you?" she yelled as I frantically tried to sweep up the shards. She towered over me. "I can't believe how you mess up all the time." Powerless against her wrath, I cowered like a beaten dog, averting her eyes to avoid further punishment.

The size of my misdeed never mattered. Mom's harsh and condescending reaction overwhelmed any possibility of me learning from my mistakes. I believed her repeated criticism. She was my mother, and I trusted that she knew everything. I came to believe something *was* terribly wrong with me.

The next year, Susie and I sat in my bedroom making large houses for our Barbie families out of encyclopedias. "Your father's been running around the neighborhood again in shorts and his white undershirt," Susie, now ten, laughed at how funny he looked.

I tightened my skate with the key, acting as if I didn't care. "So, what, Susie. Stop it! It's not a big deal." I loved Dad, though quirky and oblivious at times to social norms. I didn't like people laughing at or making fun of my wonderful father.

I had no idea why Dad ran around the neighborhood in a big, open-arm white undershirt and plaid shorts with white tennis shoes. No one ran in the early sixties unless a bear was chasing them. Dad was a cardiologist, though, and I'd later learn that he was way ahead of his time on heart health.

"What the heck is he doing that for?" The neighbor across the street, Gladys would peek out her window and watch him. She talked to Betty about it, and soon, it would be the gossip of the long block. No one understood his unusual behavior, and it mortified my mother.

Dad's health obsession extended beyond exercise. He was dogmatic about our health, and our family meals were stressful because of his obsession. Dad felt eating existed for nutrition and good health only—not enjoyment or entertainment. He insisted on a low-sugar and low-fat diet before anyone else had heard of it. It kept all of us, except Mom who always battled excess weight, healthy and lean. His resolve was enviable, though booze didn't make the excluded items list.

Mom hated cooking because she couldn't use Dad's "forbidden foods." Butter, mayonnaise, cheese, fatty meats, and sour cream were not allowed in our home long before the health risks of fats became known. These foods, however, were essential to Mom's midwestern upbringing on thick gravies, fried meats, and bread pudding. The "healthy" new miracle food, margarine, was the only fat allowed, its lengthy list of chemicals not yet examined.

One night after Mom and Dad had drunk too much, I could hear them arguing about the beef stroganoff casserole Mom had prepared. Still in his starched shirt and slacks from the office, Dad's lips curled tightly. "Why did you put sour cream in that casserole? You know that's not allowed."

Mom's face reddened, and with her hands on her hips, she said, "There isn't much in it. It's got to taste right. Why is it so important to you—everyone else I know uses sour cream?" Mom's eyes glistened as she glared at him. "None of my friends have these rules. Why are you like this?"

"You *know* fat is bad for your heart—that's why. Don't ever cook like that again—do you hear me?" Dad stomped out of the kitchen, frustrated he couldn't get his point across to his wife, much less his patients.

As a child, the conflict over food seemed endless, and I could always feel the tension. The development of tasty low-fat recipes didn't exist, and our meals were often dry and overcooked.

The food fights escalated when his mother arrived. Dad's strict rules magically went out the window when Nana came. She cooked however she damn well pleased. Our home would delightfully explode with the smells of homemade fudge, cookies, and fresh pies. Our kitchen had never seen such decadence as Nana piled shiny, homemade cream-filled eclairs onto our plates. I delighted in the delicious richness of sugary desserts.

But Mom wouldn't accept the relaxation of the rules for Nana. With my ear to Mom and Dad's bedroom door, I could hear her yell. "Why do you let her cook like that, and I can't? Too wimpy to stand up to your own mother?" The whole house could hear her tirade. Dad never answered.

One Christmas eve, I skipped into the kitchen, all smiles, to see how the holiday preparations were coming. It seemed like it had taken forever for the holiday to finally arrive. I could always trust it to be a happy time in our home. I jumped up and down, seeing our long dining room table already set with our family's finest silver, Wedgewood China, and Waterford Crystal. With the giant Douglas fir decorated and the stockings made by Nana hung on the fireplace, everything was ready for the celebration to begin. Christmas had finally arrived!

Nana, whipping up a chocolate torte and wearing her heavily splattered apron, turned to Mom, "I don't know why you don't cook better? I saw you put margarine in the Christmas cookies today. You should always use butter. You wrecked them!"

Mom shouted back at her. "Because your son won't allow butter! I'm only allowed margarine. I can't cook anything the way I want to."

Nana ignored her remarks. "That's ridiculous. You just need to learn to cook."

Mom ran to her bedroom, hurt and humiliated, and cried most of that Christmas Eve. She alternated with yelling at Dad and admonishing him to get control of his mother. The whole house could hear her rants. "Send her home right now!" I'd never heard her so angry.

I trembled with rage as I sat outside their bedroom door. Tribal rules didn't allow me to say anything. It was so special to have my adored Nana at our home as she only came a few times a year, and it hurt me to see this big fight. As I watched and listened, I learned that eating was fraught with conflict, stress, and confusion never relished and enjoyed. I had counted on my family to be happy on this special day. But that year, my trust in a predictable, joyful holiday evaporated.

My beloved Christmas had been destroyed over a cube of butter.

Besides being confused about food, I was fearful. I couldn't help it. I was sure I'd fall off and break a bone if I rode a bike. If I went swimming at the beach, a huge shark would surely get me. Anything that locked me in, such as rides at amusement parks, was entirely out of the question, too scary to enjoy. When the metal gate on the ride clanged shut, I panicked, knowing I was trapped.

I couldn't understand how being afraid was fun for so many people. As I grew into an adolescent, terror filled me if I was alone at night without Mom and Dad. Someone, I was sure, would break in and attack me. Every noise sent shocks of fear through me like an electric current, and I'd call my parents to calm me down.

Carol C. Boyce

Nightmares were the norm. Unlike my visions which I kept to myself, I would flee to the safety of my parent's room, sobbing from a scary dream. "There she goes again, always afraid of something." Mom rolled her eyes. "She was just born scared."

Taking me back to my bed, she admonished me to stay put. Dad ignored me and would go back to sleep. I had no one to comfort me, and I believed my all-knowing mother--fearfulness was just my nature. I'd been born afraid of everything.

It'd be two more decades before these unexplained fears shattered my life.

By the time I was in sixth grade, Mom had talked openly of hating raising her four children. When Dad came home from the office, she'd announce, "I can't stand this. You stay home and take care of these kids. They drive me crazy." She didn't care what we heard.

Dad took a deep breath and calmly responded, "That's what mothers do. They take care of their kids. You shouldn't have had them if you didn't want to be a mother."

Mom would only grow frustrated and yell more. Sometimes she would sob on their bed in misery. I tried hard to figure out what was so wrong. I thought we were a burden to poor Mom, but I couldn't think of anywhere else we kids could live. There was no one else who'd take us. She'd just have to keep us, and as the oldest daughter, I felt responsible for her unhappiness.

If anything, Mom's moods had some predictability. She'd be a gentle Golden Retriever in the morning, a vigilant German Shepard in the afternoon, and an angry Pitbull in the evening. After school, I could hear her muttering to herself before Dad got home. Her rage would grow the longer she talked.

Scared of her rath, I listened carefully to ensure I was safe and not in the crosshairs of her anger. As kids, we thought these full conversations with herself odd, but we never dared say anything to her. I wondered to whom she was talking so angrily but later realized she was winding up for Dad when he got home from the office. "You forgot to call me today. You don't care about me, do you?" she'd whisper to herself. Forewarned, the misery of the evening to come was inevitable.

Dad would change out of his suit and tie when he arrived home at six o'clock. He'd greet us and then prepare a large pitcher of martinis with a twist of lemon. With the endorsement of Dean Martin, Sammy Davis, Jr., and Frank Sinatra, this cocktail became fashionable at that time. With Mom and Dad's stylish brew, they'd retire to the living room. As their intoxication grew, my mother's rage at Dad would erupt like an awakening volcano. Darkness oozed out of her pores without obstacle.

"Our old neighbor, Betty, came into the office today. She seemed good," Dad casually remarked one evening as he flipped the paper open.

Mom's head shot up. "Oh, did she? Betty looked good, you said?"

He rolled his eyes. "I didn't say that. I said Betty seemed healthy."

"Yeah, I bet you thought she looked good! Just like your assistants at the office. What do you do with them, anyway?" She knotted her eyebrows and glared at him. "Huh? Answer me!" Her rage was palpable. "Ya don't care about me...do ya?" She hissed at him, now showing the effects of the cocktails. "You care about yourself and no'on else."

Like a helpless animal, Dad hoped her engulfing lava flow didn't burn him. Any response enraged her more. I thought he was a grown and powerful man capable of defending himself. Shouldn't he at least stop making pitchers of martinis? They only aggravated her.

Mom would announce, "I'm calling the attorney in the morning on bad nights. We're getting divorced." I'd worry about their impending divorce all night and carefully observed her the following days to see if she did make the call. *Where would my family, Dad, and I end up? Where would we live? Would he be gone from my life?* I knew I had to stop their fighting somehow myself. I had to keep my family together.

But I had another issue brewing. Amid our family's prosperity and plenty, I was hungry.

"When can we eat?" I'd ask. As a growing child, I felt starved during their endless drinking fights.

Dad replied. "You can't eat now. It will wreck your dinner. Don't eat anything." They'd continue arguing and I'd wait endlessly for dinner.

The next night I'd say again. "I'm hungry now. When can I eat dinner?'

"You cannot eat." Hunger was a nightly reality, a constant in my life. Deep down, I fumed over their control of my food and me. I wanted to scream, "You have kids who are hungry and need food! Why don't we matter more than your drinking and fighting?" I didn't dare reveal my thoughts--Mom would skewer me. My anger grew year after year. When we finally ate dinner, it was often overcooked and tasteless. True to the unspoken family rules, no one said a word.

I made my first solemn vow. It would have profound adverse effects on my health for most of my adult life:

No one will ever control my food again and nobody will ever decide what and when I can eat. No one!

The following morning, I would dress for school, with the smell of a warm breakfast drawing me to the kitchen. A strange and peculiar peace would appear, an odd calm belying the previous night's upheaval. With Dad's head buried in the morning paper and quietly sipping his coffee, Mom scurried around the kitchen, feeding all of us. She never missed a beat.

I'd sit down next to Dad and pour milk on my steaming oatmeal as he smiled warmly at me and gently rubbed my forearm. I'd smile back, grateful for his loving gesture, feeling sorry for him after my mother's rath. Then, like clockwork, at eight a.m., he'd rise from the table, kiss Mom goodbye and head out for hospital rounds.

Poof...Gone...I couldn't understand where the parents from last night were. It seemed surreal. The eruption that passed through our home had strangely left no visible destruction in its wake. There was no mention of the night before, no explanation or apologies, no complaining of hangovers, no silent treatment, no hurt looks, and no misty eyes. Mom's volcano would go dormant for a few peaceful hours, only to return with a full vengeance that evening.

Chapter 6

In the Closet

My troop's annual Girl Scout cookie drive had begun when I turned eleven. The soft carpet in my dark bedroom closet felt good on my bare feet on this lazy Saturday afternoon. I jumped with my petite frame to grab the pull cord for the overhead light. As my eyes adjusted, I saw a tower of my favorite delicious cookies before me.

Mom and Dad rarely gave us sweets. Not only were they not allowed, but anyone who liked them was subtly looked down upon. How could anyone like something that wasn't healthy, was Dad's thought.

I did crave sweets and dreamed of eating them as I looked at the towering boxes. I thought of how good they all looked. Eating one cookie from one package—just one—couldn't be a big deal, right? Bargaining with myself, I thought I could try one box and pay for it with my saved allowance. After all, I had agreed to sell the boxes for the fundraiser but had never said *to whom* I would do it.

No one would notice if I ate one package of cookies myself. What could be the harm? I could meet my sales goal faster, and

Mom and Dad would never know I had eaten the forbidden sweets.

I carefully pulled down a box of Thin Mints so as not to spill the tower and took out one small cookie. It melted in my mouth with an explosion of sweet chocolate and minty goodness. I thought one more cookie couldn't hurt and ate another. And another and then finished the box. Soon, I opened another package, ate the whole thing, and then opened another. I couldn't stop until I felt sick. I put my money in the manilla payment envelope for the boxes I ate and sold the rest later in the week, happy I had met my goal but with a big stomachache.

For the first time in my life, I had been free to eat as I pleased. I was in control of my food, not my parents. The sugar rush intoxicated me, and my complicated feelings seemed to disappear. It was my first experience of feeling strong and powerful. An accessible drug, sugar was now what I craved. Though I wouldn't often have the freedom to eat sweets until I was in college, the mental backdrop of my future eating disorder had begun.

It would be decades before I understood that I craved far more than sugar.

Chapter 7

Between Dolls and Boys

Somewhere between dolls and boys, Susie and I tried to find an easy, clear pathway into adolescence and a way to sneak in without anyone noticing. One afternoon, her mother, Holly, went shopping, leaving Susie, myself, and her brother alone. While sitting in Susie's bright yellow room, we opened our treasured Barbie doll cases packed with parts of once beautiful outfits. As preteens, romantic encounters dominated our play with our Ken and Barbie dolls, and we relished changing them into their many wonderful ensembles.

After an hour, we got bored and decided to play with Holly's cosmetologist work case, though we knew not to touch it. Like pirates with a stolen treasure chest, we scurried it away, ready to explore the grown-up and intriguing world of glamorous make-up.

As we opened her mother's large case, we tried to figure out what went where. We knew the lipstick went on our lips, but we weren't sure what to do with the many-colored pencils and shadows. Knowing precisely where everything went seemed especially important at this critical moment in our lives. Impressing our friends with our sophisticated knowledge felt vital to starting middle school next year. We knew our natural look was not sufficient anymore and that we needed the magic of make-up to fit in.

Getting bright red lipstick on our lips and not the surrounding skin became an important symbol of enlightenment, and we came close. We fumbled with the challenging task of drawing black liner close to our lashes without poking ourselves in the eye or ending up with smeary black streaks. Heavy-handed for an extra dramatic flair, we applied the magic and then preened, admiring our work in Susie's large dresser mirror. Our brilliant blue eyelids, dramatic eyebrows, bright pink cheeks, and the shimmering red lipstick completed our amazing, dramatic makeovers. Giggling all the way, we seemed to transform from the pure and innocent faces of childhood to masked, sophisticated marvels, from childhood to womanhood with the simple flick of a mascara brush.

After admiring and congratulating ourselves, I said, "Susie, I'm going to the bathroom. I better wash this makeup off before your mom gets home. I don't want us to get in trouble."

"Okay," Susie replied, still admiring her transformed face in the mirror.

I scampered down the hall past Bob's room as I had a hundred times before. Four years older than us, I usually avoided Susie's sixteen-year-old brother. He was mean to everyone, and his snake collection scared me.

I walked back to her room, not seeing Bob standing in his bedroom doorway. He jumped out at me from nowhere. Grabbed me and painfully constricting his strong hands around my upper arm, he pulled me into his bedroom.

"Shut up," he demanded as he covered my mouth with his rough hand. He brutally slammed my back against his bedroom wall, subduing me with his surprising strength. Frantic, my voice froze along with my body as I pleaded with wide eyes. *I'm Carol—little Carol, remember? Susie's best friend. Why are you hurting me?*

Unable to move or escape his powerful grasp, I could feel his erection press against my leg as he forced his free hand under my shirt and groped my budding breasts. Terror overcame me as he fumbled with his zipper. I was powerless.

Suddenly, Susie called out, "Carol, aren't you done yet? Hurry up! We have to clean this mess up before Mom finds out."

The assault ended as suddenly as it began. Bob abruptly released me and zipped his pants, unable to complete his assault. I ran to the safety of Susie's room, pulling down my shirt and straightening my clothes.

"What took you so long?" Susie said, oblivious to what had happened and irritated I'd been gone so long. "We have to hurry. Mom's gonna be home soon. Put the makeup back in the case."

My heart pounded as I mumbled, "Sorry." Numb, I silently stuffed the makeup back into the case and quickly went home.

I left the world of dolls and make-believe behind that day, never to return. I no longer went to play at Susie's house, too confused and fearful. In that one fleeting instant, I was merely prey, someone to use, with no other value. Bob had known me my whole life as his sister's sweet playmate. He'd watched me grow up, which I thought would make him care, even love, and protect me. But I could see the narrowed slits of his eyes were empty and dead, vacant of compassion or empathy, holding only venom.

Confused and vulnerable, I couldn't understand what had happened or if I had caused it. I had heard the basics but had no idea what sex really looked like. Bob had only touched me briefly. *What could be wrong with that? What do I call what happened?*

As a twelve-year-old, I didn't have context or words for sexual assault--what it might be like or who could be an offender. Left to my own conclusions, I only knew it felt wrong--violent and frightening. My changing body felt violated.

I never spoke about this incident to anyone, even Susie. What could I say? The confusion and shame silenced me, and the incident would remain a bad memory, protecting Bob from all consequences.

Forty years later, I made a rare visit to see Susie, who now lived across the country. As I was leaving, she looked at me questioningly. "Bob wants to apologize for what he did to you. He wanted to make sure I told you, though I'm not sure what he was talking about."

I smiled broadly as Susie looked confused, still not knowing what had happened so long ago. "Tell him… I appreciate that very much." After so much time, I couldn't believe that he spoke the truth and took responsibility for his actions.

Chapter 8

Nothing Really Happened

B ored, I wandered into my Presbyterian church group for junior high kids. I only went because Mom insisted. It was awkward, and I didn't relate to or know the other kids. They didn't go to my school, but sullenly, I complied.

We all sat down on the wooden chairs in the large, noisy room at church. Eric, our youth pastor, wrote on the chalk-smeared blackboard: Saturday at 9. Carpool to Kennedy High School in Watts. "Kids, quiet down." He paused a moment. "We've been asked to volunteer to help disadvantaged children read. The event will be at their local high school. I guarantee you'll find it an interesting experience. Many of the children come from homes with much less than you have." Eric started to print names on the board. "So, who's coming on Saturday?"

I raised my hand.

Watts was a socio-disadvantaged area about an hour's drive from my house into the heart of Los Angeles. The Watts riots had just ended and from the violence I'd seen on TV, I was a bit concerned. Looking out the car window as we drove, it was the first time I'd seen an impoverished neighborhood. Its graffitied walls, few trees, trash piled on the streets, and people hanging on corners with nothing to do stunned me. I was out of my safe bubble, leaving my affluent, insulated world behind, and I had no idea the challenges those who lived there faced.

It was a wet, chilly day when we arrived at the entrance to the high school. Being Saturday, no students or teachers were on campus. The gray, concrete school seemed deserted except for the ten high school students and two chaperones with our group.

"Mrs. Primly, the program director, eyed us as we funneled into the carpeted school library. It was a nice, well-organized room though the desks looked dirty. "Grab a napkin and donut from the tray and sit down. She straightened the pearl strand at her neck. "First of all, thanks for coming. These children could use your help with reading." She bit into her glazed donut and took a sip of tea. She wiped the crumbs off her chest. "I've paired you up so you each have your own child to help. They'll be here in a minute." She licked the sugar glaze off her fingers.

"Find a quiet classroom and read a book over there to your child." She pointed to a shelving unit on the far wall. About ten children between five and seven years old came into the room. We checked each other out. They seemed as awkward with us as we did with them.

Finding my six-year-old assignee, Lavonna, I crouched down and smiled at her. With luminous brown eyes and a huge smile, she asked if I'd read her *Charlotte's Web*. She liked animals. I found the book and held her hand as we walked down the cold, trash-laden hallway. The faint odor left by the garbage and someone's vomit filled my nose. Our shoes clicked on the deserted gray hallway as I searched for a quiet, secluded classroom. Finding one, we settled in for a morning of stories.

Sitting close together, I began reading about the young pig. In my best little girl voice, I said, "You have been my friend. That in itself is a tremendous thing." Her smiles told me she enjoyed the escapism and my undivided attention. The story was far from Lavonna's dingy, poverty-stricken world. She gazed up and captured my heart.

After fifteen minutes of enjoying reading together, my ears perked up. I heard footsteps and deep voices in the hallway, unexpected in this deserted area. I glanced towards the door, hoping not to concern Lavonna and disrupt our reading. They were walking down the hall, checking out each room. *They must be lost and will leave in a second.* With a calm voice belying my fear, I continued reading.

Five tattooed teenage guys, dressed in ragged clothes with chains on their belts, appeared at the doorway. My eyes widened as they swaggered into our room. My stomach clenched as I realized I didn't know if there were unspoken behaviors or language girls used here to protect themselves. Several of the guys leered, grinning as they eyed me. I heard a low chuckle and words between them that were inaudible. The front guy, the apparent ringleader, could see I'd be easy prey. I was clearly from a different world, with my long blond hair, cardigan sweater, and slacks.

Lavonna suddenly startled and ran from the room. At six, she knew more about what to do than I did. I took a deep breath, relieved she'd be safe. My heart raced as my throat tightened. I knew I couldn't outrun them and there was nowhere to hide. As they circled my chair, the color drained from my face.

The leader put his hand on my neck and rubbed it slowly, then moved his hand to my breast, touching it through my shirt as the others snickered. His hand became a shove and knocked me out of my chair. As the metal-edged chair clanged on the unforgiving concrete floor, I fell onto the floor. I cowered and rolled into a protective ball. He laughed as he laid down next to me and pulled my jumper up, showing my panties. I was horrified, and none of the guys tried to help me. My head pounded as I trembled all over.

Suddenly, I heard the fast-paced walk of clicking heels. Someone was coming! My heart was in my throat as the guys turned towards the sound. Mrs. Primly's stern face appeared at the door. Lavonna must have told her I needed help! The teacher grabbed my arm and lifted me from the dirty floor as the guys fled the room. I pulled my dress down and brushed off the dirt.

Brusquely, she grabbed my arm and took me back to the cafeteria, muttering angrily under her breath. "You're okay. Just a little shaken up--nothing happened." I wondered why she said that. I didn't feel like nothing happened—I'd been terrified.

Wanting to protect her program's reputation, Mrs. Primly never reported the assault to the police, informed my pastor, or notified my parents. Neither did I. The story's hero, Lavonna, went home without acknowledgment or appreciation for her heroism. This courageous six-year-old had the wherewithal to run for help. I will never forget her power and strength.

As I look back, I realize I didn't understand the seriousness of the situation, how quickly I could have been raped, or even what rape was. I learned that assaults could happen in minutes and change a life forever. As with the incident with Bob, I didn't have words or context to know what had happened or even what to call it. Only touching had happened, and as Mrs. Primly told me, "It was nothing." I realized my belief that it was a big deal must be wrong, but I knew I'd never forget these events and the intense fear I felt.

Telling no one, I buried the memories away.

Chapter 9

The Family Stew

T he stovetop was as hot as the sweltering day, as mother slowly stirred the old family stew recipe. With one cup of abandonment, one of alcoholism, one of shame, and one of anger, hefty servings of confusion were served to Mark, Debbie, Tim, and me. It left us hungry for compassion, nourishment, and love. Every child swallowed their portion as best they could and, in some ways, tasted a slightly different recipe tailored to their unique position in the family.

My siblings survived our family's emotional chaos by coping in the best way they knew how. While I obsessed over food and fixing my mother, my siblings struggled in their own ways. Like me, their feelings were irrelevant to our immature parents, who couldn't cope even with their own. Between us, we never discussed what was going on with each other—we just survived. We assumed Mom and Dad's behavior was normal, accepted it, and managed as best we could.

Mark, the oldest, wrestled with adolescence. He was handsome and a good student, but he struggled with poor adolescent decisions--partying, reckless driving, and marijuana. It caused more uproar and battles at home. Watching what Mark was going through, I decided my role was to keep the peace. I knew our family couldn't handle any more stress.

On the other hand, Mom and Dad didn't care what Debbie did if she stayed out of their hair. Overwhelmed by their own troubles, she used their lack of interest as a license to rebel. She would get their attention, even if negative. She'd gotten herself into drugs and alcohol by junior high. She didn't worry about coming home drunk or vomiting, as Mom was often in worse shape. Debbie broke into stores to steal alcohol and took joyrides in "borrowed" cars by high school, acting out the neglect at home.

One night when Debbie was twelve and I was fourteen, she arrived home acting strangely. I watched her stumble into the house and sit on her bedroom floor. She stared at her carpet, fascinated, separating its fibers with her fingers. "Look at how cool the carpet is—there are, like, a million colors in it." She had dilated pupils and her face was flushed.

Wide-eyed, I sat down next to her on the carpet and drew a long breath. "What's going on?"

"LSD is sooo cool." She smiled broadly, thrilling in her careful examination of the carpet strands.

Dread twisted my gut as Debbie ignored me, too busy analyzing the strands. This new and popular hallucinogen scared me, and I didn't know how to help her. As a ninth-grader, I felt responsible for keeping her safe. Debating telling my parents, I knew they'd only yell at both of us, so I said nothing.

Despite how much she hated it, I figured protecting Debbie fell to me. No one else was doing it, and it was a great responsibility at my young age. Miraculously, on her own, she found the strength in late high school to stop using heavy drugs and straightened her life out before suffering any long-term damage. Her recovery amazed and inspired me.

My youngest brother, Timmy, survived in his own way also. He believed our parents battled because of him. My youngest brother was sensitive, adorable, and wildly creative. He survived by hiding in his room and burying himself in art.

Disneyland was his favorite escape and on his first visit, he wanted to live in that much happier place forever. Timmy would hide in his bedroom, sketching his own versions of the magical characters and unique, brilliantly designed rides. Developing his own concepts of the epic castles, pirates, and witches captivated him, and Halloween became great fun because of him.

However, his fantasy world followed him to school and his grades naturally suffered. No amount of yelling, punishments, or tutors by Mom and Dad brought him out of this protective world. Later, drugs and alcohol became his coping method, which he also eventually overcame.

Sailing with the family at an early age, Tim would have strange, terrifying thoughts. As the boat sailed out to sea, and ocean waves slapped the boat's sides, he waited for Mom and Dad to throw him overboard, sure they wanted to kill him. Their lives would be so much easier without me, he reasoned. *Maybe I'd be better off, too.*

His heart pounded, wondering when the petrifying moment would occur during the eight-hour journey on the lonely sea. He was a young child with no sense of safety and never questioned why. Alone with his terrifying thoughts, he accepted them as a normal part of childhood.

Choking on the family stew, we all survived the best way we could.

Chapter 10

An Alcoholic

The summer after ninth grade, I had a ballet lesson one Saturday morning. As I got ready, I noticed the kitchen smelled inviting, and I went to see what was cooking for breakfast.

Set with matching placements and napkins, the table waited with our breakfast of poached eggs and steaming hot oatmeal. Mom never missed preparing a nutritious breakfast for us. Mark, Debbie, and Tim were already at the table.

Mom stared out our large kitchen patio window in her floral cotton house dress and rollers in her hair. She muttered to herself as she held a steaming mug of coffee, shaking her head back and forth. Brutus pushed up next to her and whined, wanting to be let into our backyard.

"What's going on, Mom?" I asked, blowing on my hot oatmeal.

"Cassie must be drunk again—her curtains are shut. Passed out on the floor, I bet, and it isn't even nine in the morning!" She sighed and opened the door for Brutus. He bounded out happily.

"Wow," I replied.

"I don't know what to do about her—what an alcoholic!" Mom took a sip of coffee and furrowed her brow. "We'd better start looking for her kids and make sure they haven't fallen in a pool or something."

"What's an alcoholic, Mom?" I asked innocently.

She stared at the closed drapes, hoping to see some sign of life next door. "Oh, someone who can't stop drinking until they get drunk."

I shrugged my shoulders. Cassie, a former state beauty contest winner, had lived next door for five years with her husband and two small children. Gone often on location, her husband, a cinematographer, filmed big movies and TV shows with famous stars.

Stunning to look at, she could be a vibrant mother to her two young children, and she had one of the funniest senses of humor I'd ever known. When sober, she was delightful and could get you in hysterics within minutes. When drunk, she became completely incoherent and unable to stand up.

I thought about Mom's definition. With Cassie, everything seemed black and white: she was either completely sober or passed out drunk with no in-between. I tried to process the differences. If that was alcoholism, then wasn't one, right? After all, Mom opened the drapes and functioned during the day. But Mom was drunk every night, and that must count for something, I figured. I was left confused, particularly when Cassie drowned in her bathtub during another binge, tragically leaving her two beautiful children motherless.

Strangely, my mom saw Cassie as utterly different than herself.

Chapter 11

Scouts Honor

By tenth grade, I had become a quiet, unassuming people-pleaser. I never spoke back to anyone, particularly my parents, and always did my chores and homework. I was too afraid to make any mistakes. I didn't want to be the child Mom yelled at and stayed under her radar as much as possible. I certainly didn't want to add more stress to our home.

I was a good kid and made most of my clothes--I loved the creativity of sewing. Analytical by nature and strong in math and science, school seemed easy. Painfully bored, I worked hard enough to get mostly A's and B's but not much more. I didn't see a reason.

Many of my old childhood friends were blossoming into confident, involved students. They joined high school teams, Student Council, and drama. I didn't have that confidence in myself. Most of my friends took part in cheerleading squads, but it didn't make sense. I knew girls had more important things to accomplish than jumping around in short skirts cheering on guys.

As a first-year student, I got accepted into the school chorus but was soon requested to leave without explanation. I assumed my voice wasn't good enough, and I didn't have the confidence to join any other club.

One lunch period, my friend Patti and I leaned against a brick wall. "Listen. There's this Girl Scout Troop that my mom keeps nagging me to join. She says I'll love it and that it's a great troop. I'm not so sure--sounds dumb to me." She rubbed her foot on the ground, embarrassed even to bring up the subject. "Any chance...um...you would join with me? It would be more fun with you there." Her eyebrows rose as she smiled weakly.

I couldn't imagine anything more socially appalling in high school than Girl Scouting. If I ever got caught wearing the uniform, I would die, and my already thin social life would become non-existent. But I considered the proposition, and ultimately, my empty social calendar won out. "Okay. I'll try it--but only if I don't have to wear my uniform to school."

Patti agreed.

Our troop went on a ten-day backpacking trip in the stunning Sierra mountains every year. I had never backpacked and was unsure about it. I eventually agreed to go, excited to spend time with my new friends. I had always loved the nearby Sierras, thanks to my family trips.

We headed to the Desolation Valley and stood at the dusty trailhead with our fifty-pound backpacks. I proudly wore my new hiking boots, Girl Scout official shorts, a white shirt, and knee-high green socks with their red flags with no boys around. My lack of confidence in my physical abilities spiked as I stared up at the towering mountain range, suddenly so close and intimidating. "I'm not sure I can do this, Patti." Our packs were daunting because we had to survive a long time with their contents.

At 4'8" and tiny, Patti didn't seem bothered by our heavy loads. She placed a gentle hand on my shoulder and smiled. "We'll help each other--we can do this."

I breathed deep, wanting to believe her. "Okay," I said and started the trek. I found out that I could hike long distances. I wasn't the fastest up the mountains, but I wasn't the slowest. That made me proud. I could keep going no matter how steep it got and motivate others who were struggling. I could lead.

When everyone arrived at the camp, we set up our beds under the stars. I was elected patrol leader of eight girls. I got them organized to set up a latrine, build a fire, make dinner, collect water, and set up our tents.

After dinner, I wandered away from the loud, boisterous camp to a rock outcropping, needing a little space to think. The granite precipice overlooked a pristine, glacier-carved valley surrounded by towering evergreens. A majestic eagle circled languidly above as the sunset dripped hues of amber and gold. I was in awe of the majesty before me. In the quiet, I felt something new. The overwhelming experience with my scout friends and the incredible view of nature spoke to me. For the first time, I felt the presence of God and his loving embrace.

I came to love scouts. I flourished in its all-girl environment and developed great, lasting friendships that I treasure. With our remarkable leader, who we called Bambi, I had the freedom to discover who I was and develop strengths I didn't know I had. Well-liked, I felt as though I fit in somewhere. The activities taught me I could be a responsible, hard-working, and trustworthy leader. It was a godsend to my young, lost life.

Carol C.Boyce

The troop also helped me realize I was an individual, separate from my parents. It was the beginning of my learning about life outside the chaos at home. Though no one knew what was going on there, the troop under Bambi's remarkable leadership helped me realize that there was more out there than my painful family life, and my future would be up to me.

I realized I needed a new swimsuit for Girl Scout camp one day. Mom drove me to Sears, where I picked out a few two-pieces and headed for the dressing room. "I'll come out and show you the ones I like. Okay?"

"Sure." She shrugged and sat on the upholstered bench, starting a crossword puzzle on the newspaper she had brought with her.

I hurriedly shut myself behind the door. I had been on a no-carb, high-fat diet with my overweight girlfriend and had only eaten pork rinds for a week. Though I felt sick, I tried the first suit on. Under the harsh fluorescent lights, it shocked me to see how curvy my body looked in the three-way mirror. I twisted and turned, studying myself from all angles.

I was so fat. On my five-foot-two frame, I was huge at 105 pounds. *How did I get so big? I look horrible.* Tears rained down my cheeks as I looked away. I couldn't stand to look at my body.

After a while, Mom knocked and came into the room. "What is taking you so long? I have to pick up Tim at school in fifteen minutes." She saw my reddened eyes and put her hands on her hips. "What are you crying about? This is nonsense--that suit looks fine on you. What is wrong with you?"

"I hate how I look—see how fat I am?" I sobbed in my hands.

"Hmmm. I don't know what you are talking about. You're not fat--you're thin." My body heaved as Mom's anger grew. She shrugged and dismissed my puzzling emotions as we drove home without a second thought.

That dressing room was my first memory of hating my body, though I had no idea why. My tainted perception had developed into a lens with which I would judge myself for much of my life. I would eventually make my body image match my distorted self-concept.

It would be decades before I understood that my body shame and fears were tightly connected.

Chapter 12

Another Perspective

B esides chores, school, and babysitting, I started a private guitar studio for the neighborhood kids. I'd also work at Dad's private medical practice during summers. I loved learning about medicine, and he taught me everything he could, hoping I'd follow his career path. I developed x-rays, filed charts, and helped with EKGs. It provided an opportunity to know him outside our home.

After completing his patient appointments, Dad took me on his hospital rounds and "house calls," visits to elderly and sick patients at their homes. He'd bring small instruments and pre-scriptions in his black leather satchel.

He often visited one elderly lady, Mrs. Henry. As we entered her dark bedroom, I noticed many used tissues that had spilled onto the floor. Wearing a stained satin bed jacket, Dad sat down next to her and opened his bag. Speaking loudly, he said, "How are you doing today, Mrs. Henry? I brought my daughter along. Hope you don't mind."

"I am so happy to see you both, Doc, but I'm about the same—not too good." Her large, heavily wrinkled eyes clouded over.

Dad nodded and pulled out a stethoscope from his black bag. "I'm sorry to hear that." He took his time checking her heart, reading her blood pressure, and refilling her drugs. I watched from the corner. "Sorry, you're not feeling well. Continue with your medications, rest, and take loving care of yourself, you hear?" He smiled at her and patted her hand before packing up.

Back in the car, Dad rubbed his forehead. "Mrs. Henry is in bad shape—her heart's shot. She won't make it through the month."

"That's awful," I said.

He shrugged. "Old people go on way too long. The family should break out the champagne when she dies. They'll be lucky to get this ordeal over with."

I shrugged, thinking it was an odd and cold statement, but I trusted he must know more than I. After all, he dealt with death routinely.

We went to the hospital next for his rounds. The bright white walls of the fast-paced medical center jarred me along with the antiseptic smell as we walked down the long hallway.

As Dad entered one room, I paused at the doorway and stiffened at the scene. Medical staff surrounded an elderly Mr. Lynch lying on his hospital bed. Nurses ran around quickly, touching dials and looking at medical instruments. I could hear a long beeping sound that never wavered in pitch.

Soon, a nurse threw a white sheet over Mr. Lynch's body. Another nurse handed Dad a clipboard with the death certificate he needed to sign. They wheeled his body out of the room unceremoniously. After completing the necessary documents, Dad signaled for me to leave, and we headed back to the parking lot.

In the car, Dad dropped his head against the steering wheel. Tears streamed down his scrunched face.

"What's wrong?" Leaning toward him, wide-eyed, I handed him a tissue. I had never seen him cry before.

"Did you know...uh...I lost my father...when I was five? A great man—an electrical engineer and an expert outdoorsman. He survived the 1918 Spanish Flu but never fully recovered. When he died ten years later, he left Nana with three kids to raise on her own." He sniffled, wiping his eyes. "I've always looked for a substitute father." He paused a long time. "Mr. Lynch became like one to me. He always meant so much--the way he listened and offered me advice." He stopped short and stared out the window.

"I'm so sorry...I didn't realize how much that must have hurt. It must have been devastating to lose your father but now Mr. Lynch." I leaned over and hugged him. He closed his eyes and pulled me closer to him.

I had never seen this side of my father before, vulnerable and deeply emotional. I felt closer when he shared his grief. He was fighting his childhood pain as best he could.

As I physically developed, Dad changed. He started treating me less like his little girl and more like someone he didn't like. He even stopped rubbing my forearm and smiling at me, and I had no idea why.

One day, I came into the living room where he was reading medical journals to show him the new dress I'd sown. The mini skirt was the latest fashion and I'd worked hard to make a stylish outfit. My dress was several inches above my knee.

"Look at my new dress, Dad. Do you like it?" I twirled around, showing it off.

He gave me a cold stare. "Way too short. You're not going out like that. It's awful."

I blushed and left in tears.

It also felt different when I dated. Dad seemed upset by it. Thin, petite, and curvy with long blond hair, I was asked out often, though no one particularly interested me. He'd warn me in a low, gruff voice, "They only want one thing." He had never talked so bluntly, and I realized something was different.

Dad lived to sail, his greatest passion. We owned a thirty-six-foot sailboat, and he wanted to venture to nearby islands almost every weekend in the summers. But even there, he had changed. I usually loved seeing dolphins playing in our boat's wake and the smell of the fresh, salty sea air. The six to eight hours it took to get to Catalina Island by high school seemed endless. I learned to sleep as long as possible in the galley berth to pass the time quickly.

One sail to Catalina, I was sleeping below deck when I heard Dad suddenly stomp down the stairs. Leaning close to my ear, he hissed, "You're just a JAP."

I was startled awake. "Whaaat?"

"A spoiled Jewish American Princess is what you are. You'll never amount to anything—you're lazy and worthless." After his pronouncement, he clomped back up the stairs. Trying to understand what was upsetting him, I went to the cockpit to help with the sails. If that was all he wanted, why did he have to say it like that?

His mean, antisemitic comment seemed so mean and unlike him. First, we weren't Jewish, though many of our family's best friends and Dad's colleagues were. Second, he never used to call me names and third, I wasn't lazy. I worked at his office, babysat, went to school, was active in Girl Scouts, did many chores at home, and had my guitar studio to manage. I didn't think that "lazy" really fit me.

He called me a JAP so often that I started to believe him. I wondered why his treatment of me was progressively worsening and couldn't understand what had changed.

Later that week, after getting back home, I stood in the kitchen. Dad came home from work, and I couldn't wait to tell him about my day. "Dad, guess what happened? I got to ride bareback..."

He cut me off with the first sip of his martini. "Would you just shut up? I'm so sick of your mouth running."

I ran to my bedroom sobbing. Where was my old father? Why didn't he like me anymore?

I'd understand why my growing up was a big problem for him much later.

Chapter 13

Deliriously Happy

When I was sixteen, my family took a camping trip to Zion National Park. Dad had driven the long journey with four kids in the backseat. We parked and opened our green canvas tent trailer to air it out before sleeping that night. As the evening finally darkened and cooled down, Dad lit a fire. The flames crackled and soared in the air like fireworks as the smell of smoke and evergreens enveloped us.

The martinis had flowed at happy hour as usual, but Mom's mood became joyful on this rare night--the tone of her voice told me everything. With her anger rarely gone, I became hopeful this special evening might be without conflict.

As the hours passed, she became euphoric—deliriously happy. Dad was his usual, quiet drunk self. "Kiz," she slurred, "help me find the moon. It's soooo beautiful. Come, fahlow me!" I realized she was extremely drunk.

I looked toward my brothers and sister and rolled my eyes, knowing we were in for some stupid jaunt.

Mom laughed and laughed. "Fawlow me, come on." She waved her arms wildly in the air.

I rolled my eyes and reluctantly stood up. Once again, Dad didn't say a word. As instructed, we hurriedly followed her down a dark, narrow path, watching her wobble and stumble. No one expressed concern for Mom's safety. We were well-trained in the unspoken rule. "Don't make Mom mad under any circumstances." I wanted to yell out my anger at Mom's drunkenness, but I sealed my lips tight and pressed on.

When she finally found a clearing in the trees, she wobbled to a halt and nearly toppled over, dangerously tripping over some rocks. She raised her hands to the star-filled sky and shouted for joy in a sing-song voice, "It's so beaudiful, sooo stunnin."

We all stood in the blackness, looking at the moon until she'd had enough, and walked back to camp silently, another ruined evening. I wondered whether my sister and brothers were as frustrated as I was.

This foray was crazy, and my sense of powerlessness grew with each step. I wondered why we were all so helpless over Mom's bullying and terrible behavior and why Dad didn't stand up to her. I couldn't make sense of any of it.

She passed out when we got back to camp.

Chapter 14

Love on a Battlefield

Understanding my mother's complexities seemed critical to knowing myself. I couldn't grasp the causes of her anger because it never came out as a direct, honest statement. She always wrapped it in rage at my father, and its real reason was hard to untangle. I remained hypervigilant of her every word, trying to understand.

She had a few friends that also drank and took too many sedatives. They were also angry about their lives. Sometimes, I'd envision their limited options when she and her friends married in the fifties. I tried to picture what restricted their lives and dashed expectations.

Women stood at the altar and took their wedding vows in white bouffant gowns of lace, flowing organza, and tulle, symbolizing their likely virginity and innocence. They ran out the church door joyfully after promising their lives away, holding their new husbands' strong hand. They hoped that he would understand and care for their every need. Climbing into the luxurious train headed toward the land of happy marriage, the wife waved a relieved goodbye to her single friends chugging toward the town of dreaded spinsterhood.

As it barreled along, a dress of society's choosing was fitted to her, with a full skirt, tight bodice, skinny belt, and a short strand of luxurious, perfect pearls. She gladly accepted the attire because with it came the promise of a life of emotional fulfillment, financial security, and a few children.

The bride's dress design might be perfect for her, but then again, it might be wretchedly wrong. If it was so tight, she could barely breathe, it was too late to stop the train. This track was the chosen destination, and there was no turnabout.

Along with the outfit came unreliable birth control and the women's lives quickly became engulfed by caring for too many little ones. Dreams outside of the family had to be abandoned like a rabid dog. She could not fight against the tightness of the dress and the unmovable railroad tracks that were her destiny. Society wouldn't allow for it in the fifties.

With opportunities to make more income, the husband was the breadwinner, and with it came the power in the relationship and family. The woman was financially bound to him to feed, house, and clothe herself and her little ones. With limited options and none as vast as his, the wife had little choice but to live the life chosen for her and accept any behavior he decided to show.

The dress made for Mom didn't fit her—not the expectations, not the lifestyle, not the reality of raising four children and always being financially dependent. She was brilliant, creative, and dreamed of being a journalist, not home with kids and their endless needs. Despite living in a gilded cage, the expectations of being the doctor's wife dashed away her goals and aspirations, her pretty pearl necklace strangling her.

When our family couldn't make her happy, Mom learned to sedate her dashed dreams with martinis. Of course, they didn't work—outside substances don't fix anything. We all suffered the consequences.

Alcoholism is a progressive disease, and Mom's addiction got worse every year. Martinis continued to control our lives, and I never recognized it as a disease with a name. No one ever mentioned or discussed it, a given in our lives. Deep down, I was profoundly angry.

One night I drove myself home from a Girl Scout meeting. Dad was out at a hospital conference and my siblings were in their bedrooms. I was tired and still had homework to do. Mom greeted me with a sloppy hug. She could hardly speak. "Wad ya up to?"

I rolled my eyes. I didn't have time for this.

Mom tried to walk to her living room chair. As I juggled some books in my arms, I shadowed her closely. She wobbled and tripped on the shag carpet. I tried to grab her arm as she fell but missed catching her. I heard the resounding thud as she fell to the ground.

Time stopped in that frozen moment. My usual anger drained from my heart as she lay there. It felt surreal to see my bulldog mother be so helpless and powerless. The mother I always feared looked like a small defenseless child, and I was strangely grateful for the surreal moment.

Sadness grabbed me as I thought of Mom's brilliance with her creative writing, love of literature, theater, and world travel.

My heart ached as I compared that amazing person to the tragic one before me, the woman I desperately needed to nurture, guide, and value me. I realized at that sad moment I would never see her recover and heal--the bottle would make sure of it. It was much more powerful than her.

I knelt next to her unconscious body and stroked her pale forehead with my hand. "Mom, Mom...are you alright?" I studied her ashen face, hoping she was still alive. "Wake up!" I hurriedly wetted a washcloth with chilly water and blotted her face. Finally, she roused, groggy, disoriented, and strangely sober. She looked around and asked, "What happened? Why am I on the floor?"

I shut my eyes and lowered my head. "Mom, you...uh...had a bad fall." I would never mention how drunk she had been. My body relaxed with relief--I wasn't ready to lose her. I helped her to bed as my tears fell, gently stroking her head until she was asleep. I kissed her forehead.

Love is complex on a battlefield. My love for Dad felt clear and straightforward. Though he drank too much, also, and had moments of coldness, I didn't hold it against him. Compared to Mom's demeanor, he was a saint, the rock in my life, the 'good' calm parent I desperately needed. I felt compassion for him with the abuse he took from Mom. Despite him becoming colder as I grew, I loved him dearly and had profound respect for him.

Holding him accountable for protecting us from our mother never crossed my mind. I didn't realize then that it was his job to keep us safe and set up boundaries with her. At a minimum, he should have helped us cope with living with alcoholism.

Love was more complicated with Mom. While I loved her when kind and sober, I was extremely frustrated and angry when martini time arrived. How could I hate someone who clothed me and took me to ballet lessons? What kind of ungrateful child was I to feel this way? Look at all I have. Feeling guilty about the one who birthed and fed me was constant.

I had obsessed my whole adolescence about how to fix her and make her happy to no avail. I didn't understand her addiction and the depression she suffered. There was no excuse in my mind for why she emotionally abandoned the other kids and me. I only knew that when she drank, I had no one to listen to me, teach me how to manage my emotions, or nurture my soul.

I've learned the deepest love can cause the deepest pain in life and the greatest hurt. We all pay the price, and as angry as I became at Mom, I always loved and cared deeply for her. As much as I wanted to discard, abandon, and release it, love remained firmly implanted in my heart. It's impossible to extricate completely, no matter how angry and frustrated I might get. Though the endless anxiety she created in our home shattered me, she would always be my mother.

One afternoon returning home as a junior in high school, I grabbed a glass of skim milk and graham crackers. Mom was bustling around the kitchen getting dinner started as I sprawled out on the couch, waiting for my first guitar student to arrive. I turned the dial on our new console color television, searching for something to watch on our three channels. Moving the two antennae arms, I found *The Dick Cavett Show*, a popular talk program. He was talking to a psychotherapist who was showing couple's therapy. He had a married couple on who fought over doing chores. The therapist had them each discuss their side of the issue calmly. He got them to listen to each other and come up with solutions.

My eyes brightened and I sat up straight. I'd never seen anything like it--adults that communicated and resolved conflicts rationally. If Mom and Dad went to counseling, all their problems— all my problems—might be resolved. There *was* something that would help my family. I was thrilled.

Mom walked through the kitchen with a load of dirty laundry. "Mom, please watch this for a second. What do ya think?"

She stopped and watched casually for a few minutes. Scowling, she said, "It'd never work. Therapy's not for people who are really mad at each other."

"Mom, it does work. Just watch." I scooted up on the couch.

"I'd never air our dirty laundry outside the house. It's private." She smirked. "What a waste of time." She hurried to the laundry room and filled the washer.

I stood up and slowly turned off the TV, dropping my eyes. My heart fell as the truth set in. Mom would never look at herself and take accountability for her emotions and actions. In her mind, Dad caused all her problems, so she spent her life trying but unable to change him. She had no intention of getting sober or taking responsibility for her part in the marriage and family. With her comments about therapy, my hope for peace in our family ended. Resolving my mom and dad's endless conflict would never happen, and I grieved my loss of hope.

But despite Mom's unwillingness to face herself, and though I was only sixteen, I had learned a life-changing lesson from that brief talk show. I now knew professionals existed who helped families solve their problems. Family life didn't have to be as painful as mine, and emotional chaos didn't have to define my future.

This awareness forever changed my life path because I now knew there was another way to live and communicate. I would leave this madhouse behind and never live in one again.

I made another solemn vow to myself, one that would forever change the trajectory of my life:

My future children and I would never feel like I did growing up and would live in a peaceful, sober home if it were the last thing I ever did. I would figure it out as if my life depended on it.

Chapter 15

You'll Like It

In the summer after my junior year, I wanted more money, so I began waitressing at a pizza parlor near my house in the evenings. I enjoyed the families that came in and the tips they left. The owners I worked for were kind and pleasant.

After several months, the owners asked me to work at their other location, where their son was the manager. I agreed and arrived in my crisp uniform at the small Italian restaurant smelling the warm oregano from pizza in the brick oven. Mozzarella cheese, olives, pepperoni, and dough rested on the clean countertop.

Their huge twenty-five-year-old, slovenly son, Joe, bent down to greet me. "Hi, glad you're here." He leered at me with a wet, Cheshire Cat grin.

Feeling a tingle down my spine, I tried not to shudder as I nodded a hello. I realized I was the only server that night, and he, the only cook. I'd have to figure out how to avoid him. I got busy and refilled the parmesan cheese containers, covered the tables with checked red tablecloths, and swept the floor. A steady stream of families arrived through the shift, and I managed to stay busy.

When closing time finally arrived, Joe and I were alone again. Sweat dripped from his forehead, and his damp shirt stuck to his large body as he ogled me. "I've locked all the doors," Joe assured me as he sauntered over to where I was working. "By the way, I met a wonderful girl yesterday."

"Hmmm." I ignored my new boss as I wiped down the condiments.

"She was fun." He lifted his eyebrows as he smiled.

I finished straightening the chairs, trying to ignore his greasy glare.

"She liked being tied up. It was fun watching her squirm and writhe." He was almost drooling.

Stunned, I stopped in my tracks. If this was my first shift with Joe, I wondered what he might say the second day. I could tell from his harder breathing that he was getting excited telling me about the "date." My heart raced as fear ran through my veins. I moved to the well-lit kitchen and started cleaning more counters.

"And where did you meet this woman?" I had to say something.

He announced proudly, "Oh, I had to pay her—she was a prostitute." He smiled as he picked up a large cleaver. He slowly sharpened it on an oozing whetstone. "Do you think you'd like that, too? Being tied up? Wouldn't it be fun to try?" Joe smiled broadly, looking at me.

With my pulse quickening, I remained silent. What started as an innocuous conversation now felt terrifying.

"I think you'd like it."

Oh my God, this guy is for real. My eyes darted around, frantic for an exit out of the now dark, locked restaurant. I retreated toward the back door. "It's time for me to go home now, Joe. I'll see ya later." I removed my apron and grabbed my purse hanging on the coat rack.

Joe cornered me, the butcher knife glinting in the low light. "No! I think you'd like it if you just tried it. Let me show you."

I stammered, "Please, …uh…it's time for me to go home…I… must leave. My parents are waiting for me." Did I have "victim" written all over my face? "Let's…uh…talk about it later. I'm exhausted now--how about tomorrow?" I didn't know any other way to convince him to let me leave but to play along and act interested.

Joe smiled, envisioning tomorrow's possibilities. He went to the door and unbolted it to let me out. I sprinted into the deserted parking lot, glancing behind to ensure he didn't follow me.

When I arrived home, I told my parents about the interaction. They were sitting in the family room. It was the first time I'd ever told them about a sexually inappropriate interaction, and I hoped they'd protect me and know what to do. I expected they'd at least call and admonish him or even call the police.

"Well, what do you expect from a man?" Dad responded with his frequent comment to me. He went back to his medical journal.

Mom looked up and gave me a skeptical look. "Hmmm." She stared at me a moment and then returned to her book.

That's it? That's all they're going to say? Did they not believe me or think his actions weren't important? Was I not valuable enough? I couldn't believe their lack of response.

I called Joe's parents and quit the following day. I didn't give them a reason, and they couldn't understand why their good employee was leaving so soon.

Despite the lack of support, I had stood up for myself and spoken the truth for the first time. I learned I had the power and strength within me.

Chapter 16

Just the Three of Us

S adly, Girl Scouts was ending soon because of high school graduation. At one of our last weekly meetings, a colorful flyer floated around the room about a summer trip to Scandinavia, and I was excited.

"Lucy, look at this!" I handed my long-time scouting friend the flyer. "We could go to Sweden and Norway with the International Girl Scouts—it's a chance of a lifetime! Please come with me," I begged.

A trip to Europe sounded enthralling and came at a very reasonable price. Because of my parent's frequent international trips, I got the travel bug, too. I wanted to see the world, and this looked like a fantastic way to start. Hearing of many international events through my high school scout years, I decided to go and pay for the trip with my savings. I would meet so many new girls from many other countries.

We wrote letters back and forth with the Swedish program director, Jan, all on official letterhead. She sent us the packing lists and necessary passport requirements. We filled out official registration forms and felt ready for the adventure.

After our high school graduation ceremonies, Lucy and I flew to Stockholm for a month-long sailing and camping trip through Scandinavia. Our tour group would include a diverse group of girls from all over the world, and we were anxious to make new friends and learn about their lives.

I loved the excitement of the flight to Stockholm. Descending the steep plane stairs, we saw the beautiful Scandinavian mountainous landscape for the first time. I looked for a middle-aged woman but only saw a twenty-ish, tall, skinny man wearing a Boy Scout uniform.

Wide-eyed, I whispered in Lucy's ear, "That can't be Jan... Were we writing letters to a man all this time? He's only a few years older than us!" Jan (pronounced Yan), we learned, is John in Swedish. "The other thing, Boy and Girl Scouts are separate organizations--why is he wearing a Boy Scout uniform for a Girl Scout event? Seems weird."

Lucy shrugged. "Beats me. Sweden is a different country. Maybe they're combined here."

"Hmmm." I shrugged my shoulders. "I don't know, but it must be okay since it's through the official program and they organize these trips often. Anyway, lots of Girl Scouts will be joining us today," I rationalized. "It'll be okay—he's just the organizer." With no internet back then, researching these programs ahead of time was difficult, and this lack of information made us vulnerable.

As Jan motioned us to his battered car, I said, "Don't we need to pick up other girls at the airport before we leave?"

"No...um...their flights got delayed. We'll pick them up later today." Jan bit his nails as we drove away.

It sounded reasonable to us. Bilingual in Swedish and English, Jan was our only source of translation. There was little

Carol C.Boyce

English spoken and almost no signage. He spoke confidently, and I had no reason to question him.

Jan always carried a critical, large binder with the two-hundred program participants' information. He often made lengthy calls to them in Swedish, using data from these reports, and translated their reasons for not arriving to Lucy and me. "Oh yes, as I said, there have been unfortunate delays. We'll see them all when we camp tomorrow."

Jan had many excuses for them, a new one every day: flights canceled, bus trouble, illness, or their car broke down. Telling us the others would meet up with us, we believed in the program as we continued to travel with him.

We took a long train trip to the Arctic Circle the next morning, visited with local Laplanders and their reindeer, and hiked the Swedish mountains. The experience was amazing though our families had no idea of our whereabouts. We were two pretty teenagers, sleeping in one small tent with a stranger we knew nothing about.

As the days passed, no other scouts joined us. They all had had mishaps that delayed their arrival.

We returned several days later to Goteborg on the southwest coast of Sweden to begin the sailing part of the trip. Jan insisted, "Our sailing trip up the fjords of Norway will be potentially dangerous. The Sweden Girl Scout Council insists you take a swim test with your dress uniforms on. Falling off the boat while wearing your high heels, skirt, and jacket could be dangerous, so the council needs to know you could swim to safety with them on."

I whispered to Lucy, "Seems really odd...but who knows how they do things in Sweden. When in Rome...right?"

Lucy replied, "Hmmm, he won't let us sail if we don't do it, so I guess we better. I want to meet the rest of the group."

We sailed on a severely leaky, old boat to a beautiful fjord, lush with evergreen trees near the peaceful blue water. We dove into the cold ocean dressed in our green Scout dress suits, stockings, and heels. "Show me you can swim fifty yards from this buoy to that one."

Anxious to get certified, we did the crawl across the long span, dodging many tiny jellyfish. Out of the corner of my eyes, I looked at Jan standing on the shore, excitedly snapping endless photos of us. Click, click, click, click. I wondered what was going on but continued swimming.

Afterward, Lucy and I stood on the shore in our sopping wet dresses and shoes. He continued clicking his camera. "Why are you taking so many photos of us? We already passed the test," I demanded.

"This is part of proving you did the test to the council. The photos will be evidence."

"Hmmm—that doesn't seem right." I questioned the logic but thought he must know what he was doing. After all, he was five years older than us.

Passing the test, we dried off and started the sail to Norway. Day after day, we bought all the information Jan fed us. I pumped the bilge of the leaky wooden boat every forty-five minutes, navigating the gorgeous fjords myself, with Jan resting below deck. I was so grateful to understand sailing as Lucy was vomiting with seasickness for much of the trip.

"So, where are the other scouts?" I asked as Jan came up on deck. I was tired of his excuses and growing skeptical of the lame explanations.

"The others will be here soon. You'll see." Jan repeated his favorite phrase with an air of authority. As much as Jan tried to convince us the others would arrive soon, I no longer believed him.

When he went below deck to nap the next day, I grabbed his precious notebook and whispered to Lucy, "I'm going to see who these other scouts are. Don't you think it's odd that none of them have joined us yet?" I started leafing through the information sheets as we sailed through the deep blue waters of the gorgeous mountainous fjord.

"No, they're just having problems. They'll come soon. Why would you doubt what Jan says?" Lucy was still clueless and so trusting. Her private Catholic-school upbringing made her more naïve than even me.

While flipping through the pages of his notebook, my eyes widened, and I hissed to Lucy, "Every application is in the same handwriting--Jan filled out each form himself! And there are almost two hundred of them!" His critical notebook, which kept the program participants' information, was a total sham. There were no other participants! "Oh my God, Lucy, no one is coming to join us! We're alone with a total stranger!" I shivered as the old boat creaked along the silent, lonely fjord. *Who is this guy?*

"Lucy, we must get out of here, away from Jan. We can't stay!" It had already been two weeks. I pleaded with Lucy to escape the next morning when Jan went below deck to nap.

Lucy's face was taut as she crossed her arms. "We have no extra money to eat or sleep, and we don't speak Swedish. How can we leave? He has all our money, and I can't call my parents before our scheduled flights home. They'll kill me."

Despite his endless lies, I didn't see any way out until our flights home in two weeks. We were over five thousand miles from home, alone with a sexually deviant person in the middle of nowhere with no way out. He was a voyeur and tried many times to walk in on us dressing. Without resources, we protected ourselves as best we could. We surprisingly had no thought about getting help from the consulate, police, or at least the Swedish Girl Guide Council. It never crossed our minds.

When we finally flew home, my parents were there to pick me up. Driving home, I told them the basics of what had happened.

Dad changed lanes on the freeway. "Hmmm. That's odd."

"Jan wanted to see us in wet clothes." My eyes were wide, wondering what they'd say.

"Hmmm." Mom said, checking out her manicure and then looking up at me.

Despite my attempts to engage them, there asked no other questions or made any comments. I kept trying to engage them, but they seemed preoccupied and disinterested. I couldn't understand it.

It was the last my parents and I ever spoke of the strange trip, relegated to the ever-growing 'don't talk about it' trash heap. My parents' lack of reaction to Jan and Joe from the pizza parlor taught me that victimization was a normal part of life for my gender. In patriarchal societies, men did these things, and girls were targets, was the consistent message. From what I experienced, sexual assaults and threats were expected and unimportant, even by my parents, and abusers were not held accountable. They were to be hidden from view and never discussed.

Regardless of whether they believed me, they did nothing to protect other girls from this international predator. Neither my parents nor I warned my local Girl Scout Council, the Swedish police, and the few girls going after us about Jan. I was eighteen now, a high school graduate, and should have spoken up, but unfortunately, I followed my parent's lead. I'll always regret my inaction, and I'm certain Jan continued his international schemes to lure girls. I shudder to think of what could have happened to us or whether we would have ever been found.

By the end of high school, I had absorbed much of my honorable and upstanding family's pathology, like a dry sponge immersed in polluted water. I obsessed over fixing my mother and neglected my ambitions, dreams, and emotional development. I focused my energy on staying safe, packaged within the small box my family needed me to fit in. I never looked forward in my life because I had too much drama daily to cope with and analyze.

I didn't realize the extent of what was going on.

Chapter 17

Launching

There was never a question of me leaving home for a four-year college--to my parent's credit. It wasn't an "if you go" discussion but a "when you go." While most kids were dying to get away, I was scared to face the outside world and worried about leaving Tim and Debbie unprotected from Mom. But Dad insisted I go.

As my parents dropped me at the small liberal arts college dorm an hour's drive from home, tears ran down my cheeks as I waved goodbye. What was I supposed to do? I didn't know anyone. I wandered the halls and cried for days, lost and lonely. I wondered how I could have been so confident going to Europe over the summer but intimidated being an hour away from home. College felt more permanent, I guessed.

College, I quickly learned, did have several benefits. Realizing there was a men's college next to ours, things started looking better. I stopped crying and began meeting new friends. We attended parties together and had a wonderful time partying.

Another benefit was the dorm cafeteria, with full buffets at every meal. I suddenly had all I desired--I could eat whenever and whatever I wanted without rules and scrutiny from my father. Sweets were now available all day and night, and like the cookies in my closet so long ago, no one would control me around them. The freedom was intoxicating.

So, I stopped eating.

Hunger felt good. I was in total control of myself, and I basked in that power. Not eating seemed the epitome of personal power and I dropped weight quickly. It felt right to deprive myself, overpowering my hunger. Unlike home, I no longer had to eat meals I didn't want or like; I now had a choice. I could say no to dinner or lunch if I didn't want it. I got to ninety pounds on my five-foot-two frame.

It wouldn't last long.

A few weeks after college began, I had a brief but intense romance with Dave, who I met at orientation. It was my first real relationship, and we dated briefly. I was crazy about him. Soon he broke off our relationship, and I was heartbroken.

Something snapped in me. Moving away from my childhood community of friends, family, church, Scouts, and the rejection from Dave was too much. I didn't want more male attention--it was too painful, so I reversed course and started eating. Food choked out the scared, lonely feelings. Overeating was more intoxicating than starving, and I soon discovered that donuts and cookies helped me cope and focus on my studies better. I could swallow my hurt and confusion, one bite at a time.

Without any warning or real reason, I also had fleeting thoughts of suicide. They terrified me. I couldn't understand why I was feeling so poorly just by going away to college. Luckily, I knew I could reach out for help. I remembered the TV talk show about "therapy" and decided to seek professional help. I made an appointment at the college health center.

One week later, I sat in the cold, sterile waiting room, glancing at the other students. I searched their calm faces and wondered if they felt as bad as I did. I noticed a magazine cover showing happy college students, and I couldn't understand why I wasn't like them. How could I be doing so poorly just weeks after leaving home?

A gray-haired man with a crumpled shirt called me into his office. "Hi, I'm Dr. Pitt. What can I help you with today?"

I shook his hand and sat down on a ripped vinyl sofa in his cramped office. The walls of bookcases towered over his desk, piled high with messy paper charts. "I'm just miserable and have no idea why I'm feeling like this." Tears came to my eyes as I looked down at the floor tiles. "I broke up with this guy and I can't seem to get over it. I don't understand why I feel so poorly." I wiped my eyes with a tissue from the box on his desk.

Dr. Pitt ran his hands through his thin hair. He put his arm around my shoulder in a fatherly way as we walked out. For all in the waiting room to hear, he declared with a big smile, "You just have a broken heart, is all. You'll be fine."

I glared at him and stomped out of the building. How could he embarrass me in front of the whole waiting room? His minimization of my feelings left me without direction or help. I knew I wasn't okay and that it was more than a broken heart, but I had no idea what was wrong.

Though counseling didn't help me, I started to perk up with some nice friends in my dorm suite. I even joined the college chorus. But just like my high school experience, I was asked to leave soon after joining. Disappointed and embarrassed, I figured singing was not meant to be—I just wasn't good enough. But I gradually stabilized living away from home and got used to being on my own.

Carol C. Boyce

I couldn't understand why I felt scared and anxious so much of the time, picturing someone around every corner was waiting to hurt me. I imagined my fears as a gunnysack full of snakes I carried on my back. It was as though they slithered around me, scaring me with their long, split tongues, writhing at every turn. My fears taunted me from deep down in my soul and wouldn't leave me alone. I guessed they were always there because of my strange flaw, a part of my sensitive and fearful makeup that Mom insisted I had.

Ashamed, I told no one about how much I was struggling. I knew I was lucky to go away to college and I didn't want to seem ungrateful. My first serious bout of depression went unidentified and nameless.

When I went home on holidays and summers, I was greeted warmly by Mom and Dad, and their fighting and drinking seemed better, though they probably were just putting on better behavior. I was happy to see their new, grand home and visit my siblings and friends. We had warm Christmases, and in general, it wasn't as intense as when I was a child.

Nineteen-seventy-four was a tumultuous time in the US, with Richard Nixon's resignation and the official end of our involvement in the Vietnam War. After two years of the private college, Chris, my roommate, Lucy, and I, along with Chris's grey cat Tiki transferred as juniors to the University of California at Davis, near Sacramento.

After my roommates and I moved into our small apartment in a large student-housing complex, we received an invitation from the guys in a neighboring unit for a kegger party. The invite was innocent enough, and we were excited to meet new guys at the university.

I had no awareness my life was about to change drastically. Mine would take a significant pivot that night, and I was delightfully clueless. The party would forever change my life.

Lucy, Chris, and I walked into the sparse neighboring apartment, and the smell of beer and poor housekeeping permeated the room. The carpet was dark and sticky after years of wear and tear. Rob, the party host, handed Chris, Lucy, and me a beer in a red plastic cup. "Hey, glad you could come." His beer sloshed on the matted carpet as he hugged each of us. "I want you three to meet my roommate, Michael."

We smiled at each other as I looked up from my five-foot-two height to his six-foot-three muscular frame. Averting his eyes, Michael quietly stood by my side. He had on a psychedelic body shirt and had curly shoulder-length brown hair, parted in the middle. His look yelled "hippie" to me. He's probably into macrame, tie-dye, and smoking pot. Not my type at all. We talked blandly about where we were from and what subjects we were taking that semester, awkwardly sitting on the apartment's beat-up sofa. We figured out we had Organic Chemistry together and mumbled something about seeing each other in class Monday morning.

The next morning, Chris glanced sideways at me as she washed the dishes. "So, whadya think of Michael? You talked with him for quite a while last night." She lifted her eyebrows and smiled broadly.

Carol C. Boyce

"Nice, but not my type." I grabbed a dish towel to dry the pans. "He's a hippie." I yawned, tired from the late night.

Later while lounging on our lumpy sofa, Tiki meowed outside our door. Letting him in, Chris noticed a small rolled-up piece of paper on his worn red collar. "What is this? So strange." She pulled out the note, "Carol, it's for you. It's from Mike--that guy you met last night?"

"What are you talking about?" I snatched the note from her, laughing. Mike had figured out that Tiki was my roommate's cat and hoped he could sneak a message to me in this unusual way. "Carol, I'll save you a seat in Chem tomorrow. See you then, Michael."

"Who is this guy?" I grimaced as I glanced at Chris. "Hmmm--not sure what to think." I smiled at the attention.

"He's interesting, alright." Chris grinned as she grabbed her textbook to begin studying.

Michael's roommate, Rob, ran into me in the apartment's laundry room later that afternoon. He was aware of his roommate's interest and tried to sell me on him. "You know, Michael was valedictorian of his class—he's a top student and a terrific swimmer--a great friend." He switched his laundry to the dryer. I wondered if Michael had paid him to say this.

"But is he into drugs and stuff?"

"Never. Mike's a straight shooter, but he does love to drink." Rob put coins in the dryer.

"Hmmm. Well, good seeing you and thanks for the party last night. "I grabbed my laundry out of the dryer and headed upstairs.

Michael saved me a seat in our chemistry class for the rest of the year. I tended to be late to class--okay, late to life--and he always kept a seat for me in the large auditorium. As we got to know each other and after more sweet feline messages, I fell in love with him. Attractive and kind-hearted, he was a rock I could hang onto--the calm to my inward storm. He grounded me with his quiet soul and hardworking, honest nature. I felt safe with him, a trait I desperately needed. From then on, we were a couple, and I hoped I'd never feel alone again.

I was intensely physically attracted to Michael, his tall, muscular physique and warm, sweet personality. When we began having an intimate relationship, I had unusual reactions that surprisingly didn't alarm me. I needed to always have a light on in the room. I knew it was childlike but had no idea why. I also wanted to curl into a ball at times when he touched me to protect myself. I still remember him towering over me as I was lying on the bed one day, leaving me with a sickening dread in my chest. I never questioned whether these reactions were normal or why they occurred—it was my normal and all I knew. Minimizing my feelings was normal, so I just brushed them off. Despite all, we went on to have a close, intimate relationship.

In June 1976, we both graduated with Bachelor of Science degrees, and we celebrated with our parents. Mike immediately left to work on a high-paying shrimp processing barge in the Alaskan Aleutian Islands to pay back college expenses. I missed him terribly and we were lovesick all summer.

With no specific plans for my new degree, I moved back home. I wasn't sure what to do with myself. Mom welcomed me with open arms, but Dad wasn't thrilled. Within a week of arriving, he cornered me in my bedroom. Glaring at me with a clenched jaw, he said in a low, menacing voice, "This isn't your home anymore. It is mine. Get out of here…and don't tell your mother I said this."

As he turned to leave, I fought back tears. "So, I don't have a home now? I graduate college and in one week, I'm homeless?" My mouth gaped as I stared back at him. I had never felt so discarded and lost. I didn't understand why he wouldn't allow me some leeway, and I was frightened by the thought of being put on the streets. I sobbed and sobbed out the pain. He'd always told me he wouldn't give me 'a cent' after graduation, which I thought was a good idea. I appreciated all their financial support through college and knew I had to support myself now. I wasn't expecting this eviction notice so soon.

Plus, if Dad wanted me gone, why wouldn't he tell Mom, I wondered. They had plenty of room in the house and only Tim was still at home. I didn't talk back, did many chores, and never asked for money. I had some saved but not enough to live on my own in Los Angeles without a job.

I wrote his hurtful comments off as having a difficult day and began to look for a job. I couldn't accept that my loving father needed me gone.

Understanding would come much later.

Soon, I landed a chemistry position with a military contractor. I loved the working world because it was much more hands-on than school, and I gained self-confidence. To my joy, Michael returned early from his shrimp processing job, and shortly later, when we were both twenty-two, he asked me to marry him. On one knee, with an armful of red roses and a ring, I said yes. I was so thrilled to marry the love of my life and get a direction for our future.

Three months later, having forgiven Dad's earlier comments, the special day arrived. In my cathedral-length wedding dress and veil enshrouding my radiant face, I slid my arm into Dad's and saw his eyes were full of tears. Despite his earlier comments, he was having difficulty letting go of me.

After a beautiful reception, Michael and I backpacked through Europe on a Eurail pass. So excited to start our new life together, I dreamed of a loving, unencumbered future for both of us where I always felt safe.

Little did we know what was to come.

Chapter 18

Nightmares

S hortly after our honeymoon in 1977, we moved to Phoenix so that Michael could work on his master's degree in Physical Anthropology. I worked in chemistry for a major military contractor, receiving the Department of Defense's Top-Secret Security clearance, and I finished a second B.S. degree in Chemistry in the evenings. We were able to buy our first home while there and spent our free time exploring the desert, playing tennis, and buying Native American baskets and kachina dolls at authentic trading posts. We were incredibly happy just being together.

After one long day, while eating M&M's, Michael and I sat in webbed lounge chairs in our huge backyard. We'd worked hard to tame the waist-high weeds and make the newly constructed small home comfortable despite the brutal summer heat. I had sewn rust-colored drapes for the patio window and bought furniture at garage sales for the empty rooms. The house was starting to shape up.

"I'm heading to bed. I've got to work early tomorrow." I kissed Michael goodnight. He would join me shortly afterward.

Outside our bedroom window, shadows danced from the full moon of the steaming indigo night. The heat rose from the tarred road out front as the black cicadas chirped into the night. As I drifted off to sleep, I began to dream. A shadowed man dressed in black forced his way into my bedroom. His face had no features I could make out. He started to chase after me, and I couldn't get away. I knew he was going to hurt me. *Run, run.* But I couldn't elude him, so I tried to shout. I tried and tried to get the sound out, but nothing came. Finally--ahhhh, I screamed. Ahhhh.

"Wake up, wake up, honey." Michael rubbed my shoulder to wake me. "You had another nightmare. You're okay." He put his arms around me and held me tight. My body trembled as I told him about it, though he already knew the story. He'd heard it several times. I tried to wake myself fully. *You're safe now. Don't be afraid, Carol—you're safe. Michael will protect you.*

I cuddled close, still trembling. It was hard to calm myself down after the bad dream, but I now had someone to hold and calm me. I didn't feel abandoned and uncared for as I did as a scared child. I had someone who loved me and was there for me for the first time. Being married to a trustworthy, kind, and loving husband brought me great comfort though it wouldn't be long before the nightmares returned.

Michael decided to change paths from anthropology, where he researched fossilized teeth, to the more employable field of dentistry. Accepted at the University of California, San Francisco, we moved to northern California in 1980. In a beautiful eucalyptus grove, we lived in married student housing, high above the school.

Hired by a major computer company in the early days of Silicon Valley, I was soon a Senior Engineer managing a large team, overseeing circuit board production. Significant risk existed while working in these chip manufacturing environments, with huge vats of cyanides and extremely high-temperature furnaces. I enjoyed the work, however, and was good at it. It was a big responsibility for a twenty-seven-year-old, but I relished the pace and challenge. We made lifetime friends in student housing and loved exploring San Francisco.

Stemming from our love of anthropologic ruins, we saved our money and splurged on a trip to Machu Picchu in Peru, followed by an Amazon excursion to an ecolodge. We dreamed of seeing the Amazon and the Incan citadel set high in the Andes Mountains. It would be a trip of a lifetime for us.

Our departure day finally arrived, and we sat on padded green chairs in the bustling San Francisco airport. Relieved to be checked in for the long flight to Lima, Michael and I settled in for a two-hour wait.

As we calmly read our guidebooks, out of nowhere, I felt my heart pounding and my face flushing. I couldn't contain the panic I felt. I'd always loved to fly and had taken many plane trips with no fear whatsoever. *What was going on?* Not wanting Michael to see how freaked out I was, I put my guidebook down and said, "Honey, I'm going to walk a little."

Michael nodded and kept reading, oblivious to what was going through my mind.

I struggled to catch my breath as my mind exploded with fear. *The plane will crash, drop from the sky, nose down, and I won't be able to get out. I'll be locked in--trapped behind a bolted door. I'm going to have a heart attack right here in the terminal. I can't board this plane--I'll lose my mind. Maybe there are ships from San Francisco to Lima--I could catch up with Mike in a week or two, but we'd be home by then.*

I couldn't disappoint Michael and tell him I was too terrified to get on the plane—he wouldn't even consider not going. We'd never get the money or time back. He'd think I was crazy, but my panic continued.

Michael was seated in the waiting area, calmly reading, and I said, "I'm scared to get on this plane, and I don't know why." I tried to minimize my terror.

He raised one eyebrow. "You love to fly. What's goin' on?"

"I don't know. I feel panicky, though. This fear just came over me—out of nowhere." I scrunched my eyebrows tightly.

"You'll be OK. Flying is completely safe. Look how big this plane is." He furrowed his forehead. "How about a drink? Maybe that'll calm you down."

I knew no drink or medication would touch my extreme nerves. I was miserable waiting and forced myself to get in line to board when they called us. It was like a nightmare and at the plane's threshold, I froze. The flight attendant smiled and welcomed me. Seeing I wasn't boarding, she put out her hand and unceremoniously pulled me onto the plane, angry I was holding up the line.

As I staggered to my seat, I noticed everything as though it were my first flight. Older and well-used, the massive aircraft seemed dirtier than usual, the flight attendants' appearances less than polished and pristine. The stale smell showed the plane needed a thorough cleaning.

My mind went wild. Maintenance was clearly not the priority. *If the maintenance staff can't even take care of the inside of the plane, how bad are the engines? Why are the stewards and other passengers so calm? Don't they know this plane could drop out of the sky at any moment?*

I stayed on the plane and gripped Michael's right arm as if my life depended on it. It was the start of endless terror with any flight I took, and it had come on in an instant. I went from loving to fly to terrified, suddenly and without warning.

But I wouldn't let my fears end our love of exotic travel. I couldn't do that to Mike and flying became unavoidable. Calming me down was impossible, and though patient, Michael couldn't understand this new terror, nor could I. We silently reasoned it was another one of the many fears we'd have to live with.

Chapter 19

Tell Me More

With my nightmares, strange fears, and general anxiety growing, I made a list of therapists in the area that might help me. Though my college experience with therapy wasn't productive, I prayed someone would be able to help me. Therapy was my only hope.

Arriving at a new therapist's office, I looked around and entered Dr. Hammond's office. The room was wood-paneled, and I loved the pink tiger lilies in a shiny black vase on the desk. With the doctor's back to me, I grabbed some of the wrapped chocolate mints he had in a bowl and shoved them into my purse for later enjoyment. I sat down on the stiff couch, a bit uneasy.

"Nice to meet you." Dr. Hammond smiled at me as we settled in, and he took down my history. I noticed a window open above his head and felt a chill. "Okay. When you called, you said you were struggling with fears. What do they look like?" He sat forward in his chair.

"I have weird fears and I don't know why. It just feels like something's wrong with me." I explained in more detail about the planes and nightmare experiences. Papers fluttered on his desk from a gust of wind.

"Okay. Tell me more about your childhood?" He smiled at me, looking intently into my eyes.

I squirmed. "I had a good childhood--full of enriching activities, focused on my education--good friends and neighbors." I rubbed my cheeks, not thinking of anything else that might be pertinent. "I... uh...had a lot more than most kids." I smiled feebly as a garbage truck rumbled outside.

"What about your parents? Tell me about your father?"

"Dad— well, he was a nice and decent father. He was always there for dinner and family events. Nothing was out of the ordinary, except he was an internist and heart specialist. People raved about how wonderful he was." I looked down, squeezing my hands together awkwardly.

"Hmm. How about your mother? What was she like?" He scribbled some notes on his coffee-stained yellow pad.

"She was good. Mom made sure we had three meals a day and she always had the house neat and clean. She got us to our activities, which was a lot of work. She took us to see lots of theater--Sound of Music, West Side Story, and My Fair Lady, which I loved. She was great but drank too much. I wished she didn't drink..." I smiled weakly and sipped my coffee. I didn't understand why he was asking about my childhood. His probing questions made me feel vulnerable. My parents had nothing to do with my depression.

"Well, I'm glad they were good parents, not perfect but decent. At least your fears aren't related to them. I noticed you got married not too long ago. Are you sure you want to be in this marriage?" Dr. Hammond looked me squarely in the eye.

A flicker of irritation came over me. *Why would he think it was my marriage?* "Yes, I love Michael. We're very happy together."

We talked a bit longer and I left the session, once again, with anger bubbling up inside. I knew there was no connection between my childhood and my fears. I was lucky to have grown up in an affluent, privileged home. Dr. Hammond clearly wasn't getting anywhere with me.

When I got home, I took out the list I'd made of potential therapists and crossed Dr. Hammond's name off, decisively, with a sharp pencil. Though he was pleasant and professional, I wouldn't go back--he had no idea what was causing my fears. My second foray into therapy proved expensive and unsuccessful, but I still knew it was my only hope.

I minimized my family background in those early sessions. I knew many children had much worse situations than me, so I felt guilty saying anything disparaging about my parents. I had so much enrichment as a child—I felt silly complaining. I was the lucky one.

Having learned not to trust my feelings or emotions, I'd discounted the pain I felt throughout my childhood. No one else acknowledged or talked about what I saw growing up, so my observations must have been wrong. My life followed an orderly path with college, marriage, a house, and an excellent job, just as I'd hoped. How would anyone believe something was wrong with my past? Childhood must have been much better than my feelings told me.

My relationship with food had been out of control since the day I left for college though I wasn't too aware of it. Coping with my anxiety, I would regularly binge eat cookie dough. At that time, I had no idea why I did it. I knew it was wrong but couldn't help myself—no big deal. But since getting married, I had gained thirty pounds and was embarrassed about it. Michael also shared my desire for sweets but exercised vigorously every day, never gaining weight on his tall frame.

I thought I hid my excess eating from everyone, though anyone looking at me would know I had a problem. Dad wanted to admonish me for the increased weight when I visited home, a huge concern for my heart-obsessed father, but Mom would hush him up. She had always battled weight and didn't want him to hurt my feelings.

Chapter 20

One Beginning, One Ending

G rowing up, Mom had told me many times, "I'll never take care of your children. I've done my time--I don't want to care for anyone else's kids. Don't think I'm going to babysit for you--don't even ask me."

"Ok, Mom. I won't ask you to--I get it." I thought it sad that she didn't want to sit for her grandchildren, but it was not surprising. She had never been nurturing and was overwhelmed raising her own kids. Why would she want to help with mine?

After being married for six years, our first child, Andrew, was born and seemed to soften Mom's stance. We were beyond thrilled, and after I delivered, my elated parents flew up to meet him.

The fog enveloped our student housing apartment building on a high San Francisco hill. The cool air felt refreshing as the tall eucalyptus trees rustled in the light wind. Inside the warm apartment, Mom stood over the white bassinet. With Andrew cooing, I carefully put him in his grandmother's arms for the first time. I'd never seen her so happy. "He's just precious. What a beautiful baby! I could hold him forever." She couldn't stop studying him. "To think I'm finally a grandmother!" She enveloped him with great love and care, warming my heart.

Dad held Andrew stiffly when I handed him his first grand-child. "He's a beautiful baby--looks healthy enough." He handed him back to me quickly. He flew home the following day, but Mom stayed with me longer. It was the first time I'd ever seen her stay anywhere away from Dad.

"Let me feed him, and I'd love to bathe him." She helped diaper him, trying to learn disposable diapers and how to warm his bottles in a new invention, the microwave oven. "Things have changed a little, I guess." I couldn't get her to put Andrew down except when I nursed him. Mom rocked Andrew to sleep, nuzzling his tiny head under hers.

While learning how to take care of a newborn, we enjoyed a precious, happy time together. Mom didn't drink much, something I hadn't seen in a long while. My whole face lit up, thinking of the years ahead, hoping we'd feel closer as I watched her love grow for my son. She was mellowing, and a baby might be just what our relationship needed. I hoped for a new beginning.

A few days after Mom got home, she called me. As I held one-week-old Andrew in one arm and the corded phone in the other, I could hear a catch in her throat. "I have breast can-cer...metastatic...stage four, they think." Left speechless, a silence screamed through the phone.

I gasped as my mouth dropped open--I couldn't catch my breath. I remembered that my mom's mother, the grandmother I never knew, had died from breast cancer at age fifty-nine. Mom was fifty-nine. How could this be? It was too strange.

I broke the silence. "Oh, Mom. I'm so sorry--so, so sorry to hear this." The diagnosis couldn't have been worse. In 1983, treatments weren't particularly effective and little hope existed for her recovery.

"There are some new drugs that they'll give me...I'll, I'll be...okay. Don't you worry. Just focus on Andrew and being a new mother."

"Right, right. Thanks for letting me know. I'm sending you a big hug. I'm always here if you want to talk." I put the phone on the cradle and wept into Andrew's blanketed body.

A few months after Andrew was born in 1984, Mike graduated dental school and we moved to Sacramento. I left my engineering position in Silicon Valley to care full-time for our baby. As thirty-year-olds, it should have been a happy time in our lives, but as Mom's cancer progressed, my life became consumed with visiting and caring for her. I took over twenty trips to L.A. with Andrew, her greatest joy. Beaming, I'd watch her play with him, a Mom I'd never seen before.

The incredible majesty of life and death is beyond our control and never follows our timing. As a unique and precious new life entered our lives, another was leaving forever. The paradox, the Ying and yang of the opposing situations, was my first realization of how precious and unpredictable my life could be. I had to accept life on its terms, not mine.

Andrew brought us tremendous joy, but Mom's brutal diagnosis devastated the family. She was too young to die. I'd had renewed hope my mother would become a wonderful grandmother to my kids and we would improve our relationship, but by Andrew's first birthday, Mom only had weeks to live. Debbie was newly pregnant, as was Mark's partner, and she'd never get to meet these and her other soon to arrive grandchildren. The tragedy was incomprehensible and left my siblings and me stunned and reeling in pain.

On one trip home, Dad and I attended services at our family church. I felt a little space to grieve with Andrew at the nursery. While sitting in the back with Dad, tears streamed down my face, thinking of Mom's imminent death. She was on her last days and in the hospital.

Dad hissed in my ear. "What is wrong with you? Why are you taking this so hard?"

Brokenhearted, I tried to stop crying but couldn't. I wiped away my tears.

Dad muttered, "Knock it off. You're overreacting again. Church is all a bunch of crap anyway."

My face dropped with his cold, compassionless reaction. I felt alone in my despair. It was *his* wife of thirty-five years who was dying. I couldn't understand why he wasn't grieving or allowing it in me.

I soon found out why. Dad had begun dating Betty and Sally, long-time single friends of Mom. Apparently, these 'friends' were excited that an affluent physician would soon burst onto the singles scene without regard to his family. Only she was still alive. As my mother fought for her life in the hospital, he started dating and looking for new love. Despite their marital problems, Mom and Dad were still married. How could he disrespect her and our family so much? I didn't know this man anymore

That night, when he casually arrived home after a date, I waited in the kitchen, ready to pounce. Crossing my arms, flames shot out my ears. "What are you doing? Mom is dying. Your children are grieving...and you're dating? Are you kidding me?" I wanted to knock him over the head with the greasy frying pan I held. "Your family needs you. Mom needs you now—she's dying, Dad."

In a low, deep voice with empty eyes, Dad answered, "Stay out of my life."

I walked the long hall to her hospital room the following week, carrying Andrew in a front pack. Mom had suffered several small strokes related to her cancer and had been very confused the last few weeks. As I walked the hall, I could hear her yelling for all to hear. I wondered who she was mad at now in her confused state. Listening carefully, I could hear she was angry again at Dad, though he was nowhere near her. She berated him mercilessly, so all of Dad's colleagues could hear. The family façade was crumbling before my very eyes. I tried to look away as I crept past the nurses' station. I couldn't imagine Dad's humiliation at having his personal problems displayed, and I shared in the embarrassment.

In her sterile, antiseptic room, I sat beside Mom's head and stroked her thin, silver hair. Her eyes glowed as she calmed and

Carol C. Boyce

stopped yelling, coming to life seeing Andrew. Despite all the tubing, I put the spirited toddler on her bed as she asked me to. As I gave her a sip of water, she beamed at her oblivious, bouncing grandson. With her hazel eyes, his tow-headed exuberance brought her immense joy, if only briefly.

Despite the pain in the past, I found the troubled times melting away and unimportant. I thought about what our last words should be, and the ones we'd never spoken became clear.

I leaned over the cold, metal bed railing and looked into her pale green eyes. Misty-eyed, I whispered the words that were so difficult to say aloud. "I love you, Mom."

She gently squeezed my hand and gave me a weak smile. "I love you, too." I wondered how it could have been so hard to say those critical words for our thirty years together. Hearing Mom's love for me for the first and last time, though the ministrokes left her a shadow of herself, touched me deeply. I desperately needed to hear it at least once in my life from the woman who brought me into it.

Tears streamed down my face, knowing our time together on this earth was over. This complex woman who'd had so much influence and control over my life was leaving this earth forever. I couldn't begin to understand her life, our relationship, and the massive loss I would soon be experiencing.

As I slowly walked out, I hugged Andrew tightly to my chest. I looked back and stared in silence at my mother's now peaceful and frail body, realizing it had no power over me anymore.

She died the following morning.

Chapter 21

Get Out of My Life

Two weeks after Mom's death, following a memorial service attended by hundreds, Andrew and I returned from Sacramento to Dad's house. Still in shock and grieving, I wanted to help and support him through our profound loss. Surely, he had come to his senses and was grieving also. I needed help and hoped the family would rally around each other.

Arriving in the morning, I relished the beautiful oak trees on the property and the wooded community. It was a beautiful sunny day, and I could hear the nearby horses whinnying. Seeing the beautifully decorated home, I thought about how Mom's touches remained.

I put our bags in the upstairs bedroom and arranged Andrew's things. When I headed down the ornate staircase, I took solace in the constancy of the house. I was hopeful for a quiet time with Dad after the busyness of the memorial service and the scattering of her ashes at sea. The friends and family had all left and we could have a peaceful visit.

I was clueless.

In the morning, while I held Andrew at the base of the stairs, Dad walked over to us casually, wearing a new open-throated shirt and flaunting a heavy gold chain. "I'll be with Brianna and her daughter all day. See you later." He grabbed his keys and headed out the door.

Do you mean your new girlfriend is Mom's hairdresser and good friend of thirty years? How long has this been going on? Dumbfounded, tears rolled down my cheeks. With Mom barely gone and a new grandson to play with, Dad had no interest in seeing us. The family I relied on for support had evaporated.

I sat stunned in the empty, quiet house all day, not understanding his actions. The family had meant everything to me, and Dad had always seemed to feel the same until recently. Where was my old father?

I walked around the quiet house and noticed other changes he had made. Within two weeks of Mom's passing, he had elevated their king-size bed with three carpeted stairs and had a huge mirror installed on the ceiling above it. His sexual agenda seemed clear, and I didn't want to accept any of it.

Hacking on onions for dinner with a sharp knife, I stared out the kitchen window, remembering happy times on the big wooden swing in the large backyard. The azaleas and camellias Mom had planted reminded me of her. I had hoped in future years, my kids would play there and visit the neighing horses in the neighboring stables, but it wasn't looking for that way anymore.

I continued making dinner, hoping to share it with Dad before Andrew and I drove home the following morning. Soon, I heard his car pull into the garage after his day-long date. As he walked into the kitchen where I had Andrew in a highchair, I tried to sound casual. "I'm making dinner for us. Andrew's already eaten." Despite my hurt and anger, I hoped to spend time with him that evening and redeem something positive from my trip.

He looked at me with a cold emptiness in his eyes. "I'm not your father anymore. Just get lost." He set his wallet and keys on the granite kitchen counter. "Get out of my life. You're not my daughter anymore." Without a second glance, he stomped upstairs.

All the air left my lungs as I sat in shock. I wondered if I had heard Dad correctly. He didn't want to be my father anymore! He didn't want me, his oldest daughter--his only grandchild and son-in-law, too? How could that be? This man wasn't the father I'd known for thirty years though I had to admit he'd been behaving strangely recently. I wondered what could be going through his head and what the hell was going on. He was throwing away my family and me like a sack of rancid garbage, never wanting to be seen by him again.

I got Andrew ready for bed and then laid down on the bed. Stunned, I realized I had lost both of my parents in two weeks. I couldn't stop crying. What wasn't I getting here? He didn't reject my siblings like this. He never told any of them to get out of his life. Why did he want just me gone and not the others?

I packed in the morning, numb, just going through the motions. I couldn't wait to get home.

Arriving in Sacramento, Michael could see something was terribly wrong. With a crumpled Kleenex in my hand, I picked at my dinner. "Dad doesn't want me anymore. He told me he wasn't my father anymore." The tears flowed down my cheeks.

"What are you talking about?" His eyes knitted together.

"Yep." I wiped my eyes. "He doesn't want me, Andrew, you—any of us--in his life anymore. He said I was...no longer his daughter." My shoulders heaved as I sobbed out my grief, covering my eyes.

"I can't believe it. That doesn't make any sense. So odd—he's a completely different person than who I used to know." Michael got up and hugged me. "He wants to miss his only grandchild's growing up and be out of all our lives? He's been a family man his whole life--he never even missed a dinner."

"That's what he said." I blew my nose.

"And after you just lost your mom." His voice trailed off. "I can't imagine what is going on with him, but we'll be okay, honey. He'll come to his senses soon."

"I don't think so. Dad meant what he said. How could he just throw me away?"

"That must hurt so bad."

I cried for weeks, clueless about the cause of Dad's cruel words. The loss of both parents overwhelmed me. Compounded by the confusion and fears I had already wrestled with before Mom's death, I didn't know how to handle my profound grief. Chaos grew in my mind.

Dad and I had no contact for the next two years. I never called him to talk about it—there was nothing to say. He never apologized or made excuses for his behavior. He was okay with it, while I was devastated by the loss. I had clung long and hard to my image of a loving, gentle dad because of my intense need for a "good" parent. I had fought my denial for way too long. I finally had to be hit with a two-by-four to accept the truth, and it hurt.

The reason Dad so desperately needed me out of his life would become clear soon. It wouldn't be long now.

In 1984 after Mom's passing, I was a new mother in Sacramento without any friends or family support. Luckily, I had Michael, but he focused on starting his career and I didn't want to burden him with my endless emotional problems. My fears and anxiety worsened, and grief pulled me into an interminable quicksand.

Dad remained unrecognizable and my siblings had all seemed to move on with their lives. Nothing made sense: not my chronic fears, not my father's rejection, not Mom's death. The older I got, the more I began to look backward. I knew something just wasn't right with my past, though I had no idea what it was.

Life went on and by the second year after Mom's death, our family was blossoming. Andrew was a rambunctious, curious toddler and I loved being home with him. Pregnant again, I started making new friends with other mothers and their children in our new city. Mike's career was going well, and we enjoyed life in Sacramento, close to the Sierra Mountains, Mike's family, and San Francisco.

I changed my career focus from technology and electronics to management, completing a Master's in Business Administration. Finance was a good fit for me, as I loved business and economics. Numbers made sense and were definitive—no gray area.

There was only one correct answer, and I loved the simplicity. After graduation, I started teaching finance part-time at a local university, focused on the enormous gifts I had in my life, and tried to move on.

In 1985, Mike and I had been married for eight years when I made an appointment with another therapist on my list. Dr. Fuller was an eating disorder specialist who worked with anorexics, bulimics, and compulsive overeaters. Since I couldn't stop eating, I thought he might know the cause.

He greeted me with a confident, strong hand. He looked like he worked out a lot in his slim-fitting suit as he sat in his oversized vinyl chair. The coffee table overflowed with worn-out magazines and the bright windows let in lots of light. I told him about my constant eating and fears.

Dr. Fuller confidently straightened up in his chair. "You have unusual fears, which is common with eating disorders. All we must do now is get rid of your fears and you won't have this eating problem anymore." He was almost arrogant.

"Really?" I took in a sharp breath as my eyes widened. It was the first I'd ever heard of a correlation between eating disorders and fears. It shocked me. I wondered why no one else seemed to make this connection. Embarrassment and shame were all I knew about overeating. It was a character flaw in most people's minds, including mine, and came from a lack of willpower and control. But I had to admit, I had a full plate of both issues.

"Tell me a fear you're struggling with."

"Okay, well, uh, I'm afraid I could be dropped in a city where I don't know anyone." I shocked myself, blurting out something I'd never spoken of before.

Dr. Fuller smiled broadly, happy to have such an easy example to fix. "Good, good. That's a great fear to evaluate. Obviously, it's not true. Why would someone drop you in a city?" He seemed amused. "Do you see how this is a silly, false fear?"

"Well, it feels very real... but yeah, I guess it's silly." After being vulnerable with him, I winced at this minimization, but I played along.

"You know, though, it's not true." He was sure he had "fixed" this one. "See how quick and easy that was?" He continued with more quick responses to other fears I suffered.

He's obnoxious and condescending. Does he really think that was helpful? "Gee, thanks." I rubbed my forehead and begrudgingly wrote another check for useless therapy as I left.

"And be sure to buy my book." He waved a copy at me as I walked out the door.

I cringed as I left. Selling the doctor's book during a therapy appointment seemed unprofessional. I made a batch of cookie dough at home to stuff my anger and frustration.

Connecting excess fears with eating disorders was unheard of back then and Dr. Fuller was, in fact, way ahead of his time. However, something significant was missing in his approach, like *why* I had so many anxieties in the first place and that it was much more difficult to get rid of them than just telling me they were silly.

Frustrated, I crossed this therapist off my list and began to believe no one could help me. As my therapy bills mounted, I was nowhere closer to getting desperately needed guidance.

Our daughter, Carrie, arrived in 1986 to our immense joy, completing our family. She was a joy, and we loved her dearly. When I first brought her home, I cradled her in my arms with Andrew next to me, recalling my vow from long ago. With a firm jaw, I whispered to them both. "You two will never feel what I did growing up. I will love you and keep you safe with every breath in my body." She and her brother would live in a happy, emotionally healthy environment if it were the last thing I ever did. Andrew looked up blankly and continued to poke at his new, exhausted sister, oblivious to the meaning of my words in his life.

From the beginning, I devoted my entire being to setting up an emotionally healthy, secure, and safe environment for my kids. I read every parenting book I could find, participated in their education, and learned everything about healthy family environments. Though far from perfect, I wouldn't allow my painful childhood to bleed into their lives. They would always know they were cherished and never experience the feelings I did.

I never questioned why I felt so strongly about this. Many kids grew up in alcoholic homes and had other painful things happen. Why I felt so incredibly passionate about my children's upbringing never crossed my mind.

I wasn't facing the truth.

Chapter 22

My Endangered Children

By 1988, four years had passed since Mom's death. Both thirty-four, Michael and I had relegated Dad's hurtful words to misdirected grief and momentary insanity. I never shared my other significant emotional struggles with Dad- he had nothing to do with my fears. My relationship with him started to mend, though it remained fragile and tenuous. I still desperately hoped to have a parent, a rock, to ground me. I had these two beautiful grandchildren that I wished he could know, and they could get to know their "good" grandfather.

My neediness and false hopes blinded me once again.

Since the late fifties, my cousins, aunts, and uncles on my father's side enjoyed an annual camping reunion. With many of us living long distances apart, about thirty of us camped at a California State Park every year.

Arriving at Calaveras State Park for this year's gathering, I opened the van door as the warm, pine-shaded campsite enveloped me with the intoxicating smell of fresh evergreens. The cinnamon-colored dirt complimented the green trees as if in a beautiful painting. Andrew, a busy five-year-old, and Carrie, now two,

After the three-hour drive, the kids couldn't wait to get out of their car seats. Jumping out of the minivan, they ran to hug Granddad, who was talking nearby with his older brother, Allen.

Dad kissed us all hello, as did my uncle, the revered patriarchs of the family. "We'll take Andrew and Carrie to my campsite so you can get your site set up. Sound good?" Dad offered.

It was nice to have Dad and Uncle Allen help me since Michael wouldn't arrive until the weekend, still seeing patients in Sacramento. "Sure, Dad. That would be helpful."

He put Carrie on his shoulders, and Uncle Allen held Andrew's hand as they headed to Dad's secluded campsite. I got the tent up, secured our food in the bear box, and positioned the old Coleman stove over the plastic-covered table. I laid out the well-used sleeping bags and everyone's pajamas to make bedtime go smoothly.

Walking over to his campsite, I could see Dad was bouncing Andrew on his knee, singing, "I'm bringing home a baby bumblebee," to gales of laughter. Carrie jumped with glee.

"Thanks for taking the kids—it was a tremendous help."

After lunch, we went gold panning, and the kids had a fun time with their grandfather. I quietly told him, "It's nice to see you with the kids. They need to know you." The week was going well, and I was glad to see he was finally interested in his grandchildren.

Having fun together, I was hopeful my estrangement from my father might finally be repaired. Andrew and Carrie were getting to know him, and the father I used to know seemed to be returning. I smiled, leaning back into our hammock, and watched the kids play nearby. *Maybe, I still have a parent.*

Little did I know that my neediness had endangered my own children.

Chapter 23

Caving In

everal months later, with our dusty tent pitched again and everyone's sleeping bags unrolled, we camped at Lake Shasta, several hours north of Sacramento. The hot, quiet campground near the vast blue lake was great for boating, swimming, and general family fun. We put the stove and lantern on our table in the scrub and pine-covered campground, looking forward to the big sky evening. We'd sing folksongs as I played my guitar, and the kids would roast marshmallows around the evening's campfire.

Lake Shasta Caverns, a popular tourist attraction, was near our campsite. Michael and I were excited to show the kids this natural wonder. I had loved cave spelunking at summer Girl Scout camps and wanted to show the kids the marvelous stalagmites and coloration of these large caverns. The cool air would feel good on this hot afternoon.

After paying for the tour and holding hands, we walked up the dry, dusty path toward the darkened entrance without a second thought. Walking casually, I smiled at the kids knowing they'd have fun with this adventure. The young guide had us move into the cave when the tour started. I gathered the kids around me so they wouldn't be frightened by the dark. We huddled together as she shut the metal gate behind us with a loud metallic clang. The sound reverberated through the inky blackness.

Like turning on a light switch, my heart raced with blind terror. Total panic engulfed me, and my thoughts were in disarray. I'm locked in... I can't get out...Darkness, darkness, I must get out of here...now! I pushed through the group with my heart pounding and quietly pleaded with the tour guide to show me the exit. Mike looked at me with questioning eyes. She pointed to the door marked "Last Exit," and I sprinted for the daylight, leaving my confused family behind.

I found a deserted area next to the back exit in the fresh air outside. I threw myself down on the lonely hillside and wept out incredible pain and terror. I couldn't stop sobbing, though I had no idea why. There seemed to be no bottom to my unknown profound grief. It was like a balloon I didn't know existed had burst for the first time, flooding me with anguish.

What's happening to me? A cave? I used to love climbing through them. What is this sudden change in me? I cried so hard my eyes were almost swollen shut. I could hardly see when everyone finally exited the tour after an hour. Keeping my sunglasses on, I hoped no one realized my extreme reaction to a simple cave tour.

The kids were confused when they exited. "Why did you leave Mommy? It was cool with bats and everything." Andrew's bright hazel eyes looked up at me with concern. "I thought you said you liked caves."

I hugged him and picked up Carrie. "I do like caves, but something made me very sad, and I needed to cry. I'm so sorry I missed it, but I feel better now. Tell me all about it, please. I can't wait to hear about the bats you saw."

It was another strange, sudden fear to add to my growing list of unexplained reactions. Michael saw my swollen eyes and knew something was terribly wrong. This fear was a brand-new terror that came out of nowhere, and we were both worried.

Several months after the cave incident, I decided to have a day in San Francisco with a friend. We'd do some shopping early at Union Square and see Phantom of the Opera in the afternoon. I couldn't wait to catch up with my girlfriend and have some adult conversation. Kissing the kids goodbye, I headed out to drive to San Francisco, a two-hour trip I'd done many times. Michael would play and take care of the kids for the day.

It was a bright, sunny day and I was happy to have a few hours to myself. I welcomed the time alone to sort through my thoughts. I drove over the bridge crossing the fast-moving American River near our home and thought how lucky I was to live in such a beautiful area. I merged onto the freeway and put on my favorite news station, heading west in the fast lane.

My heart suddenly felt like it would explode in my chest. My skin flushed hot and my hands trembled. The pounding in my chest was terrifying as I clutched the wheel and tried to slow down and exit the freeway. Somehow, I got off and pulled into a gas station, trying to calm down and catch my breath.

I didn't know what had just happened. I'd managed this drive many times alone and never had anything like this happen. I drove back home on side streets, shaken, abandoning my trip.

The panic attack scared me to my core with its intensity and sudden onset. My severe reactions increased and took a significant toll on my life without any clear cause.

Over the following months, more panic spilled into my life. I didn't know what was wrong and worried that I'd eventually be unable to cope. I continued crying uncontrollably with deep grief, many times for unknown and unidentified causes. I wondered if I'd be able to take care of my children if I continued to worsen. Racking my brain, I tried to figure out what was happening to no avail, but something was terribly wrong. I was a healthy, active, and young mother of two who should be thriving, not incapacitated by unpredictable reactions to routine situations.

Petrified, I knew no way out.

In my mid-thirties, I finally lost my mind.

It was a lazy summer day with Andrew and Carrie, now six and three, happily coloring in our ranch-style, suburban home. I had a few lovely moments of rare quiet and ventured into our attached garage. We could fit two cars in our double garage, though the stuffed overhead storage bin hung overloaded above. It was stifling hot and smelled of Andrew's Cub Scout painting project.

I yawned as I walked into the garage, still in my bathrobe and slippers, holding newspapers for the recycling bin. Suddenly, I realized someone was in the garage. In the dark shadows...a

Carol C.Boyce

man... a man was there, glaring at me. Dressed in all black, I couldn't make out features on his greyed face, but he was evil—I could feel it. He was there to hurt me, just waiting for the right moment, and I was alone with my kids! Ashen, trembling, I froze and dropped the papers.

I came to my senses and backed out of the garage, slamming the door behind me. Breathing heavily, I tried to act calm and not alarm the kids. Luckily, they didn't notice anything. I opened the garage door again when I caught my breath, garnering my courage, but the man was gone. Was I seeing things?

I shuffled into our indoor laundry room with an armload of dirty clothes the following day. It was dark in the utility room--I hadn't yet flipped on the light switch. The same faceless man was staring at me in the dim room. I threw the laundry down, terrified by this strange vision. *I'm losing my sanity. Why am I suddenly seeing this terrifying man? What the hell is happening?*

I warned myself not to tell anyone about this, or they'd know I was crazy. Even telling Michael wasn't smart—he didn't need a mentally ill mother for his children. It would be my secret. I knew I had lost my grip on reality. I was sure I was crazy, and I couldn't let anyone know. The consequences would be too great.

The man in black haunted me as the weeks went on, descending me into my own kind of madness. He showed up in the quiet, dark moments and always without a discernible face and covered in black clothing. As quickly as he appeared, he was gone. He became my dark, shameful secret, reminding me that someone was always waiting to hurt me, and I was never safe.

Chapter 24

Please Help Me

Later that fall, the kids and I walked to our neighbor's house on a chilly, rainy day. They tried to avoid the sidewalk cracks as they hopped and jumped in their rain boots and coats. The kids darted in to see their friends when we arrived.

Desperate for someone to understand my psychological problems, I got my nerve up and reached out to my neighbor. She had a degree in psychology, and I thought she might be able to point me towards help. Sue and I watched my two and her three young children play Ninja Turtles in her family room. We chatted about the weather and how the kids were changing.

With trepidation, I began. "Sue, could I share something with you?"

"Sure." Her eyes widened in anticipation. "What is it?"

"I've been having horrible fear and panic attacks. They're getting worse." I told her about driving to San Francisco, my cave experience, and my fear of flying. "I'm at the end of my rope and don't know what to do. I feel like I'm losing my mind."

"Hmmm, that's strange. You don't feel stable?" She crossed her arms over her chest.

"What do you think is happening? I don't know what to do."
I pleaded with my eyes as she looked away.

She looked at me suspiciously. "I have no idea." A few
minutes later, standing up, Sue protectively grabbed her children.
"It's time for naps for my kids. Time to go home." Her face looked
frightened as if to say, "Get away from my children!". Sue quickly
showed me the door and we walked home in the rain.

Sue never contacted me again, apparently thinking I was too
unstable and scary to be around. It had been a mistake to be open
and vulnerable. I never felt so lost and lonely.

Michael and I had a glass of chardonnay on our covered
porch several months after my experience with our neighbor. The
breeze off the nearby delta cooled down the sultry skies. "You
know, it was so fun to see the kids swimming this afternoon."
They gleefully played killer whales, Shamoo, and Shamee, with
Mike, a favorite game. I smiled, remembering.

"They loved performing 'tricks' for the 'crowd,' didn't they?
It's great, but, boy, they're growing up so fast." Michael grinned,
slowly sipping his wine. We sat in silence for a while.

Looking down at my hands, I scrunched my face. I decided
to open up. "Honey, I still don't know what's wrong with me. It's
like I have a deep, dark gash from an unknown dagger." I stared
in space. "Not a single therapist knows what's wrong." Michael
knew about my strange fears, but I had told no one about the man
who haunted me. "I don't know what else I can do." I covered my
moist face with my hands.

Michael slapped a mosquito on his leg, then turned and looked intently at me. "I'm scared, too. I don't get any of this either. But I'm always here for you. You know that. No matter what." I put my head on his shoulder. The support felt so good. "Try again. Someone's gotta be able to help. Don't give up."

I looked into his eyes with a lump in my throat. I couldn't believe he still loved me with all my problems. I wondered how he could think I was worth the trouble.

I sat in the busy HMO lobby two weeks later, waiting to hear my name. I felt like a number at the clinic with cold white walls and gray plastic chairs. I could smell burnt coffee from the dirty pot in the corner. I grabbed a cup, anyway, needing the caffeine's strength and support. With music playing in the background, I wondered if these other people in the waiting room felt as desperate and crazy as I.

"Carol? Please follow me." The friendly assistant smiled and opened a door.

I surveyed the room as I sat down on the faux leather sofa, brushing crumbs off the small chair. It had obnoxious 'uplifting' sayings on the walls for which I was in no mood.

"I'm Martha. So, tell me, what is on your mind? How can I help you?" The tall, older woman smiled at me.

I studied her as I straightened my jacket. With her blonde hair and blue silk jacket, she seemed nice enough. I knew by now, though, nice wouldn't help. I was desperate for someone to diagnose what was wrong. My fears screamed at me. What if no one could help me? What if there was nothing behind this pain and I was simply crazy?

Scratching my nose, I sat up and began my story again. "I had a good childhood with lots of enrichment. My mother was always drinking, however, and Mom and Dad fought constantly." My eyes started to burn as I thought about the drama unfolding every night. I was admitting to more of my childhood pain. "I have nightmares and I'm unusually fearful."

"Interesting. Tell me more about your fears," Martha probed.

My vulnerability surprised even me. I started talking about my recurrent fear. "I'm afraid I'll be left somewhere, dropped off. I'd have no parents in a strange city and I'd be unable to take care of myself." I wanted to crawl into my skin at the thought, but I was relieved to release more of my feelings.

"What do you mean you'll be left somewhere?" She wrinkled her face with confusion.

"In a big city like San Francisco. There'd be no one to help me." I looked down and rubbed my hands together.

"You mean like you're going to the moon or something? That sounds nuts." She smiled as if she'd break into a laugh. "That's really crazy sounding? It's ridiculous. You're grown-up--how could anyone drop you off somewhere." She chuckled as she wrote notes on her yellow pad. I guess she'd never heard of this before.

I straightened up, at once regretting being vulnerable with her. I thought I could trust her, but instead, she judged me. My biggest fear was going crazy, and she was rubber-stamping me with the dreaded label. It was the last thing I needed to hear in my unstable condition.

When the hour was over, I stood up and left. I couldn't believe how lousy a therapist she was. I crossed another therapist off my list.

I grabbed a package of Oreos and stared into space sitting in the kitchen. I realized I had bigger problems to face. My weight kept rising. As I sat in the kitchen looking at my pile of Weight Watcher booklets sitting on my desk, I realized I could be awarded a ribbon for the most starts with no finishes as I'd eventually gain more than I lost every time. My attempts at Jenny Craig, Nutrisystem, Slim-Fast, South Beach, the grapefruit diet, and the keto diet ended similarly. I couldn't keep to the prescribed regimens or understand why I always failed.

I had eaten my way through most of the pain and confusion I was experiencing. I'd gained lots of weight over the years, eating sweets over every worry, and I couldn't stop. I became morbidly obese, adding one hundred pounds to my once thin, five-foot-two frame. I had no idea why I craved sugar all the time or that I depended on a substance outside of me…just like Mom had.

By 1988, I tried to remain hopeful in my desperate search for emotional help. I kept searching for another professional. My fears continued to cripple me, and I felt more certain there was a cause. It was something about my childhood, something I couldn't figure out. I made an appointment with a new therapist on my list.

Arriving at her office at my HMO, I sat once again on a cold, plastic chair in the sizeable sterile room with gray ceilings, walls, and dingy linoleum. I watched the clock as the seconds clicked by.

When she called me in, I noticed Dr. Dorta's warm, kind face when we shook hands softly. She invited me to sit on her corduroy sofa across from her velveteen chair. After some preliminaries, she asked, "Tell me about your childhood. What was it like?"

I started into my story one more time. *How many times do I have to go through this?*

"What was your mother like when she drank?" She killed a spider on her desk with a tissue.

"Hostile, argumentative--drinking brought out Mom's anger. She yelled at my dad every night." I grimaced at the memory.

"Did your father drink?"

"He drank lots but was mellow when drunk. He could have trouble walking, and he'd drive that way. He got in a bad car accident while driving drunk with Mom, and she was severely injured. He didn't change personalities as she did." As she asked more probing questions, tears flowed down my face. Incredible pain poured out of me as I talked in depth about my family with growing honesty and awareness.

Dr. Dorta paid close attention and never looked away. After several sessions with this kind, concerned woman, she summed up her thoughts. "What I see with you is that you're in enormous pain. You came from an alcoholic home. I get that."

I looked up at her, relieved she had listened well and understood the intensity of my emotions. "Yep."

Flicking her brown hair back, she cleared her throat and looked me in the eye. "What you're describing...just doesn't match the intensity of what you're telling me." She scrutinized my face with her large brown eyes. "Being in an alcoholic family, you had many problems, but your pain level is way beyond that." Her eyes met mine. "Something is missing here--something you're not facing."

My eyes widened. What did Dr. Dorta mean 'something is missing here?' How could something have happened that I wasn't facing? I had looked at every square inch and honestly couldn't think of anything I'd overlooked.

I couldn't stop thinking about her words as they simmered in the back of my mind.

Carol C.Boyce

Chapter 25

Leftovers

B y 1990, we hadn't seen Dad since the campout two years earlier, although we talked briefly on the phone every few months. With him living seven hours away, Andrew and Carrie never had much time with him. I tried to forget and pretend all was well when we spoke. I was always the peacekeeper in the family. Six years had passed since Mom's death and his devastating comments. I couldn't let go of my dream of one big happy family and returning to a normal father-daughter relationship. Maybe if he spent time with us, he'd realize how important we were—I was--in his life.

So, I invited Dad to Thanksgiving.

I woke up the Monday morning before the holiday and casually opened the daily newspaper. The nutty, caramelized smell of coffee enticed me to join the new day as the kid's played cowboys with their stick horses. As I ate my oatmeal, a headline caught my eye, "Repressed Memories Questioned." The story said that new research was coming out about delayed memories of sexual abuse.

Having no recall of bad car accidents, war atrocities, and other traumas was well-documented. I'd heard of that, but I'd never heard before there could be memory loss from sexual abuse. The article highlighted accused parents who doubted and fought the accusations. The topic caught my attention, though I didn't think it too important. I continued reading about the latest news on the new Gulf War.

Closing the paper, I began preparations for a hopefully lovely holiday. Maybe if everything were perfect, Dad would want to come to our house more often. He might even come for Christmas some year, and just maybe I'd feel loved by him. I could remind him of the good old days of big holidays with Mom and the whole family together, and it might bring back his old feelings for me-- if Thanksgiving--if I--were perfect enough.

On our front door, a crimson, gold, and orange wreath greeted Dad, heralding the arrival of the holiday season on this chilly evening. Turkey decorations and cornucopias were on display. Feathered turkeys the kids had made decorated the table as they jumped with excitement about Grandad's visit. They knew how vital grandparents were because Michael's parents were wonderful to them---super involved and remarkably close. They hoped this grandfather would be the same.

After Dad settled into our den with a double sofa bed, we sat down for a grilled salmon and wild rice dinner. The fireplace crackled on this crisp evening. Buttering my roll, I thought how happy I felt having the family together, seeing Dad included at our dinner table. Michael poured the chardonnay and we toasted

Dad's arrival. The kids thought it fun to clink the glasses. Gravy seemed to be everywhere.

He started right in with business. "Carol, I've decided to make you the executor of my trust. You have the best background for this with your MBA and you are good with money." He took a sip of wine. "How does that sound?"

"That's fine with me, Dad. I'll be happy to do it." I felt complimented that he trusted me with his substantial assets, but his faith in me seemed strange after not wanting me in his life. He thought our relationship had healed more than I realized.

"Good, I'll let my attorney know when I get back home. I'll send you my financial information." He went back to his turkey.

With stiff conversation, we survived dinner watching the kids and talking about trivial matters. Michael got them in their flannel pajamas, and I cleaned up the kitchen as Dad read the paper.

Carrie bounced up to her grandad in her nightgown and hugged his leg playfully, so excited about his presence. He shot her an irritated look and pushed her off. Jumping up and down with excitement, Carrie blurted out, "Can I sleep with you tonight?" She reasoned there would be enough room for her to snuggle with him in his big bed, a nod to how special she thought he was. Crawling in bed with Michael and me when she couldn't sleep was not unusual.

In a sing-song voice, Dad smiled and pointed his finger at her. "I'd be accused of molesting you." He gave her a strange, creepy grin.

My head snapped. What did he say? I'd never heard the word "molesting" come out of his mouth. His response stunned me. What would make him say that---and to a four-year-old, no less? I wondered why the word came to him from such an innocent question. Carrie scrunched her nose with disappointment. For the first time, her innocence and vulnerability left me unsettled.

I hugged Carrie and firmly said, "Not tonight, honey. You need to sleep in your bed, and Granddad needs to sleep in his bed." She looked down with tears in her beautiful brown eyes. "We have a big day tomorrow. Time for bed. I love you guys-- just the way you are." I gave both kids a big hug and kiss as they trotted off for a bedtime story with Michael.

The following morning after a holiday breakfast of warm pastries, hot sausages, eggs, and fresh pineapple in our dining room, It smelled so good. I cleared the table when everyone left the room. I was glad I used disposable plates

Dad appeared and cornered me between the table and wall, blocking my path to the kitchen. He had something important to say, it seemed. In his plaid wool bathrobe, he wanted me alone. "I was a good father to you," he said, staring at me intently, "except for a few things." He chuckled with an odd, cold look. Our eyes met uncomfortably. He carefully studied my reaction to his question.

I didn't know what to say. "Um…right." I looked into Dad's eyes, wondering where this discussion was going. I had no idea what he was talking about but could tell it was important to him. I wasn't interested in discussing this, and last I checked, the menu didn't include "Carol's Childhood." I gently pushed him out of the way--I had to get the turkey in the oven.

As I filled the bird with Mom's famous stuffing recipe, my mind filled with new questions. What was Dad talking about, 'except for a few things,' and why did he want the conversation private? The intense look on his face while questioning me about the childhood he had provided was something new. What could he be referring to? His words weren't inherently alarming, but they seemed interesting, but I brushed it off.

Every corner of the house smelled of turkey and sage. I proudly presented the splendid turkey I'd managed not to dry out on the festive dining room table. My cousin and her family of five joined us at the long table. The conversation was light and full of laughter. After devouring the pumpkin, the guests left. I rubbed my brow, relieved I had survived another family holiday.

When everyone had gone to bed, I snuggled with Michael, exhausted from the long day. "Dad said some bizarre things this weekend." I told him in a hushed voice about the 'molesting' comment to Carrie and the 'childhood' comments to me.

"That's weird. Maybe your father saw a show about molesting kids or something like that. You know, he's never been the same since Mom died." Michael never overreacted to anything.

"Yeah, maybe." I set my alarm for the next day to return Dad to the airport first thing. His whole visit felt odd, and I was happy he was leaving soon. I had plenty of leftovers to think about.

In retrospect, Michael and I were clueless. As educated, protective, and aware parents, what should have been clear left us completely blindsided. Dad's façade as the good, successful doctor for thirty-six years of my life overtook logic and proved impenetrable, even to me.

As the depression returned, an all-knowing black raven with enormous outspread wings seemed to hover over me. He filled every crevice of my clouded mind with suffocating darkness. Taunting me, he knew all: the cause of my pain, the cause of my terror, and the cause of my madness. Though I tried to hide from him, deny he was there, conceal myself with a busy,

happy exterior, he would not relent, and his talons dug firmly into my bloodied back. He wouldn't let me go until I knew all, too.

I couldn't run and hide any longer. With blind faith, it was time to fight my invisible demons head-on.

Chapter 26

The Devastating Truth

In 1991, several months after Dad's Thanksgiving visit, I sat alone at a McDonald's outdoor playground on an overcast, chilly February day. The brisk air felt good, with a faint smell of hamburgers cooking. He and Carrie, now seven and five, had begged me to take them to their favorite play structure, and they shrieked with delight as they went through the tubes and slides. I pulled my sweater tight, watching them climb and play, unrestrained and emotionally free like I hoped all children could be.

After winter break, the children had returned to school, and with it, my depression and fears, too. I spent every free moment looking backward, trying to figure out my problems, worried about what new fear would engulf me next. I couldn't go on much longer, and my family's future was in peril.

Playing with Andrew's leftover French fries, I tried to reframe my problems. I remembered watching Helen Keller in *The Miracle Worker*. As a young deaf, dumb, and blind girl, her teacher, Annie Sullivan, tried to get her to understand that all the signs she was doing in her palms meant something. Helen thinks they're unrelated, a game without any significance. Annie famously splashes water on Helen's face to "wake her up" because they're all connected. Annie pleads, "Make the connection? W-A-T-E-R. These signs aren't a game. There's a connection between every letter and hand gesture." Helen finally makes the connection to words, and it changes her whole life.

Just as Annie tried to teach Helen, I wondered if my fears and phobias might be from one common cause, with one unidentified relationship. But I couldn't figure out what could connect fear of flying, nightmares, big cities, a scary man, and caves. It made no logical sense.

I decided to make a list of what I knew for sure--maybe something would click. I pulled a pen and scrap of paper out of my purse and began scribbling my long list on the ketchup-smeared table: I am terrified by routine experiences; my anxieties are worsening; a faceless, dark man haunts me; I was scared to go to sleep as a child because of nightmares and visions; I cry inconsolably for unknown reasons, and I abuse my body with food.

I looked over my notes. It felt like I was playing Clue©. I knew the victim was me, but I had to roll the dice and figure out what the weapon had been. I had to figure out who had done the purported crime and where it occurred. Did Colonel Mustard do it with a wrench in the Billiard Room? Or was it the candlestick by Miss Scarlet in the Conservatory? I wished I had a definitive gameboard in front of me.

Watching the kids, I inhaled deep breaths of fresh air to clear my thoughts, leaning on the cold, sticky table. The fears during childhood, the body shaming, the nightmares, and incredible grief all suddenly started to meld together. The cases of forgotten sexual abuse that I had read about recently in the newspaper came to mind. Some people don't remember sexual abuse. *Hmmm.*

Carol C.Boyce

It all swirled in my head until it suddenly stopped. In one instant, it all came together for me. I realized, to my horror, that sexual abuse rang true. My list of symptoms would make sense in the context of sexual trauma. Was this the missing puzzle piece?

I closed my eyes in disbelief. Oh my God--this can't be. Please, God, no! No, my problems couldn't be from sexual abuse. But in that instant, I knew that was what had happened, and I was horrified. To my horror, the truth was like a neon sign in front of me for the first time. Immediately I knew the cause of my fears and anguish.

My thoughts at once wandered to who could have done this to me. If my abuser was a man, as in my visions, who was it? I realized that only Dad had frequent and consistent access to me. No other man was regularly in our home. There was no one else but him.

Please God, not my father! No, no, no!

My heart pounded as I sat alone on the cold bench. I couldn't steady my hands as an incredible adrenalin surge overtook me. I trembled uncontrollably as my brain screamed in horror. *No, no, no... Oh my God, this can't be. Please, no! Not my father! Not my family! Not the parent I trusted! Not me! Sex.... with my father?*

Shaking from shock, I gathered the kids and drove home. Making a box of macaroni and cheese for their dinner, I loaded a VCR tape of Mr. Roger's Neighborhood into the TV and prayed they'd watch it.

I lay on my bed and hugged my soft pillow, staring out the window. The reality of Dad's incredible betrayal started to sink in. A waterfall flowed down my face as I tried to grasp my realization. So many emotions went through my mind, but I knew that this was the truth in my gut. The cause of my endless fears and terror was the person who should have loved and protected me more than anyone.

My thoughts raced as I bargained with myself. Sexual abuse couldn't be what had been causing all my problems—I'm not one of those people, nor is my family. Pedophiles were creepy, oily-haired men that anyone could identify. Clearly not my highly re-spected father. I remembered my ancestors' photos on the wall, their incredible accomplishments, my ballet lessons, my educa-tion, the classical music—this couldn't be my family!

My ignorance, arrogance, and prejudice showed up at once. I had my long-sought-after answer, and I didn't want anything to do with it. My confused and scattered puzzle pieces had suddenly locked together, creating one ugly, hideous picture.

I had been molested...by my own father.

Michael arrived home from work and found me sobbing on our bed. After greeting Andrew and Carrie, he said," What is go-ing on?" He put his hand on my heaving back.

"Dad...Dad...molested me!" My shoulders slumped as I wept. "I've finally... finally...realized what happened." I took in a deep jagged breath. "Dad was molesting me!" I wailed again. I wanted to crawl out of my skin telling my husband. I'd had a sex life that Mike, and I, knew nothing about. It felt like a dirty secret.

"What? Are you kidding me? Your own father caused all these problems you've been suffering with?" Michael sat down beside me, shocked by my news. It had never crossed either of our minds. "I'll kill him."

"Good, I will, too," Revenge sounded wonderful. "Dad had said strange remarks before, but not this. I trusted him." I shook

Carol C.Boyce

my head in disbelief, and we sat in stunned silence for several minutes. "I've lost my father forever. He will never, ever be part of my life again."

"You got that right."

"I can't face all this--how will I take care of the kids?"

With his brow tightly furrowed, Mike's throat tightened. "I'll have to do more. I'll just have to cover for you—we'll get through this together, somehow." He stared into space at the shock of the news.

"I can't go through this alone--I'm so scared." Surviving the pain looked impossible, already drained from the emotional rollercoaster and depression of the past years. I wept until I fell into an exhausted sleep.

Michael would have to be the main strength behind our family for a while. I was so thankful I had someone to lean on and hoped he'd always be there. I didn't know what I would do without this amazing man to lean on.

I would forever mark my life as being before or after that day. My life as I knew it collapsed. I had pushed aside a massive *Do Not Enter* sign and opened an old, deep mineshaft in my brain. My first acknowledgment of the abuse was the only permission my brain needed to reveal its buried secrets.

I realize now my subconscious knew all along what had happened. I just had to allow for the life-threatening emotions and memories to come and finally feel capable of facing it. One moment I had no conscious idea, and the next, I knew exactly what had happened, and the terrifying mineshaft couldn't ever close again.

Over the decades, I've reflected on this pivotal moment many times, trying to understand how it happened. I realized that

I'd always had the answer with me, just like Dorothy had with her red shoes in the *Wizard of Oz*. With a loving husband, home, and young children, I subconsciously decided I now had enough glue to hold me together for the life-threatening emotional flood that needed to spill out. When the terrifying symptoms I was having became increasingly intense, the scales tipped from the heavy terror of not knowing to the devastation of knowing.

Over the years, criticism about how I recalled the abuse was routine, as if I had any conscious choice. Some have decided that I should have had a cataclysmic memory having all that had happened with Dad's face front and center. Some believed suppression was ridiculous, and I made the whole thing up for some unknown motivation. I'd have given anything to have this not be true. I was just opening the floodgates, and that's why "I knew" in only a split second.

In truth, I did have pieces of memory first, but they were in a confused form called PTSD, Post Traumatic Stress Disorder. They were non-sensical, without faces or context. I was clueless about the many visual fragments and whether they were related. I had never put them together with sexual abuse. I'd have had to face the truth. I hadn't been ready.

Carol C.Boyce

Chapter 27

There is Always Light

*"There is always light if only we're brave enough to
see it. If only we're brave enough to be it."*
Amanda Gorman 2020

I ncredible fear, confusion, and complex trauma poured from
me when the *Do Not Enter* sign moved away. If I thought my
emotional problems were difficult before, they multiplied ex-
ponentially now, and I had no idea where I was heading. I was
already fragile emotionally and knew I could easily collapse.
Flashes of my unprocessed past began arriving as if the assaults
were occurring at that moment. The emotions from one sexual
assault would be terrible to process, ten would be horrible—but
hundreds, as I now know I endured, were incomprehensible. My
'new' past left me shattered on a bed of a million jagged shards,
and I didn't think I could live through it.

The profound grief and despair for the tragic loss of my father struck me first. I had loved him for thirty-six years as a different person. Though the last years had been rough, I had trusted
him while ignoring signs that something was very wrong. My

childhood fantasy of someday having a happy family and the parental love I craved blinded me.

Dad was no longer the hero I'd written about in elementary school. He was no longer the man who taught me to waltz and love music. My father was now a felon, a liar with no moral character, and had a Jekyll and Mr. Hyde personality. It felt like he was an ax murderer and the only one who could see the blood dripping from the blade was me.

I had dreamed that Dad and I were healing our relationship after the turmoil of Mom's death, that we might have a future. I had naively envisioned celebrating birthdays and holidays with him, enjoying watching his grandchildren and great-grandchildren grow up together. I pictured inviting him for Christmases, graduations, and weddings through his old age, with loving Hallmark cards on Father's Days to come. He would play the beautiful music I remembered on the piano, sing with my kids, and encourage their music education. But in one cataclysmic moment, my dreams evaporated into a dirty graveyard of horror and shame, which was a tremendous loss.

I was mad I had hidden these memories from myself. I envisioned an angry, accusing conversation with my brain: *How did you not remember something this horrible? Amnesia wasn't the deal we had. I'd picked "Normal Memory" from the drop-down brain-setup menu, not the "Forget Critical Events" one. You were supposed to remember everything important, no questions asked. I shouldn't have had to remind you to record my life events and give me access to them. Was there an instruction sheet I didn't read? You failed me horribly, brain. Now look at the mess we're in.*

I couldn't let my siblings know about the tragedy I was experiencing. I couldn't begin to understand the disaster and its full

Carol C.Boyce

ramifications myself. My childhood problems looked so different now, spread wide open before me. The roles I had known were upside-down, where Dad was now the aggressor, not Mom, and I, not him, was the actual victim.

Through the new lens of sexual abuse, I had the massive job of reprocessing all I'd known about myself, my family, and every comment or action I remembered from Dad. I had to redefine all my memories under the new context of sexual abuse. Dad had handed me a tragedy of profound darkness and terror on a silver platter, and I wanted to shove it back in his face.

Because of my shame and confusion, my friends wouldn't be told what had happened and couldn't support me, either. There would be no typical death traditions—no lovely memorial service, no guests speaking highly of Dad, no large soprano singing Amazing Grace, and no gravesite to visit and mourn his passing. Friends would not offer me warm hugs, deliver beautiful flowers, or bake gooey casseroles. I had to bear the loss alone.

I worried I'd never recover, but I had to honor my vow to my children. Somehow, with Michael's help, I'd have to keep a consistent, emotionally healthy environment for them. Though I wanted to stay in bed all day with a pillow over my head, I would get up and get through each hour as best I could. I'd be the best parent I could be to my beloved children.

The future of our marriage became a huge concern now. With the tremendous personal change I was facing, I couldn't imagine how Michael and I could remain married. I didn't even know who I was anymore, and I doubted whether I could recover at all. Michael had married a different person, not one with the tremendous baggage I had. I wondered if he would handle my long recovery and love me through it. No one had ever loved me like that before. I was terrified.

One day shortly after remembering, I dropped the kids at school and left feeling despondent. I headed to the empty chapel at our family church. I'd never done this before, but I was so low and desperate that I didn't know what else to do. Luckily, I found an unlocked entrance and walked into the quiet, beautiful building. I could feel a sacredness and peace. The smell of the candles and the site of the beautiful stained-glass windows enveloped me with a sense of awe and strength.

I slipped onto a wooden bench and slid onto the kneeler feeling safer. I began to release my anguish quietly. Through my copious tears, I prayed like never before and begged God for relief from my incredible pain. I begged for understanding, strength, and direction forward.

As I quietly wept alone in the beautiful chapel, I heard a small voice. "Have hope for your family and yourself. You'll heal if you're brave enough to face this. Go right through the fire. I promise you that you will survive."

Though barely there, I could feel a small spark deep down in my core, a spark of hope. I knew life was good and worth living, though it was anything but right now. I would heal and improve if I could just find the courage to face the burning flames. My family would thrive, and I would find the strength I needed. I realized that God would always be there in my deepest despair, supplying a lifesaving hope no matter the size of the fire I faced. I regained my hope.

I thought about a book I'd read earlier on my way home. In *Man's Search for Meaning*, a Jewish psychiatrist, Dr. Viktor Frankl, imprisoned, starved, and tortured for years in a Nazi concentration camp, studied survival. He observed that hope was the distinguishing feature of those who made it through the camps. Hope was the characteristic that decided whether one lived or died.

Though vastly different circumstances, hope became my savior through my life-threatening emotions. It showed me a pathway out of the engulfing black mud of depression, and I made a critical decision: I would fight with everything I had.

Chapter 28

Pound, Scream, Cry

I had begun seeing a new therapist, Laura, whom a friend had recommended. My HMO wouldn't pay for more visits, so I couldn't return to Dr. Dorta. My recovery would take years of care and medical insurance for long-term therapy wasn't available then. We'd have to figure out how to pay for my extensive treatment.

I parked on Laura's quiet cul-de-sac and enjoyed the hummingbirds near her porch feeder. She worked out of her home office. Her multicolored roses were in full bloom, and I could smell their sweet fragrance as I walked up the driveway. Entering her beautiful, Asian-inspired living room, I remembered why I was there and trembled. Where would I start? Would she even believe me? Maybe she'd bring up more issues that I couldn't handle.

Laura greeted me with a warm smile, a tall, older woman, inviting me into her office after a few pleasantries. The room was a cheery yellow with floral wallpaper. As I sat down on her soft sofa, I held my head with my hands, covering my already wet eyes. Laura sat down on her leather recliner. "So, tell me what's going on."

"I recently realized my father sexually abused me as a child. I had no memory of it before now." I explained my overwhelming despair. "I feel like I can't function—I can't handle this." She listened intently.

"First, I believe you. I have no doubt this happened." With an unusual warmth, she looked directly into my eyes. "And I know this is an incredibly tough time in your life."

"I'm also trying to care for my children and home, so I'm overwhelmed." I sobbed into my hands.

After more conversation, she could see my incredible level of pain. She straightened her chair. "I'd recommend we have you admitted to a mental hospital. It will give you time to process the incredible chaos without the distractions of your children and daily life. I think it would be best for you."

I straightened up with a jolt. *Really? A damn mental hospital—for me—you must be joking. That's for ill people, not me.* I had seen the movies. Visions of Nurse Ratched, straitjackets, and shock treatments came to mind. I could see sterile, locked wards with no key and slumped over patients wailing in cold, gray halls. "I don't think so at this time. Thanks, but no—not now. I have a husband and children that need me." I didn't want to show her how terrified I was.

Her gray cat ran into the room. Folding her arms, Laura acquiesced, raising her eyebrows. "Okay, but know it's always available to you. It would be good for you to have some space to process this tremendous upheaval in your life."

When I got home, I told Michael what Laura had suggested. "The thought of a mental hospital terrifies me. Strange people, being locked in, being given medications I don't want, not seeing you and the kids—I couldn't handle it." I wiped my tears away.

"I can see what you're saying, but I doubt modern mental hospitals are that bad. We'd be okay. Do whatever you need to do." He hugged me as Katie, our Cocker Spaniel, jumped in his lap.

"The truth is I need you and the kids near me. I need you all more than you need me right now. The normalcy of daily life kinda, ugh, helps ground me." My old world seemed so distant now, and I needed as much normal routine as possible. "The kids need stability—I can't leave them."

"I got it. It's okay," Michael smiled at me. "Whatever you need to do. We'll just take one day at a time."

For months, I trembled arriving for my therapy appointments at Laura's office. I didn't know what emotions might come up for me or what I had to face. It was overwhelming and terrified me. Confronting my unknown past and talking about it was the last thing I wanted to do, but it was my only hope. I had to trust Laura's expertise and professionalism.

Sitting down in her cheery office, the bags around my red eyes were more pronounced than usual. I looked down at my stained blouse and wrinkled pants, my hair barely combed. "I'm so depressed. I can hardly get out of bed." I hung my head, embarrassed by being unable to cope.

Laura looked intently at me. "Your depression is from holding in unexpressed emotions. Your mind can't manage the pain and shuts down to protect you from the overload. You must identify your feelings and release them. Say what's bothering you aloud, yell it out for the world to hear, and hit something. You'll start to feel better. You *can* face this."

I rolled my eyes. "If you mean I must yell or scream, that's just not me. I'm not one to be demonstrative—I'm a pretty private person."

"You're gonna have to learn to do it if you want to get through this." She handed me a blue foam bat. "Physically work out the emotions--pound your bed with your rage, scream out the terror from the assaults and cry the grief away—you'll be much less depressed. It's the only way to get to the other side of this."

The bat and I looked at each other. *I don't know about this.* "I'll try, but this isn't me—I'm just not that person. I've barely uttered an angry word—to other people. For me to scream and yell would be a real stretch."

"Try it—it'll help you."

I left with the bat. I'd have to learn to release my enormous emotions somehow. I was in so much pain that I'd try anything.

A new normal emerged when I had private time. I kept Andrew's and Carrie's lives as normal as possible when they were at home, but when they were at school and Mike at work, I spent every moment working on my recovery.

After dropping the kids at school one morning, I carefully checked that the windows and doors were tightly closed to not alarm the neighbors--I didn't want to censor what I said. Thankfully, our house was well-insulated and some distance from our neighbors, so I could be free to express myself privately. I lay down on my soft comforter, clutching my pillow. I stared out the patio window and viewed our shaded yard with two towering oak trees. It was a beautiful day, but I couldn't enjoy it. A deep painful knot in my chest was always with me.

My mind drifted back to my childhood bed, where I found all the pain arose. I could see myself as a little girl, terrified and alone, and I forced myself to say aloud how I felt. *It's dark and I'm frightened. Someone's going to hurt me. He's coming toward me, and I can't move. I'm all alone--no one can help me. No one keeps me safe. Ahh! Ahh!* I screamed and screamed.

I stood up, grabbed the foam bat, and lightly hit the bed. Then again, a little harder, and then harder. It felt good to release the anger. *You asshole—how could you have done this to me? You fucking bastard!* I pounded harder. *How could you have hurt me so badly? I was your goddamn daughter!* The more I beat the bed, the more I needed to do it.

I felt like a different person acting so aggressively--it was completely against my nature, but I beat the bed until my shoulders ached and yelled until my voice was hoarse. I stopped exhausted, and the unrelenting emotional pain would be tolerable for the day. The lion that roared within me was my 'child within' that never grew up, still frozen in my pink canopy bed. I had been powerless, unable to move, and unable to let out the screams of terror then. They all had to come out now.

I pounded, screamed, and cried through every devastating memory and realization, trying to get my life back. Envisioning my childhood bedroom, I'd burn my house down repeatedly in my mind. As I pictured my dark bedroom with Dad standing over me and experiencing the horrors of the sexual assaults, I recreated the scene and changed the setting to daylight, an essential issue. I'd envision God, the police, Michael, and my close friends surrounding and protecting me when Dad appeared in the doorway. I'd imagine him arrested and taken away, or beaten until he couldn't hurt me anymore, anything I could do to recover my power and control from these terror-filled assaults. The techniques were a lifesaver, helping me feel safer and more powerful. I did it over and over…and over again.

I was so thankful to Laura for teaching me this lesson and handing me the bat. It reconnected my brain and body, which was critical to my healing. The distress wasn't on the surface and talk therapy didn't touch the deep level of my anguish stored in my body. To survive, I had to jump into the inferno and run right through the terrifying, burning flames.

Because of the decades of amnesia, running from the trauma, I finally was facing the truth. 'Pound, scream, cry' was my mantra, my guiding solution to the pain, the only relief I found from the rage and terror buried within me.

When done, I'd change my clothes, brush my hair, put on a bit of makeup to cover my swollen, red eyes, and drive to school.

"Hi sweetie, how was your day?" I gave seven-year-old Andrew a big hug.

"I got to play with Stinky today! It was my turn." He bounced beside me, so excited about the class hamster.

"Oh, how exciting! That must have been special." I smiled at him. "Here comes, sis."

Five-year-old Carrie ran up and hugged me. "Hi, Mommy."

I hugged and kissed her. "Did you have a good day at school?"

"Yep." She jumped up and down.

"Let's go home and have a snack. I have a fun craft project, Sound good?"

"Yeah," they said as they piled into the minivan.

I created a strong structure for their day, focusing on home-work, crafts, and a family dinner where we were all together. But after everyone went to bed, I'd have to face my demons again. I was often awake until early morning, sorting through the confusion and betrayal trauma. Never one to write, I began journaling to identify my terror. I'd write out my every thought and try to make sense of it by reading it back to myself. Learning to express my angst through writing in the quiet of the night became critical to my recovery.

The next day, I'd do the process all over again. Rinse, repeat. But the trauma kept coming relentlessly and I didn't know if I'd survive.

Chapter 29

Who Am I?

A bout two months after I began to remember, I sat in Laura's office for my weekly session. She smiled and handed me a paper with information on a local group. "You should join a support group for sexual abuse survivors. It would be good for you to have the encouragement and assistance from others going through recovery."

"I'll try it. Maybe it will help," I forced a smile.

The following Monday night, I arrived and sat down awkwardly on a cold, plastic chair in the church's sterile narthex. The large gray room belied the intimate nature of the conversations I expected. Coffee, made many hours earlier, steamed in the grimy pot next to the Styrofoam cups and stale cookies. I got up and poured a cup, grabbing two cookies to help me through. I stole glances at the twenty other survivors in a circle and wondered if I was one of them.

Tina, a short woman with a warm smile, welcomed us. "Thanks for coming. I'll moderate the group today. Let's go around the circle and give everyone a chance to speak."

One young woman wearing a baseball cap pulled low on her face and dressed in men's pants and work boots began. She bent over, staring at her feet. In a monotone voice and with no expression on her face, she explained that she was left alone at a ranch with her uncle when she was eleven. "I need to teach you a lesson about being a woman,' her uncle said. He tied her to a nearby oak tree and pulled out a baseball bat. He forcefully inserted it into her vagina with a smile on his face. The pain and bleeding from the extreme tearing were horrific and she was left suffering, tied to the tree for hours.

She shared no other part of her story, and I was amazed she showed no sadness or anger as she spoke of the horrific assault. Now, fifteen years later, she still seemed in shock, frozen in time emotionally as she began to process the incident. I will never forget the terror and empathy I felt for her hearing the heartbreaking story.

Curled up on her plastic chair, the next woman to speak tightly hugged her ankles and rocked back and forth. "I'm a multiple," she exclaimed with a smile and a giggle. "Janet is here today, I think."

Another woman joined in, "I am too!" She laughed as if it was a dirty secret finally released. "I'm not sure which personality is here today," she said with glee, hiding the pain of sexual abuse underneath.

What are they talking about? I had read the controversial 1973 Schreiber book *Sybil* years earlier, and it came to mind. It was a disturbing tale of a severely sexually abused woman crippled by sixteen distinct personalities. I shuttered to think that having multiple personalities might be normal for incest and sexual abuse victims. I wondered if I had this too. Nothing was off the table in my mind as I watched these fellow survivors in horror.

These stories showed me the enormity of the recovery and the overwhelming obstacles ahead of me. I wasn't ready for this new reality and left terrified. I didn't want to accept I was one of them—I just wasn't prepared.

I walked out with my legs wobbling. Arriving home and lying on my bed, I hugged my pillow and sobbed for hours. Exhausted, I fell into a deep sleep.

I looked sideways with an ashen face at my next session with Laura. I felt numb with grief. After describing the stories I'd heard in the support group, she exhaled and rubbed her forehead. "Sounds like it really upset you…. Tell me more."

With misty eyes, I shrugged. "I don't even know who I am anymore. A few months ago, I was this married lady in suburbia raising my kids and now I could fit into a severely mentally ill category." My damp cheeks creased with pain. "Who am I? What does survivor even mean? Will I ever be me again?" My well-defined identity had become sand in my hand, slipping through my fingers. I was so lost.

"Are you forgetting all the problems you had before you knew? Tell me--was that really you?"

"Good point. I don't know who I really am. But this group scared the crap out of me. I don't want to become one of them. I want to be me, not a 'survivor.' It's like a new identity has attached itself to my back, and I don't want anything to do with it."

I worried I'd never see my old life again and was so scared of my new one.

"Developing multiple personalities, or dissociative identity disorder is a devastating coping mechanism for some sexual trauma survivors. They unconsciously separate their personalities to protect themselves. You also don't have it." Laura's eyes locked onto mine.

"Okay, but a massive chunk of me hid for decades. What will more jump out at me? What else don't I know about myself?" I closed my wet eyes tightly as I rubbed my hands together. "I'm just overwhelmed." Clammy skinned, I trembled. "When will I step on the next devastating land mine? Will I--can I--ever re-cover? It's like nothing is real anymore."

"Remember how much confusion and pain you had before? You're going to get better. You've already survived the worst of it, and you're recovering." Linda explained.

I didn't believe her.

In truth, I got much worse before I began to improve. The terror of the memories kept me unstable emotionally. I could only hope I'd recover quickly.

At another session, I asked, "So, Laura, how long will this recovery process take? How long do I have to go through this misery? You think this will be over by the end of one year?" I brightened, thinking about an ending.

Laura stifled a smile. "This will take a long time. I don't know how long, but it is not a quick process."

Her vagueness irritated me, and I responded strongly. "I can't manage this much longer. It's got to end soon. I'm giving myself one year from when I remembered to get over it and that's it!"

I had promised myself in my toughest moments that this horror show wouldn't last long. It would end soon with a clean and decisive death knell. I'd put a pretty bow on the devastating chest of abuse as quickly as possible and shove it under my bed for perusal in my old age. Over. Done.

It would take decades to grasp the devastating reality that my old life, the old me, was gone forever, and my recovery would take a lifetime. I would never be the same person again—I'd be better.

Looking back at my early years of recovery, I realized I had tried to deny all that I was facing and minimize the enormous psychological damage. I was too scared to face how hugely damaged I was. There was so much I didn't understand.

I always thought if I had to get a disease, I'd want one from which many suffer. The illness would be well-understood and researched, so I'd have a clear path to recovery. Instead, I got a disorder, traumatic amnesia, which was highly unpopular, not well-known, nor believed. The science was in its infancy in the early nineties, when I first remembered. Like me, most people had no idea memory loss could result from severe sexual trauma.

I had no orientation, terminology, or instructions about healing from this highly controversial "new" disorder. I had no path or timetable for recovery, no role model, books, or reason to believe I would ever see an end to the pain. There was no #MeToo movement, social media, or internet to access support or information. Researching my disorder was impossible. No one, not even my therapists, had a roadmap for my recovery, much less an example of someone with a successful outcome. I was in uncharted territory.

As my journey continued and I uncovered more of what had happened, it became clear to the professionals that I had survived extremely severe, young, and long-term sexual abuse. My methods of survival alone showed this. I had done everything I could to survive, including suppressing all memory of it. I had dissociated in many ways to protect myself from the reality of living with my attacker. Recovery would be a long and daunting undertaking with no guaranteed outcome.

But healing came along with the devastation. I finally had the cause of what was so wrong with me mentally. I knew now that sexual abuse was at the core, and it was a great relief for Michael and me to have a diagnosis. I wasn't trapped in an unknown disorder anymore, and I was surviving.

Chapter 30

Touching Me

I had a headache that had grown worse throughout the day. The kids were finally asleep after a seemingly endless story time, and I fell into bed next to Michael, exhausted. The vice on my head still pounded with pressure on my eyes—I knew I wouldn't be able to sleep with the pain. I reached for him, now sound asleep. The feel of his strong arms beside me always grounded me and helped me to feel safer.

Slowing down from the hectic pace of the day, soccer, and Carrie's Girl Scout troop I led, I realized the headache was from the trauma. I knew this wouldn't go away until I faced the cause head-on and let the memory come.

Figuring out what the pain represented was always the challenge. My fear was incredible, and my anxiety sky high. I wanted to run far away to a land where I was free from the endless tyranny of my father's actions. But it didn't matter how scared and overwhelmed I was. The memory had to come. I couldn't run away anymore.

I couldn't lie quietly in my dark room any longer in pain, so I tiptoed into the garage, flicking on the light and shutting the door as quietly as possible. Closing all the windows, I sat in the driver's seat of my car where, without waking Michael and the kids, I could process what I needed to in privacy.

I tried to relax and let down my defenses, taking a few deep breaths. *Just let it come, Carol. You're safe now. You've already survived the assault. Just release the memory that needs to emerge for you to heal.*

Hands...I see so many hands. Everywhere. Large, man-size hands. They come at me like an octopus with gripping tentacles. They are, at once, touching me all over my chest, stomach, legs, and pubic area. I want my gross and vulgar body to implode and disintegrate into pieces, become shattered fragments that no one can touch.

My body feels like it is several feet to my side, completely detached from my brain. The softness of my flesh gives license to the evil man to hurt me. My soul collapses, becoming a speck of what it was as I feel the assault for the first time. I disappear into the bloodbath of shame, wanting to punish my battle-weary body for participating.

Stop! Get your hands off me. Get your damn hands off me! Ahhhh. Ahhhh. I screamed out the terror and pounded the passenger seat until my arm hurt. All the cries I could never make as a silenced child began to loosen up.

When I was exhausted and depleted, I tiptoed back to my warm bed, thankful for the privacy I'd had in the car. No one had woken up. I shut my tired, wet eyes, trying to process this new horrifying truth.

I fell asleep, happy my headache was gone at last.

To this day, this recollection is still difficult for me. I can never truly remove the hands from my body despite tremendous work to the contrary. I can't make the hands stop touching me

Carol C.Boyce

when triggered, and it can still be deeply disturbing. I wish there were a way to remove this trauma.

Chapter 31

The Stranger in the Doorway

T hroughout 1991, I gradually got more flashbacks from the severe trauma that occurred in my childhood bedroom. It was usually me as a child looking from the doorway or closet into my room. I didn't feel safe enough to get closer to my bed for many years. I was too terrorized.

It was always very dark in my room, and I shut down from the horror. Eventually, I began to see a figure, a silhouette in the dim light of my bedroom's doorway. I asked Laura to help me work on it at our next session. I would feel supported and safer facing my past with her there.

I closed my eyes and took a few deep breaths. "What do you see?"

"There is a person there ... a person in the darkness. Someone in the glimmer of my bathroom nightlight." I squeezed my forehead with both hands. I hated this. "It's a man's silhouette--dressed all in black. There is a dark opening, but his face is flat and gray. I don't know him—he's…he's a stranger." I shuddered, reliving the utter terror. "He's coming to hurt me…he's going to hurt me..." I panicked and covered my mouth to suppress my screams, then stopped and tried to calm down for a few minutes. I kept taking deep breaths.

"Keep going. What else do you see?" Laura leaned forward, knowing I was making progress.

"Blackness...blackness. Don't come near me! Get away!" I silently screamed in my head. "Don't move, or he'll hurt you!" I feel the terror as if it were happening at the moment. My muscles tense, and I freeze with fear as if I was still that child. Tears rained down my face, releasing the pain I'd held onto for decades.

Laura remains calm. "Keep going."

I squeeze my temples. I can't take any more of this. "I'm done. I don't want to go any further." I open my eyes, devastated by my new image. I "knew" intellectually that the man was my father, but I never identified him as a child. I would have had to face the truth if I had, and I subconsciously knew I couldn't handle living daily with my assailant.

"You did an excellent job today. You've found more of the trauma. Be good to yourself, and I'll see you next week." She hugged me as I got up to leave. "Will you be okay to go home?" She knew how upsetting this was for me.

"I'll be okay." I thought of picking my kids up from school. "I have to function in an hour." I got in my car and wept, sobbing uncontrollably. The tears felt endless, and my body felt slimy and dirty. It was disgusting to think my father terrorized me with his sick sexual desires.

I spent the next week feeling disoriented and depressed from the revelations. My daily anxiety and debilitating fear kept me working at home and going to my weekly sessions.

My life went on for many years in this fashion, getting bits and pieces of what had occurred during the assaults but never a clear, cohesive narrative. I hoped that would come later. My mind was still doing everything possible to protect my conscious mind from my knowing my brutal past.

I realized the same haunting man in my garage that followed me was also a distorted replica of this man in the doorway. Laura taught me he was a form of post-traumatic stress syndrome (PTSD). The stress response created a representation of this unknown, faceless man, taunting and reminding me I had to face him. My traumatized mind had played a never-ending 'hide and seek' game with me, never telling a clear, understandable story. It just hinted that something was terrifyingly wrong and then hid again in the recesses of my mind.

With Mike new in his dental practice, kids to raise, car payments, and a mortgage to pay, the costs of private therapy were challenging to absorb. I felt guilty spending so much of our budget on myself, but I desperately needed a professional's help. My HMO wouldn't cover any long-term therapy needs, leaving survivors abandoned. I had to heal from this horrible betrayal trauma, no matter the price, and luckily, I had the resources. So many others didn't.

Sitting on Laura's soft floral sofa one week, I put my Starbucks on the end table and braced myself for the session. She sat down on her chair next to me. "I want you to truly relax and allow whatever is in your mind to come out. Close your eyes. Breathe deeply and relax." She shifted in her seat and waited several minutes. "Where are you? What do you see?"

I breathed slowly and deeply, trying to clear my mind and feel safe. My thoughts always returned to my childhood bedroom when I shut my eyes. "Blackness.... blackness.... it's dark...shadows...I'm hiding in my closet. I won't come out." My breathing accelerated and my heart pounded. "Something horrible is going to happen. My bed..." I squeezed my temples with my hands, shaking my head.

"Tell me what is there."

"My bed...I can't--I can't see what's happening." I caught my breath as my forehead clenched tight.

Over many therapy sessions, I tried to get close to my pretty, pink canopy bed, but my mind couldn't go there, too terrified to know what was happening. I was often only in my closet, looking out. I eventually realized that my trauma occurred only in my bedroom late at night—it was always pitch black. The fears were a big block to my recovery.

Sitting in another session, I was able to get closer to the crime scene. I started feeling a bizarre feeling as I got mentally close to my bed. "I'm suddenly floating in the corner of my bedroom ceiling. It's all dark but peaceful up here--I am not afraid anymore. I'm floating.... floating...at the top of my room and safe now.

"What's happening below you?"

"I can't see anything. Nothing is going on below me." Sereneness engulfed me.

"Okay. Let's finish here for today." Laura looked happy I was making progress.

I wondered what had just happened. It was the strangest sensation, like entering another world. "What was that about?" The bizarre, sudden out-of-body phenomenon shocked me. It was surreal--I'd never experienced anything like it before.

"You dissociated from the violence below to the safe, calm world of your ceiling. You could pretend no assault was happening. It helped you survive."

"Hmm. I have never felt like that before."

Laura leaned forward on her knees to look me in the eyes. "This 'ceiling' escape is a way severely abused children flee from sexual assaults. It's a type of dissociation called depersonalization. It's part of the fight, flight, freeze, and collapse responses. Severe, life-threatening trauma caused you to have a collapse reaction to your father's assaults.

"Your brain is still trying to protect you. Sometimes you must let it." She encouraged me to trust my defenses. Laura explained that collapsing is a survival method where you go into total passivity and shutdown. Your brain, she explained, is no longer looking for ways to endure and instead enters a state of physical and emotional disconnect. It was a way to live through a vulnerable situation where you were utterly helpless.

The ceiling escape was terrifying. To have this intense, strange, and surreal feeling of being on the ceiling was shocking. I wondered if other frightening survival mechanisms would appear of which I knew nothing. Strangely, instead of relishing being mentally protected, I was frustrated about not knowing what happened during the sexual assaults. I wanted to get the pain and horror over with and not have the prospect of memories returning randomly. I didn't want the possibility hanging over me. It was a complicated and daunting hurdle and would take years to accept the reality that so much was forever inaccessible.

I also questioned whether there were full memories in my brain and whether I could recover without them. I wondered what could have happened that was so traumatic I couldn't even face it now as an adult. I believed cohesive, linear memories were hidden inside me, waiting to reveal themselves. I hoped I would know my whole story one day and not wonder what was hiding in my mind for the rest of my life.

Chapter 32

I Can't Breathe

Laura moved to Colorado, so I transferred my care to Peter, a licensed psychotherapist near my home. She highly recommended him and said he was an exceptional therapist well-respected in the local psychology community for decades. He had a doctorate and licensing as a marriage and family therapist. I questioned whether I would feel comfortable talking to a man about such personal issues but made an appointment based on the lofty recommendations.

Peter, a man with gray hair, a neatly trimmed beard, and a short, slight build, welcomed me into his office. He smiled warmly at me, and his gentle demeanor made me feel comfortable right away. The pictures of his pretty wife and sons were comforting. He had a rippling waterfall in the corner that softened the sounds in the room and a bowl of colorful, flowering succulents. As I sat down on his soft brown couch, I noticed the pretty yellow carnations on his desk and wondered whether this new therapist would know how to help me.

After pleasantries, I shared my background. After listening to me explain my experience, Peter said, "I believe you. I don't question at all that this occurred." I relaxed. The words felt so good. I didn't have to convince him of anything because he'd seen it several times before. He updated my history and described how our work together would proceed.

After several visits, Peter suggested, "I want you to breathe deeply and feel yourself relax. Close your eyes." Though terrifying, he knew I needed to keep going back to my bedroom and horror show to get at the trauma.

"When you're ready, tell me where you are," Peter said calmly.

I shut my eyes, breathing deeply, calming my anxious brain. "I'm in my twin bed. It's dark. It's so, so dark and quiet." I scrunched my face with tension, my eyebrows so tight they hurt. "Debbie is asleep in the bed next to mine."

"How old are you?" Peter asked.

"Maybe five or six—young." I keep focused on myself in my bed. After a few minutes, I start shaking. *What is this I'm seeing? Don't look. Don't look, Carol.* I don't want to re-experience this. I'm terrified but stay with Peter's directions. "I'm in a twin bed by my big window and Debbie is asleep in her bed. Daddy is on top of me. There's a pillow... over my face...a big pillow covering my nose and mouth that he's pushing onto me. He doesn't want me to make noise and wake my sister, but I can't breathe."

Peter was strong and calm. "Keep going. What else is there?"

"A tunnel. There's a long, black tunnel in front of me...with a white, brilliant light at its end. I just watch the light--it's so peaceful."

"Go on. Stay relaxed and tell me what is happening?"

"I only see the light. I know I'm dying," I inaudibly say as I shake my head.

"What is your father doing?"

"Uh…I don't know, but he's on top of me. I'm just watching the bright light." I focus more. "It's like I'm not there. I've left the world, but I'm so peaceful." Taking a deep breath, I dropped my head in shock. How could this have happened? My own father had almost suffocated me, a sweet little girl. My mouth gaped open as I processed the unfathomable.

"I'm glad you're facing more of the trauma," Peter said when I opened my eyes.

"I don't understand why I felt so peaceful. You'd think I'd be squirming and fighting back." I wept as the reality of the horrific incident began to register.

"Your brain knew your situation was hopeless. Perceiving that your death was imminent, it sedated itself with enormous amounts of opioids, giving you that peaceful feeling. It was another drastic survival method."

The hour was over, and I left Peter's office horrified by my new memory. Suffocating at my father's hands was unbelievable and it would be years before I could understand the ramifications of that early, severe trauma. I wondered how often he put the pillow over my mouth when he abused me—once--ten times—more. I'll never know, but his technique worked—it kept me quiet, and Debbie never woke up.

The near suffocation memory has never changed or left me, and I still struggle with the near-death experience. But there is an irony in this disturbing experience. I learned that dying is not scary. I'd seen the brilliant light of death's threshold, and strangely, I never felt more serene and peaceful. It was as if something bigger than me had taken over the care of my helpless child's life. I will be forever thankful and in awe of that. I assume now that even in the most brutal deaths, people can experience this flood of cortisol, releasing the fear and giving our loved ones a feeling of peace and calm. I'm grateful to know that.

But also, that day, I realized that underneath the pain, I finally had a therapist in Peter, with incredible skill and compassion. It gave me hope. He was extraordinary, able to listen, support, and guide me in areas in which few had knowledge or training. After so many therapists without these qualities, knowing I had a safe place to be vulnerable and vent my confusion was invaluable. I had someone I trusted fully to provide strength and direction. I would need it much longer than I ever realized.

Tragically as a young child, day and night meant two completely different things occurred. During the day, I learned to read and sing "Twinkle, Twinkle Little Star," but I faced brutal sexual assaults at night. Dad had the same drastic difference between night and day, healing patients during the day and attacking me at night. It was craziness. I could clearly see a Jekyll to Mr. Hyde type personality change in my father.

Another benefit was that I now knew why I was so fearful, and it wasn't because I was born that way. I had good reasons to be terrified. I learned early to be in a constant state of alert--that I was never safe. With no context or vocabulary about sexual assault, I had no choice but to dissociate to the ceiling and mentally leave, setting an effective survival mechanism I used for the rest of my childhood. Sometime after the assault, I put the memory in a deep, encapsulated place in my brain and lost all conscious awareness.

It got me through my childhood.

Chapter 33

No Greater Honor

On a hot afternoon in the summer of 1991, I dropped Andrew off at his piano lesson and headed out for my weekly therapy appointment. I plunked down on Peter's sofa, furrowing my forehead. "I need to confront Dad. It's been months since I remembered the abuse. I haven't said a word to him about it." I bowed my head. "Maybe I could...uh...handle it now." I was not looking forward to confronting him. Since remembering, I had refused phone calls and contact with him and never explained why. I'd been so shocked and overwhelmed I couldn't begin to confront him before now.

"I agree it's time. Do you want to write a letter or talk directly to your father?" Peter sat forward on his chair, looking at me steadily.

"Uh...send him a letter. It'd be more under my control...than having a conversation. At least he'd hear my complete thoughts."

"That's true. You'll have much more control of the narrative if you write a letter." Peter brushed his slacks. "Do you think your father will be surprised you didn't know?"

I rubbed my temples. "Yes. It's so strange. Dad had no reason to think I didn't know anything about his molesting me. I'm sure he thought I just wasn't talking about it, even as a grown woman."

"Well, it's only recently that scientists suggested that sexual abuse victims could have no memory. Amnesia would probably never have crossed his mind."

I shrugged. "Yep, and along those lines, Dad's behavior makes more sense now-- why he asked about my childhood at Thanksgiving. I didn't know what he was referring to, but he wanted to find out if I remembered. He must have read the news reports, just like I did." I closed my eyes at the madness. "The articles must have been his first realization that I might not remember anything."

"It might have been great news to your father, or it could have scared him to death." Peter's eyebrows rose.

I rubbed my eyes. "I bet it scared Dad. He thought I knew about his assaults all along and, for some unknown reason, wasn't ever going to say anything. He had no idea how I'd respond to the knowledge or how loud I'd yell about it if I'd forgotten."

"Hmm," Peter said.

"After Mom died, he suddenly needed me gone. He seemed to think that Mom somehow protected him---I'll never understand that. Dad's solution was to tell me to 'get lost,' 'you're not my daughter,' and 'I'm not your father anymore.' He had to get me out of his life. His strange behavior all makes sense now. He'll be set straight with my letter—he won't be confused any longer." I smiled broadly.

Peter sat forward on his chair, folding his hands in his lap. "I'll be anxious to see the letter you write."

"It'll be so difficult to write." I frowned, looking sideways. "Despite everything my 'bad' Dad did, it will be an official goodbye to my 'good' dad, the one I loved." My eyes glistened as the grief came. "I'm dreading the loss in my family when I start speaking openly about his abuse."

"It will be hard to confront him, but you'll be glad you did. You can do this."

I shrugged.

Sitting down that night with my feet on a chair, I sipped a cup of hot black coffee out of my favorite moose-shaped mug. Katie was a good companion, with the rest of the household blissfully asleep. Petting her soft fur, I gathered my courage. I had to get this letter written.

It felt surreal and unbelievable as I started to write. I couldn't believe incest was in my family. I was confronting Dad's Mr. Hyde, a stranger that had done everything he could to destroy me. How did I get to this place in my life, I wondered--saying goodbye to my own father? It was difficult, but it was long past due, and I was anxious to tell the truth. It would be the first time his horrible sexual assaults would be in the open after thirty years.

I suddenly wanted to cling to the past, so afraid of my future. Somehow at this moment, the old days looked so much safer. I forced my fears away and grabbed a sheet of paper. I had to write the letter now

Dear Dad,

I remember now. You were molesting me! You were having sex with your own daughter! What the hell is wrong with you? With my recent memories, I am horrified. You caused so much suffering in my life. It is beyond my capacity to understand how my own father could have done this. I had no idea this had occurred until this year and I'm appalled by your actions. Your job was to protect me at all costs, and instead, you hurt me deeply. The suffering I'm going through now is incomprehensible. I wouldn't wish this pain on my worst enemy.

I only have fragments of what occurred, so I need to know as many details as possible. Please have the courage to admit to what you did. How old was I? When did it start and when did it stop? How could you live with yourself after destroying your daughter?

You were alone with Andrew and Carrie several times. Did you molest my children? My nieces and nephew? You are truly an evil man, a felon who, so far, has gotten away with your massive crimes but no longer.

I beg you to acknowledge your horrible abuse so I can fully heal. I want a profound apology—that's the very least you can do. I want you to take responsibility for your vile actions.

You taught me always to be honest and trustworthy. I'm being as honest as I've ever been in my life now. After answering these questions, don't ever contact me again. You are as evil and vile as anyone could be. You no longer have the privilege of being my father.

Carol

I dropped my head down on the desk and wept into my folded arms as I finished. My grief over losing myself, my family as I'd known it, and my 'good' father shattered me. I had no idea how he would react or who he might tell. I could barely handle what I was already dealing with and knew I couldn't take much more.

That evening after dinner, I leaned emotionally on Michael. "How can I send this? I'm saying goodbye to my 'good' father and everything I know about my family. It will be like a bomb hitting them if he tells Mark, Debbie, and Tim. I never saw myself in this horrible position."

"Yeah, you're in an awful position. That you had amnesia will be shocking to your dad. But I'm proud of you. Confronting him takes huge guts." Michael hugged me for a long time as I nuzzled into his shoulder. My tears and mascara dirtied his white shirt. "Remember, your father is to blame, not you. He already knows what he did."

"Yep. I better send it right now while I have the nerve."

I jumped in the car and drove to the post office. I stared at the open mailbox drop as I held the letter in my shaking hand. Should I let it go or just tear it up? I hated my indecision and finally let go of it. I knew my life would never be the same again, but I did what I had to do.

Sending that letter was one of the hardest things I'd ever done, but it was also one of my life's most significant accomplishments. I was proud of my courage to face my perpetrator directly and speak out about the horror I had survived at his hands.

There could be no greater honor.

Carol C.Boyce

Chapter 34

You're a Liar

Andrew, now seven, and I played with his beloved wood trains on the family room floor on a hot August afternoon. Five-year-old Carrie tried to join him. "You can be the caboose, but you have to go fast like this." He showed her how speedy his long train could be.

"Okay." She smiled big, so thrilled her brother would allow her to play. She yelled, "Choo, choo," trying to make the caboose keep up with the engine.

I was hungry from my new grapefruit diet as I headed to the garage to gather our mail. I was always on a diet, though I never lost weight for any length of time. It had been a week since I sent the letter to Dad, who was still living in southern California.

Dad's perfect cursive jumped out at me in the stack of envelopes. How could he have written back so soon? Didn't he need to think about this? I didn't want a fast reply—I'd barely recovered from sending my letter in the first place. I dreaded his potential response. I hoped he'd give some deep thought to my allegations.

My hands trembled as I slowly opened the envelope.

August 3, 1991

Dear Carol,

You are lying

I have never touched you or any of my grandchildren ever. I have never touched a child or infant in the entire world ever. Your letter was just a rambling mess. If anyone had touched you while at home, I may have killed that person.

It has been my experience that persons having problems see psychotherapists that blame the parents instead of psychiatrists who blame the patient themselves.

I am a very uncomplicated, open person. I have spent 40 years in medical practice helping people, not tearing them down. I also fixed things at your house for you.

Your mother and father loved you, and although we made mistakes, we gave you an enriched childhood. Your mother worked at the church nursery school for years to get your names on the pre-school list. I remember camping, taking you to the ER when you broke your finger, and taking you to college.

I hope you improve.

Dad

Michael arrived home soon after and saw me lying on our bed, curled in a ball. The kids remained occupied watching *Sesame Street* in the family room. "What happened?" He pulled off his tie. "Oh…you must have heard from your dad…"

"Yep." I caught my breath and handed him the letter. "To see Dad's handwriting…he called me a liar! My own father." The white pillowcases were wet, and Michael grabbed me more

Kleenex. "With everything I'm going through, he didn't acknowledge anything. Nothing! Dad could care less about me, only himself." I blew my nose. "I guess I should have already figured that out."

Michael sat down next to me on the bed and rubbed my back. "It's like we expected...and it must be so painful."

"Somehow, I hoped I meant more to him. I'm his daughter! Doesn't he know I'll never have a relationship with him again? That it's over?"

"You'd think he'd get it." Michael looked down. He had a friendship with Dad over the sixteen years he had known him and was sad also that I'd lost his presence in the family. He knew that the kids were losing a grandfather in addition to their grandmother's death years earlier, and he knew how essential grandparents could be. Though he respected him as a successful physician and a good, stable father until the last few years, he'd never done many activities with Dad and wasn't particularly close to him.

I wiped my face with a wet, crumpled tissue. "Dad stole my childhood from me, and he won't even admit it. I dreamed of hearing, 'I'm so, so sorry, Carol. I don't know how I could have done this to you. Forgive me? How can I make it up to you?'"

"Unfortunately, I don't think you're ever gonna hear that." He changed into a t-shirt and jeans. "I wish I had more control over the situation, that I could magically remove your pain--make this go away." He looked warmly at me.

"I wish you could, too." Sitting up, I blew my nose.

His eyebrows squeezed together. "I'll write him a letter and tell him what I think. I'll let him have it. How dare he treat you—us---like this. It's appalling. And to think I thought he didn't have a mean bone in his body."

"Michael, please don't write him. You deserve to vent, but it'd make it that much messier for me--harder, not easier. Right now, it's between him and me." I hugged him. "But thanks anyway."

It was strange to see my father's handwritten, official response to my accusations. I had something tangible and real in my hand for the first time, though I could see he had no guilt, regret, or remorse. I should have expected this response, but I'd been hoping for an apology. How much his actions had destroyed my life and my incredible suffering didn't matter to him. His only care was about himself, just as when he abused me. As horrible as I felt, I had finally confronted him and was glad the abuse was out in the open between us.

With his denials of molesting any child, Mike and I worried deeply about whether he'd hurt my kids. Watching them for unusual fears and behaviors became our only possibility. We lived for years without knowing whether Dad had molested them, and I carried guilt and horror for allowing a pedophile around my children. I berated myself for not having the slightest inkling of what had occurred between Dad and me.

That said it all. Dad was willing, once again, to use and blame me, despite his high moral character and teachings on truth and honesty when I was growing up. My future with him was heartbreakingly clear--it was over. I was still in such denial and his gaslighting was a powerful weapon. I wanted my fantasy good father back and for all of this to just go away.

Chapter 35

Not My Kids

T rying to parent while in a deep depression and battling PTSD was tough. I wouldn't transfer my anger and pain to Michael or my children, as my mother and father had to my siblings and me. Mike worked with the kids as much as possible when he was off work, playing baseball and swimming, and helping keep a healthy normal home environment. I wasn't as emotionally available to them as they needed me to be during those years, but I gave them all the love and care I could muster.

One afternoon, as I stared out a window, seven-year-old Andrew asked, "What's wrong, Mommy? What are you looking at? Don't you want to play trains?" He peered up at me with his big hazel eyes.

Tousling his blonde curls, I replied, "I'm sad right now. It's not about you or anything you've done. But I need time to think."

I didn't want to tell my innocent son the truth--he was too young to understand it, but I worried my depression was affecting him. How could it not? I didn't want my trauma to involve the kids, but there was no way to avoid the fall-out; I could only minimize the damage. The best I could do was talk about my feelings honestly.

My parents never understood the critical distinction between a child's and a parent's feelings and that they were responsible for the healthy handling of their emotions. I had to shoulder my pain entirely and not transfer it to my children.

I explained to Andrew so he could understand, "Grandad hit me when I was little, and he hurt me. I'm angry and sad about it." I hoped this gave him something concrete to understand. "My sadness has nothing to do with you and I'll be better as soon as I can. It happened a long time ago." I hugged him tightly and kissed his forehead.

Andrew could relate to how hurt he would be, and my simple explanation made sense to him. He never asked again.

The following week, I sat down on Peter's oversized couch, next to the ever-present box of Kleenex, and scowled. "I've tried so hard to keep my issues to myself, but Andrew has asked me about my depression. It's not fair he has to suffer, also. This damn abuse bleeds onto everyone!"

Peter pulled up his chair. "All kids experience some pain in their childhood. It wouldn't be normal if everything were perfect. That's not real life." We'd gone through this issue before, and Peter wanted me to understand that all kids experience problems, and mine would be okay.

I leaned forward and glared at Peter. "Not my kids. They are not going to feel this pain if I can help it! I'm not going to let their grandfather's deeds spill into their lives, too." I couldn't bear them feeling my angst. I had enough pain for all of us. I thought of my vow to them. "They won't ever feel what I felt. I'll do anything to keep their childhoods happy!"

"They won't feel how you did. Your children will never have the severe trauma you had, the lack of love and nurturing. They can still have a happy, emotionally healthy childhood, even with some problems." Peter explained.

Breathing deeply, I sat up straight. "Maybe I'm blinded by what happened, but I will be as protective, loving, and encouraging as possible with them. They deserve a happy childhood."

Peter rolled his eyes. He knew he hadn't convinced me.

Chapter 36

Go Outside

Despite all my work and professional help, the constant pain, terror, and confusion of recovering remained overwhelming. Reliving the emotions from hundreds of sexual assaults was destroying me, overpowering all my coping skills. I was losing the battle.

After dropping the kids off at school one morning, I, once again, lay on my bed alone, hugging my soft pillow. I knew I couldn't go on any longer like this—there was no more fight in me. I stared out the window with glazed eyes. Like a Sherpa who hauls a climber's gear for treks on Mount Everest, I desperately needed someone to help carry my load, but no one could. I prayed for help but couldn't feel any strength coming back at me.

A bluebird swooped down on a small table outside my picture window. Laying on my stomach, he was at my eye level. I watched him for a long time, fluffing his beautiful, azure feathers, enjoying his glorious grandeur.

He seemed to sense my grief, staring unflinchingly back at me. As we looked at each other, a message came to me in his silence. "Come outside--it's a spectacular world out here. Look how beautiful it is!"

The message made me chuckle, coming from a bird, but it roused me from my depression, and new thoughts came to me. *Go outside--the world is breathtaking. Fight on--you are worth it. Don't give up--an entire life is waiting for you. Draw strength from others. Leave this isolation and get outside.*

It became a turning point in my recovery. The beautiful bird reminded me to stop being so isolated. I needed to leave my house and get outside to see that life was still going on. There was beauty in the blue skies, the green plants, and the budding of dogwoods and hydrangeas. I could gain strength and normalcy from the happy children at parks with loving parents, grandparents, and family dogs, unburdened by depression. I needed to know that others were still functioning. It would also give me a sense of safety to have people around when I didn't want to live anymore.

I changed my daily coping method. Slowly, I'd drive around my quiet neighborhood for a while and then park in a shaded, secluded area when overwhelmed. The feelings I faced were intense and not something I could talk out rationally. In my car's privacy, I was able to let out all my pain, all my frustration, all my terror, all my anger, all my lost childhood, and all my broken dreams.

I screamed at Dad. "You fucking jerk, how could you have done this to your own daughter?" As Laura had taught me, I pounded the passenger seat with as much strength as I could muster. "You fucking asshole, you asshole—what the hell was wrong with you? How can you live with yourself?" To Mom, I yelled, "Where the hell were you? Why didn't you stop drinking and realize you had children that needed you? I loved you so much, but you never realized it."

On another drive, I grieved. "I loved you. Dad. Why couldn't you love me back? You did everything you could to destroy me and then just walked away." I'd start with my rage, which was easier to acknowledge, go to my fears, and end with my profound loss and sadness. I sobbed deeply and uncontrollably many times, as I desperately needed to release the pain.

Remarkably, no one ever noticed my strange behavior. Nobody knocked on my car window to ask if I was okay, questioned my sanity, or called the police for the 'losing it' woman. It was amazing.

These forays outside restored my will to live, to fight on for my family and me. The enormous task of getting out the emotion became attainable and helped move me forward from the quicksand of depression.

It is still my go-to when difficult emotions arise.

Chapter 37

Nothing but a Good Father

In 1992, not long after confronting my father, I knew it was past time to tell my sister and two brothers about my memories. Now thirty-eight and Dad sixty-seven, I felt like I had enough clarity and strength to face them for the first time. Interestingly, Dad had not said anything to my siblings about my contentions. I needed to explain my sudden attitude change toward him and warn them to protect my nieces and nephew.

There would be significant hurdles to my sibling's understanding and acceptance of my news. Sexual abuse by Dad, as far as I knew, remained limited to me--none of them had come forward. I prayed I was the only one, but questions remained. Why was I the only child? Or was I? Did they not remember, too, or were they just not saying anything? It would be unusual for a perpetrator to stop with one child when there were four and molest only one daughter when there were two. I also knew that my memory suddenly returning would lead to doubts as this survival method was not common, understood, or accepted at that time.

Another challenge would be Dad's gentle and calm demeanor. How could they believe who he really was without seeing his other side themselves? In therapy, Peter had warned me early on that no one wanted to know about sexual abuse in their family. He advised me that they would do anything to deny the truth: blame the victim, therapist, and anyone possible to protect the family perpetrator.

He couldn't have been more prophetic.

At one time, I had believed, as my brothers and sister did, that Dad was the composed, good guy, the victim of Mom. As adults, we had discussed Mom's drinking and anger several times and there was no illusion of happy, carefree childhoods with any of us. We had all suffered and coped in our own ways. It seemed clear that Mom carried the blame for our painful family story.

I now knew Mom's anger was only the tip of the family's painful iceberg with my new recollections. Hiding beneath icy waves was the massive blue base holding the dark family secrets of incest and terror. I worried the base's sheer size might cause my siblings to deny my revelations, but I believed my good character would be enough to convince them I was telling the truth. As difficult as it would be, I hoped they'd trust and support me. I was desperate for some compassion from my family.

Because my sister's and brothers' homes were far away, I rarely saw them. Since I couldn't tell them in person—I'd have to call.

On a rainy February evening, I put the kids to bed, dreading the calls I had to make. They would forever change our family. I dialed my oldest brother. "Hi, Mark. I hope you're doing well. I…uh...need to talk to you about something important."

"What is it?" His voice sounded curious.

"Dad molested me...uh… I've just recently remembered it and it's been horrible." *Oh my God, I actually said it aloud.* My heart pounded, realizing that it was now on the table for all to know. I took another deep breath. "You must protect your daughter from him."

He responded quickly and curtly, "Dad's been nothing but a wonderful father to me. I don't know what you're talking about." As the oldest, Mark idolized Dad. I could hear at once in his voice that nothing I said would shake his belief. He asked no questions and did not acknowledge my suffering.

"Take care, Carol." Click.

That phone disconnecting seemed so final, so deafening in its coldness. *That's all Mark's going to say?* I stared at the receiver. He meant so much to me and all he gave me were a few short words.

His lack of empathy and interest unnerved me. I worried that all my siblings would react in the same defensive way. But I had to keep calling the others, knowing my courage would only last so long.

"Debbie, it's Carol, uh," I stammered. "I need to talk to you about...uh... something terrible that's happened."

"You're scaring me. What is it? Did somebody die?" Debbie's voice rose.

"I... I was molested by Dad...for a long time." My voice trailed off, sad to cause her pain. I hated being the messenger of painful news.

"What are you talking about?"

"I survived terrifying sexual abuse by him." I shivered from the adrenaline rush. "I've recently remembered it--it's been horrible."

Her silence showed the shock she felt. After a lengthy pause, she said, "Why would you remember now?"

My voice cracked. "I got memories last year. I had no idea this happened, but it's not uncommon for people to forget sexual abuse."

Another long pause. "This doesn't sound right. Dad would never have done that. He's a good person—you know that.'

Calmly, I said, "Above all, protect your kids."

"Goodbye." Debbie ended the call abruptly.

Tim, my youngest sibling, understood better than the others that our father and mother had significant emotional problems. As the youngest, he had paid a higher price for Mom's increasing alcoholism as the last one to leave home. My brother had plenty of his own childhood pain and confusion to resolve. I hoped he might understand better than the others as I continued my calls.

Tim answered on the first ring, and I told him my news. "Carol, this was a long time ago. Leave it alone--sexual abuse happens all the time."

"So, because it happens frequently, does that make it okay?" I could feel the anger surging into my head.

"No, but don't stir this up—Dad's just an old man."

"Yeah, an old man who committed atrocities."

I had needed so much love and compassion from my siblings at this horrible time in my life but got nothing. I comforted myself by saying they were in shock and hoped they'd call me back soon to offer support. But as the years went by, no help came.

I hadn't expected this total denial. I hoped my siblings would be the ones I could lean on in times of crisis, but this was too close, too difficult to understand. Defending 'poor' Dad became their primary focus. I wept at this new loss, feeling isolated and alone.

Debbie called me several months later. Her children were now five and seven. She updated me on her life. "We had a nice visit with Dad last week. It was great weather--we went sailing."

Rage pulsed through my veins. "You can't take your kids around Dad. He's a pedophile!"

With a calm voice, she said, "It's okay. Dad never molested me."

She wasn't getting it and I was sick with fear for my niece and nephew. "Whether you believe me or not, please don't risk their safety. Dad isn't safe!"

Mark also brought his daughter on visits to her grandfather, and I was horrified that my siblings would allow their precious children around a pedophile. I had no idea what Dad might do or who he would target next, but I had little control. With Dad living four hundred miles away, I had few options to intervene. I warned them, however. "If I hear the kids have been near Dad, I'll notify the police." I meant every word.

Despite my threats and pleas, their visits never stopped. They just hid them from me, hoping I wouldn't find out. In their minds, hurting Dad's feelings more than I already had, seemed cruel and unjustified. To my horror, their denial was so profound that their kids became pawns in a dangerous game of protecting Dad.

Decades after informing Tim of the sexual abuse, he shared, "you say one thing and Dad says another. I can't tell who is telling the truth." That gave him license not to choose who was telling the truth.

"Do you think we have equal motivation to lie, Tim? Do you realize Dad has a great reason, but I have none? I'm getting nothing from this except pain. Going through this hell is not entertainment." I was livid.

Around this time in 1992, Dad's only sister, Judy, called to see me. My aunt was always so kind and was someone I admired for her many musical accomplishments and loving demeanor, but she didn't usually visit. I knew this would be about my accusations.

It was a sweltering day and the gardenias blooming on our porch smelled heavenly. I grabbed Katie, who was barking loudly, and opened the door when she knocked. The air conditioning in the house felt good as I brought out a tray of iced tea. "Hi, Aunt Judy. So good to see you." We hugged and kissed each other on the cheek.

Sitting on the living room sofa, she got down to business right away. "I heard about your accusations against my brother. You can't be serious! Walt's nothing but a fine, kind man. He loves you dearly."

I looked down and shook my head. "I am serious. Your brother molested me for years." My eyes burned with tears. It was still hard to hear it aloud and I hated that it was causing her pain— she had nothing to do with it.

"Maybe these memories are from your therapist? You know, a lot are introduced by them." She continued pressing me.

I squeezed my wet eyes shut. "They're not from my therapist." I couldn't believe I was hearing this old belief again. "This happened. He was molesting me through most of my childhood."

Aunt Judy sipped her tea. "You know our friend had memories of sexual abuse with her father, and she forgave him and moved on right away. She didn't dwell on it like you are."

My eyes widened with her minimization. *Forget about it? What a joke. I'd like to see you forget about it. You try to recover—let me see how long you 'dwell' on it.*

Here I was, barely surviving and no one in my family even cared. Defending Dad was, once again, the primary concern. With a clenched jaw, I replied, "This was severe, prolonged abuse that started when I was young. It's not something I will forgive and forget. I'm just beginning to heal now, and he must be held accountable." I looked away in disbelief. "My relationship with Dad is over. And I'm not dwelling on it!"

She rolled her eyes. "How could you say this about my wonderful brother? I've known him to be kind and truthful for sixty years."

She finally left frustrated, unable to change my mind. My heart broke from the pain it was causing my family. I knew Aunt Judy meant well, but she could not fathom Dad's dual personality like my siblings. She couldn't believe her kind and respected brother had an evil side. It's extremely hard to believe something you haven't seen yourself.

A few months later, Aunt Judy called me again. "You know, your father is going to die someday! You can't continue to be this cold to him!" She continued, "He will die, and you will never see him again. How could you do this to your own father?"

I rubbed my forehead firmly, closing my eyes, repeating my earlier statement. "Thank you for caring, but my relationship with Dad is over. I must hold him accountable." My anger grew as not one word of compassion for me emerged. I wondered how she could not understand how devastating this loss was for me, the last thing I ever wanted in my life. I shuddered, wondering how long my family would respond so cruelly and naively to me.

Like gold and red leaves falling to the autumn ground, my family's support of me dropped with each denial. My empty branches shivered with their nakedness, rustling alone in a chilly wind. I couldn't understand how they could support a perpetrator over me--it was madness. I already battled my sanity daily, and this rattled me even more. That Dad was a pedophile was unfathomable to these well-educated, intelligent people. They condoned my father's criminal behaviors, their own sister's attacker, letting him off scot-free.

Dad continued to join in all the family birthdays, holiday celebrations, and weddings. My allegations remained ignored, and he enjoyed the compassion shown for his daughter's horrible treatment of him.

I felt discarded, extremely hurt, and unimportant seeing the smiling photos from events without me. My character, not Dad's, became questioned, trampled, and doubted amongst my relatives. Their unwavering support of Dad felt like I was more expendable, the identified sick family member with all the emotional pathology. It was appalling.

It took me decades to understand my family's painful position Dad's abuse had placed them in. They had a horrible choice—him or me. They desperately wanted to keep both relationships intact—they loved each of us dearly and didn't want to choose between us. They just didn't want to know and couldn't handle the truth.

Everyone paid an enormous price for Dad's assaults, regardless of whether they believed me. Over the decades, the situation affected everyone: grandchildren, children, siblings, nieces, nephews, aunts, uncles, and cousins. The closer people were to Dad, the more trouble they had believing me. They, like juries, wanted hard evidence before they trusted me, but there wasn't any. Incest and sexual abuse damage are primarily emotional, not physical.

I was in the same position as victims in the sexual abuse cases I'd heard about in the news. People didn't believe the first, second, or third accusers of Larry Nasar with the Olympic gymnasts, Michael Jackson, Bill Cosby, Jeffrey Epstein, and the priests in the Catholic Church. Countless children and adults experienced sexual assaults because no action occurred with the first accusers—they were too nice, wealthy, or kind to believe it. Those who spoke out were criticized and rarely supported. People can't believe that molesters are often charming, kind, and trusted community members. This must change.

My family may never believe me and continue to blame me for the family pain. They never asked for this horror in the family, nor did I. They didn't deserve this in their lives any more than I did. Dad never thought or cared enough about the enormous problems he created for *everyone* in the family. Extraordinarily self-centered and cruel, he was only interested in his immediate need for sexual gratification and power. He has no remorse or conscience for the devastation and victimization of our incredible, innocent family.

Chapter 38

Law Flaws

It was 1992, one year since I recalled the abuse as I sat down in my local police station's reception area on a cold plastic chair. A young woman paced up and down the dirty vinyl floor with spiked hair and a black leather jacket. I tapped my foot as I watched the large clock click over the door, wondering how long I'd have to wait. Curled paper signs and notices covered the walls.

After ten minutes, the burly officer in charge called me up. He looked at his paper in front of him and loudly asked, "Whatcha here for?" Privacy didn't seem to concern him.

"I want to charge my father with abuse...uh...sexual abuse." I looked down at the old stickers on the counter.

"Okay." He opened his desk drawer and pulled out a padded form. So, give me his name, address, and phone number.

I gave him the details as he filled in the form. "What day did this occur?"

"In the late '50s and 60s."

He looked at me and laughed out loud. "That was waaay too long ago. The statute of limitations is long over. We can't do anything." He crumpled and tossed the form into the receptacle, calling the next person's name in line.

"Wait a minute. I can't believe this. Do you mean my father is a free man? After what he did to me? It's a profoundly serious case."

"Well, why didn't you press charges earlier?" The officer gave me a sideways glance. "It's your fault you waited so long."

I leaned into the counter as my blood pressure rose. "I only remembered last year. I had no idea this had occurred before then."

"Yeah, sure." The officer sneered, curling his upper lip.

I brusquely gathered my purse and glasses and headed to the car, slamming the door behind me. I couldn't believe there was nothing the police could do.

Months later, I consulted a family law attorney to file a civil suit against Dad. He needed consequences for his actions. I walked into the attorney's beautiful, wood-paneled office and sat on the walnut and leather chair. I noticed the framed degrees on the wall and the hundreds of law books on the mahogany bookcase as his assistant brought me a cup of coffee.

The well-dressed man shook my hand as he entered the office, sitting at his large desk. "Hello. How can I help you today?"

"I want to sue my father for molesting me."

He fiddled with his tie. "Tell me more about this."

I explained the situation that I'd only become aware of the assaults in the past several years.

His heavy brows lifted. "You mean you had no memory of it? Seriously?"

"I had no memory of it until recently—absolutely none. My father seriously abused me, and it's been devastating to remember it." I looked down, embarrassed to speak to a stranger about incest.

"How about your siblings—would they corroborate your story, validate, and support you?"

"No, my brothers and sister would not support me at all. They think our father is wonderful." I smirked and shifted in my seat. "What recourse do I have? Recovering from this abuse has cost me tens of thousands of dollars in therapy bills and lost wages, and he's never paid one dime."

He put his notepad away. "You'd be laughed out of the courtroom. You have no hard evidence and no corroboration from anyone. A court would eat you up and spit you out the other end."

"How could this be? The police won't prosecute him, and the civil courts won't do anything either. He walks away a free man? He should be spending the rest of his days in a jail cell." I was seething with frustration.

"You can do what you want but know a good defense attorney will attack your mental health from every angle. They will subpoena all your therapy records." His eyes never wavered. "Plus, it was way too long ago. Your father's lawyers will use all of it and any sexual past you have against you. They'll rip you apart."

"So, am I getting this straight? Survivors develop mental injury *because* of the perpetrator's actions and courts use this against them?" I couldn't believe how uneducated and outdated our judicial systems were in trauma-informed care. "And just for the record, I don't have any lurid sexual past to worry about." I crossed my arms. "What other crimes happen where courts look at deep knife wounds and use it to deny the victim was stabbed?"

He cleared his throat. "I know it's hard to understand, but that's the law today."

"Because it was years ago doesn't make it any less criminal. If it was last week or fifty years ago, is it any less felonious and devastating to the victim?"

"Well, whatever...the statute of limitations is long past."

"And why would there be a statute of limitation with sexual abuse? People often don't remember it for decades, and it takes years to process it after that. They cannot quickly deal with it and face our legal system simultaneously." My heart was pounding.

"Nonetheless, it would be futile to try civil recourse or criminal prosecution. Don't waste your time or money--your father will win. I guarantee it." He sniffed and straightened his tie. Shaking my hand, he strode out of the room.

Dad had won all the legal battles without stepping foot in a courtroom.

There was no way to prosecute my father, and he would never spend one day in prison or pay any monetary damages for his heinous crimes. Without any legal ramifications for the incredible financial and emotional destruction to my life, I felt further victimized. Because of statutes of limitation, lack of supporting evidence, and disbelief in traumatic amnesia, I became one more victim failed by our flawed legal system. Another perpetrator went free. As the primary financial support of a large family and given the era, Dad could assume at the time that he wouldn't face prosecution.

He was correct.

Because delayed recall of developmental trauma is highly controversial and often lacks outside corroboration or evidence, no jury would prosecute Dad at that time or even today. Courts are often under the dated belief that nothing as traumatic as sexual abuse could ever be forgotten. However, scientific research clearly shows sexual abuse can be more traumatic than war or accidents. Thankfully today, most psychological professionals accept amnesia from sexual assault as a normal response to trauma.

Research shows that returning memories are explosive and devastating to the traumatic amnesia victim, no matter the cause. Overwhelming emotion, anxiety, and PTSD, both before and after remembering, create mental instability in victims. Defense teams use this to negate all victim credibility though it was the perpetrator who caused it. When the accuser is struggling mentally, courts must realize that they're seeing more evidence of the crime, not an excuse to exonerate the perpetrator. (Salmona, Muriel, 2018)

Considerable stigma exists about how survivors "should" or "shouldn't" respond to severe trauma. Dr. James Hopper, an expert Harvard psychiatrist in traumatic memory, has shown that the brain takes over during highly traumatic assaults, and no one has a choice in how our bodies react. Responses are automatic and out of the survivor's control, as with me. I had no choice in how my brain responded, yet its subconscious decisions condemned me. If I'd been a victim of war or accident, none of these problems would have existed. Education is the only hope for people to believe and understand normal fear responses. (Harsey, 2017) (Hopper J., 2014)

Carol C.Boyce

I learned that statutes of limitations, the maximum number of years after a crime is committed that the victim can press charges, are significant deterrents to prosecuting sexual perpetrators in our patriarchal society. These statutes exist for most offenses. Based on current law, the only crimes without them are ones that courts consider 'serious,' specifically murder, embezzlement of public funds, and treason. But sexual abuse *is* a profoundly 'serious' crime and cases need evaluation on a case-by-case basis. These statutes must never close the doors to the prosecution of sexual predators.

The nature of sexual abuse is that there is rarely outside evidence or corroboration to prove the crime. Convictions based only on memories or recollections are never enough in other types of cases and are questionable in any legal proceedings. This requirement, however, becomes a high hurdle in most amnesia-related sexual abuse cases because the physical evidence often doesn't exist. Therefore, successful prosecution today is still at merely eight percent of perpetrators. Ninety-two percent escape scot-free, resulting in more assaults and more victims. The primary evidence is the victim's statement and emotional and mental damage. Adults like me who recall long-ago abuse rarely have physical scars, nor is there evidence from the long-ago crime scene. The most severe cases are often not recognized until decades later, if at all.

Traumatic amnesia can take decades to appear, and our courts must allow for that. The victim does not choose their method of survival. Amnesia chooses them. It is a sign of severe trauma and all professionals, teachers, lawyers, judges, law enforcement, and medical personnel require trauma-informed training. The fundamental principles taught are safety, choice, collaboration, trustworthiness, and empowerment, all critical concepts for finding and treating survivors.

One tangible source of evidence has emerged with MRI brain scans. Permanent changes to the abused child's brain can now support a survivor's case. MRIs are a meaningful change for victims of early sexual abuse, and the science continues to grow. Severe childhood maltreatment is associated with remarkable functional and structural changes, even decades later in adulthood. The brain scans are physical corroborating evidence that could help court cases. (De Bellis, 2011; Crum, 2021)

The high rates of sexual abuse will continue until we educate about the nature of the crime, the perpetrator's countenance, and how memory stores assaults.

Even though I couldn't prosecute him, my father still paid a hefty penalty. He lost me, his oldest daughter, and my family. All the joy they could have offered him was gone. He lost contact and connection with two of his five grandchildren and, eventually, his only great-grandchildren. He lost the relationship with my husband, which had been enjoyable for fifteen years. I'm glad some profound consequences existed for his devastating life choices.

Chapter 39

Someone Else

In 1993, Dad was vacationing in northern California with his new wife, Ellie, when he called to ask if he could attend a therapy appointment with Peter the next day. Surprised by his request, I called Peter to see if he'd agree to it on such short notice.

"Do you want to have this conversation with your father? You don't have to. It could be very tough," Peter advised me.

My foot tapped on the tile of the kitchen. "Dad said when he called that he wanted to 'figure out what this nonsense was about.' It doesn't sound good, but I haven't seen him since I remembered. I want to see his face and connect my two fathers--the good and bad. I want to look into his eyes and see they're both there." Though I questioned how it would go, I thought the meeting would be important.

"You need to be strong—he'll try to manipulate the truth."

"Dad will deny everything, but I want to see him in person—we've never discussed anything eye-to-eye." My voice trailed off as I stared at the floor. "The hardest part will be that it'll be the unspoken in-person end of our relationship."

After some silence, Peter said, "Okay then—I'll see you and your father at noon tomorrow." He had never met any members of my family, and this meeting represented a significant risk. He had no idea whether Dad might react physically or verbally to my accusations.

The following day, I bounced my knee and fidgeted with my hair as I sat in Peter's reception room. I didn't know how I would react to Dad or if I could hold my emotions in enough to not beat the crap out of him. My hands were shaking as I sat down in Peter's office. I prayed I could do this.

Dad parked his rented motorhome outside, and I could hear Peter's door creak as he entered. He had gotten lost coming to the office and seemed agitated and flustered as he sat on the chair between Peter's and mine. I made brief introductions, and Dad sneered without acknowledging either of us. "So, what's this garbage all about?"

"You know what this is about. You molested me for years and I just remembered it." I was shaking, having my first direct conversation about his abuse with him. Saying it aloud made it seem more painfully real. I wondered how I had gotten here. It felt disorienting and surreal saying these words directly to his face. I had never stood up to him or talked back growing up--it had never felt safe. Even as an adult, breaking this taboo felt uncomfortable, like I was still a child. These words now came from a new, powerful adult, someone I didn't know.

"Yes." He responded quickly in an authoritative voice. "As a doctor, I believe you were molested, although it wasn't me. I don't know who could have done it...uh...but it certainly wasn't me."

I screamed inside my head as my heart raced. What is Dad talking about? "What other man would walk around our house at night? Who is this unknown person you're referring to that molested me? Who, Dad, who?" I sat red-faced, my jaw clenched. I was losing it. I yelled, "No one else was in our house. It was you and you know it and you've lost your daughter and grandkids because of it!" I wanted to kill him and sob hysterically at the same time, but I knew I had to hold it all in.

"Carol, take a deep breath." Peter shifted uncomfortably in his seat.

"No, it wasn't me," Dad replied calmly. "It was someone else. I have helped people as a physician my whole career--I am a healer. I would never hurt anyone." His eyes never wavered. "How could you say this after all I've done for you? I just hope your kids do this to you someday."

Staring intently, my back straight, I replied. "My kids would have no reason to." I felt near hysteria. "It was you, Dad, and you alone, and it devastated me." I glared at him, fighting the chaos of many emotions. Thank God Peter was there to mediate this explosive conversation.

"Why would I hurt someone?" He was convincing himself of his innocence. After a moment, he glared at Peter and, insulting him, exclaimed, "You do everything first class, Carol, except medical treatment."

The session was over, and Dad stormed from the office, furious he hadn't "straightened me out." I had held my ground and though I was still shaking, the confrontation was behind me. I'd survived, to my great relief. I thought about how much easier it was to show my anger rather than the profound grief I felt.

Peter smiled at me. "I'm proud of you. Despite what he said, you were strong and never wavered or compromised your position. You made it clear that he had molested you, lost you and your family, and that you wouldn't put up with any of his lies anymore. You stood up for yourself...and were powerful."

"Thanks so much for standing by and supporting me. I'm sorry my father was so awful."

I had a lot to process. I left Peter's office dazed and overwhelmed. The weight in my chest overpowered any feelings of pride, but I had face-to-face told Dad what he'd done and how I felt. He had leaned heavily on his professional credentials, made no apology, and tried to make me feel guilt, reversing his responsibility. His gaslighting amazed me.

Dad's agreement that a stranger had molested me at night in our home was unexpected and laughable in its own way. It was the first and last I would ever hear him suggest that theory. Oddly, he must have realized soon after that it couldn't be true, as no other man was in the house routinely. After he got home, he quickly returned to his narrative that no sexual abuse occurred.

Confronting Dad at this meeting remains one of the most agonizing moments in my life, realizing the man before me I had so loved had caused my devastating visions, nightmares, and fears. Connecting this person and the 'dark man' was almost impossible during that brief hour. This meeting represented the only in-person farewell to my 'good' father, and grief overwhelmed me.

It would take a lifetime to accept.

A week after the session with my father and Peter, I picked the kids up from their Scout meetings. Carrie, now seven, had learned some new knots, and Andrew, now nine, had built a small wood boat for the Rain Gutter Regatta. They proudly showed me their projects, and I admired them.

After settling in, I picked up the mail in our garage slot and found a letter from Dad in the stack. So soon after the therapy appointment with Peter, I was surprised to hear from him. I guarded myself against more pain. I pulled the letter from the envelope.

July 1992

Dear Carol and Michael,

I arrived home at one A.M., utterly exhausted after leaving you on Monday. We had little time for sleep, having to return the rented RV. However, I was glad for the opportunity to meet your therapist.

My impressions of his operation were very disturbing and did not inspire confidence. A successful professional doesn't practice in a shabby storefront building. The surroundings of a professional person reflect how he feels about himself and his profession. I'm sure Michael will confirm this.

I'm sorry to hear, Carol, that you are so opposed to medication for relieving your symptoms. Patients often resort to using these symptoms to manipulate and control their families when crises arise. They can be a convenient escape mechanism for getting on with life. I hope you won't fall into this trap.

Post-traumatic stress syndrome improves with or without treatment. Your therapist sympathizes with you but has not helped you in the two years you have seen him. I would strongly urge that you contact the largest ER in the city for a referral to an MD psychiatrist and get started on definitive therapy.

The tension this situation has created is evident to everyone. It affects every member of our family. Your accusation has caused me great pain and I look forward to the time when our differences can be resolved.

Dad had developed innovative, innovative ideas. According to the doctor, a miraculous medication would make all my trauma evaporate. I'd have loved to know the name of this magic drug, but of course, it didn't exist. He didn't assume any responsibility and assured me my husband would agree with him, as if Mike supported him. In this letter, he again leaned heavily on his expertise as a physician. Dad made it clear--a psychiatrist would fix this problem in one or two visits and that trauma would go away without any outside therapy. He flipped the growing family tension to me.

As I continued to grieve and fight for my life, Dad transferred his accountability to Peter's office decor. It was so odd. The office was comfortable, clean, and ideally suited for private therapy in a historic part of town. Peter, he reasoned, didn't know what he was doing because of the location and style of his office. To him, it strangely proved Peter was incompetent and had constructed my abuse memories, a strange and illogical connection I would hear about for decades. Dad was grasping at straws, pointing the blame at anyone and anything other than himself. For decades, he would continue to use Peter's office location and décor to convince the family of his innocence.

And my family believed him.

Dad would also convince the rest of the family that Peter made up the sexual abuse and put it in my mind. They believed my therapist was an incredibly powerful charlatan who duped me into believing the abuse occurred. He never stated why Peter might want to do this or his motivation--there was none. In his mind, I was incapable of deciphering truth from fiction, a helpless pawn in a delusional therapist's game. It was so ridiculous and insulting.

Instead of thanking Peter for saving his daughter's life, Dad attacked him. In truth, he was an incredible therapist with an excellent, long-term reputation. Because of the severity of the abuse, my professional relationship with him was to last over twenty years. He helped me face the incredible trauma I needed to address, walking by my side through all the horrible times and providing direction when I had lost my way. I attribute much of my healing to his unfailing guidance, constant care, deep faith, and knowledge. I felt safe and had complete trust with him, traits critical to my recovery. Instead of attacking him, my family should have profusely thanked him for saving me.

I didn't respond to Dad's letter or any of the others I would receive from him over the years. I had said what I needed to say. It was too painful and not worth my energy to engage in any back-and-forth. I wasn't asking him--I was telling him the truth.

Michael brought in the mail on a cold November evening in 1993. Standing by the kitchen counter, he noticed a beautiful panorama of Hong Kong on a postcard. It had been six months since my confrontation at Peter's with Dad, and there'd been no communication between us since his last letter.

"Carol, there's a postcard from your dad. Do you want to read it?"

"You tell me. Do I?" I said, coming into the kitchen after bringing our hungry kids home from soccer practice. We never discussed my father's abuse around them, and Michael pre-read all mail from Dad now, per my request.

As the kids changed in their rooms, he smiled broadly. "Yes, it's about a trip he and Ellie are on."

I cautiously took the postcard from his hand, wondering why he was smiling.

Dear Family,

Having fun! The view from where we had dinner in Hong Kong last night was beautiful. We love China and its interesting sites. We are having fun shopping but doing little buying.

The dim sum brunches are interesting. The young Chinese use forks and wear Levi's—they're very westernized. It's been a great trip. Wish you were here.

Love, Dad

I felt flames shooting up my face as I whispered, "What the hell is this? Is he living in a fantasy world? Does he think this will all go away if he just ignores it?"

"It's crazy-making," Michael rolled his eyes. "He's hoping everything will miraculously go away, I guess."

"How does he go into total denial?" I fumed over the audacity he showed, minimizing his horrendous actions. I shook my head in disbelief, thinking my words hadn't fazed him. I was starting to see he lived in an imaginary world. It wouldn't be the last time he showed me this made-up world.

The postcard had said everything by saying nothing at all

In 1994, three years after I remembered, Dad sent another letter. Mike was out of town at a dental convention, and I decided to take a chance and read it. I should have left it for Mike to censor. *Maybe he's reconsidered and will confess. Perhaps he'll even apologize.*

Carol,

How could you try to destroy me and separate me from my children and grandchildren? Every accusation you have made is a venomous lie, and I will no longer tolerate this abuse.

I had made you the executor of my will. You are too unstable for such an important job. Therefore, send back all the financial papers I sent you; I'll make other plans. Until you treat me with the respect and the dignity I deserve, don't contact me or write to me ever.

Dad

I smirked, thinking how he wanted respect and dignity, precisely the qualities he took from me during the assaults. Behind his words, though, I realized that Dad was worried about his money and estate. After years of thinking about his actions and accountability, Dad's only concern was that I knew all his financial information.

I showed Michael the letter when he got home. He grinned and said, "It's almost laughable that he thinks you're unstable now after doing everything possible to make you that way."

"All of it is so ironic. Glad you see the humor in it." I frowned at him. "Now that I'm starting to recover mentally, Dad blasts me as unbalanced--and he was the cause. "

My eyes glistened with tears with grief for my once-beloved father. His obvious cruelty and total lack of caring was a reality I still didn't want to embrace.

Chapter 40

The Diagnosis

I had run a few errands and then drove to Peter's office. It was a glorious morning in the spring of 1994, and I'd much rather enjoy the sunlight today, but I knew my therapy was more important. The area of town was famous for its many roosters, and they always hung around Peter's office in this semi-rural area. I tripped over a red, yellow, and brown rooster squawking outside, catching myself on the door before spilling my cherished coffee. I was happy to grab myself before falling--smashing my face on concrete wasn't in the plan this morning.

I sat down, slightly shaken, and looked intently at Peter. I still had unanswered questions and wanted to ask a few. "So, I'm wondering what my actual diagnosis is? What do you call what I've been through?"

"Well, your primary diagnosis is Major Depression from Traumatic Developmental Amnesia and Complex Post-Traumatic Stress Disorder (CPTSD) from sexual abuse.

"That's a mouthful--sounds horrible."

"Complex PTSD means you have repeated assaults over months or years, rather than one or two events. With repetitive incest, it becomes more complex and harder to recover. Peter grabbed a handout that explained it.

"Well, it's certainly complicated. What about the Traumatic Developmental Amnesia? What is that?"

"It is a memory disorder primarily found in victims of severe sexual abuse during their childhood. These boys and girls survived by 'forgetting' what happened."

"So, it's not unusual to have amnesia as a kid, huh?"

"Not with a primary caregiver's severe and prolonged sexual abuse of a very young child."

"I'm glad to…uh… know there are names for what I've gone through." My eyes glazed over as I tried to absorb the information.

Peter shifted in his chair. "Researchers such as the psychiatrist, Muriel Salmona, have documented that the memories return as they did for you---' brutally, uncontrolled, unintegrated, and fragmented as if the assault is occurring now, not in the past.'"

"It's interesting to hear someone accurately describe what I went through, finally. I just thought I was losing my mind." I looked intently at Peter. "So, then, who is my father--in a clinical sense?"

"Well, your father has an antisocial personality disorder. He is a high-functioning sociopath. He has no remorse, compassion, or empathy for damaging others, and he easily lies." Peter sat forward in his chair.

"Hmmm...that makes sense. Anybody who could continually and severely hurt their own child, without any accountability or compassion must be missing basic human qualities." I looked away. "Hmm...I thought sociopaths all were violent--murderers."

"That's the popular misperception, but many perform very well in normal society. People around them have no idea who they're dealing with. Your father was high-functioning and socially adept. No one could tell what was going on underneath his veneer."

Rubbing my forehead, I shifted in my chair. "No wonder people can't believe the dark and cruel sides."

"He's also narcissistic. You can see how he and his money are all that matter to him. Narcissists also lack compassion and have a grandiose sense of self-importance and entitlement."

"Well, he certainly felt entitled to use me any way he wanted." I stared out the window in silence, grasping how I had to spend my entire childhood with a sociopath. "I guess I could see his callous side, but I didn't want to face it. My need for a 'good' parent blinded me. When he visited that Thanksgiving and said, 'You had a good childhood, except for a few things.', he'd laughed as if the abuse was a joke--funny and minor." I shuddered at his audacity.

"Those were all signs of his pathology." Peter looked at me intently. "He was a master at covering it up, as all good sociopaths are—they're very tough to identify until their actions reveal themselves."

I found out that Dad's technique for defending himself had a name—Deny, Attack, and Reverse Victim and Offender. The DARVO concept by researcher Jennifer Freyd, Ph.D. at the University of Oregon, described this perpetrator defense mechanism that enforces victims' silence. Through the perpetrator's denial and attacks, the tool flips the responsibility to the victim. The gaslighting is effective, confusing, and silencing to survivors, and exactly the technique my father tried to use against me.

Dad's decisions were shortsighted and confused. During the day, I was important enough to educate, but at night, disposable. He behaved as though I would never grow up and confront him or press charges. He couldn't see how his actions would impact our future family—he just didn't care. I wasn't a person to him, and my future was immaterial at night.

Jumping from the top of a high torrential waterfall to the unforgiving granite below, believing the truth of my father's character, became a slow-motion dive. Accepting the facts would take a lifetime.

Chapter 41

Finding My Voice

B y 1994, my family life in Sacramento was going well, despite my challenges. We enjoyed Sacramento and made many friends. Andrew and Carrie were now eleven and eight, and Michael needed help managing the business side of the growing dental practice. Utilizing my MBA, I started to oversee the practice's financial and personnel requirements. We made a good team, as we had different strengths. Most importantly, self-employment gave me the flexibility to deal with my recovery. If I had a difficult day, I wouldn't go to the office. I did most of my work from home, anyway. I'd always thought I'd go back into electronics and engineering, but I couldn't manage a full-time job with my recovery demands. I wanted to focus on the kids.

We were busy and spent much of our time with Scouts, baseball, and Michael's family. His parents always welcomed us to their home and were loving, involved, and adoring grandparents. I was so thankful they were part of our kids' lives. With my family in total turmoil, my mom gone, and no contact with my father, these moments were particularly precious. Michael's family knew nothing of my trauma. I'd awkwardly mumble something when they asked about my family without telling them the truth. I felt ashamed and embarrassed and didn't want to explain what I hardly understood myself to his many relatives.

Coming home from visiting with his family one evening, Michael and I sat in our den reviewing our day. The sun was setting and there was a chill in the air. I pulled the throw blanket over us. "You know, I think I'm finally starting to get better. The emotional pain is lessening. I'm functioning better. All my pounding and screaming must be working."

Giving me a big smile, Michael hugged me. "That's the first I've heard you say that. I'm thrilled!"

"Yep." I pressed my lips together. "I had to believe I could get through it. I had to feel safe, trust myself, and believe the horrible reality was true." I shrugged and gave a slight smile. "This optimism feels great--like there is recovery. I might finally get my life back." We enjoyed a long hug. I still had so much to face, but I was happy the initial craziness and trauma had improved.

"I need something new. There's an article about a local voice teacher in the paper. I think I'm going to see if she'll take me as a student. It would be fun." Since middle school, I had sung folk music while playing the guitar but had continued to dream of singing classical music despite my earlier choral rejections.

"Sounds great—you've always had a pretty voice."

Excited and nervous, I opened the door to Kathy's beautifully appointed studio. The black grand piano stood nearby, and a big stack of music sat on it. After getting comfortable, she introduced herself and said, "Sing this scale. La, la, la, la, la, la, la, la." She played the notes on the piano.

I sang the scale, followed by more up and down the octaves.

She stopped suddenly. "You have an incredible voice—unbelievable and big. You know that, right?"

People had liked my voice in the past, but I only hoped it was okay. "No. I had no idea. Really? " I said wide-eyed with excitement.

"I'm sure," Kathy looked me straight in the eye. She accepted me as a student and I began studying in earnest with her, learning voice for the first time. Thrilled to sing beautiful classical repertoire, I was so grateful for the invaluable piano lessons my parents had insisted on. Through lots of work, singing brought joy to my difficult years and a new focus to my life.

Months later, I auditioned for our regional opera company chorus. After singing an aria for the conductor, he said, "Thank you. You have a world-class voice. You could sing lead roles on any opera stage in the world. Are you aware of that?"

"No, sir. I'm ...uh...surprised. Thank you so much."

In a stern voice, he said, "We'd like to offer you a contract for next season. We will be performing Aida and La Traviata."

I bubbled with excitement as I signed on the dotted line.

Since that beginning, when I was forty, I have never stopped singing professionally. The opera would bring me extraordinary experiences--a great diversion from my difficult recovery. I would go on to sing many personal recitals, grand operas, symphonic concerts, backup Andrea Bocelli, and many other musical events, along with studying and lessons.

But it was also ironic. It was Dad's beautiful voice in my throat, the voice that I had loved to listen to as a child, his talent always inspiring me. Despite the connection to my father, I decided to develop my voice as best I could. My drive was more significant than the tragedy I lived in. It was something good about my body, something vital, and something I could be proud of regardless from whom I'd inherited it.

In working hard to speak my truth, I had finally found my true voice, a voice of power, strength, and beauty.

Chapter 42

Everyone's a Stranger

O ne day, settling into Peter's couch for my weekly visit, fresh lavender carnations brightened his office, cheering me. He sat down in his oversized brown chair after we greeted each other.

"You've talked many times of your fear of being abandoned in a big city." Peter looked back in his notes about this topic that had plagued me for so long "I thought we could work on this today. Tell me about it."

I tried to relax and calm myself by taking deep breaths and closing my eyes. This would be painful. "I'm little—four or five. Um...I can see myself alone on a grimy, cold sidewalk in a big city. I have no food or water."

"Keep going."

My forehead tightened at the memory. "I was bad, so Dad dropped me there. I don't know anyone, and no one stops to help me. Cars and grown-ups pass me by." I felt so vulnerable and sad about this fear I had lived with for so much of my childhood. "I was garbage thrown away on the sidewalk."

"That must have been terrifying to you." Peter looked at me with soft eyes.

"To be all alone--I knew I wouldn't survive. I would die on the streets. I never knew when Dad would dispose of me." Tears fell down my cheeks as I paused. I thought it was strange that I had no sound or words in any flashbacks, though my emotional reaction remained powerful and terrifying.

"So, you believe your father threatened to abandon you like this?"

"Yes, I think if I didn't cooperate and do what Dad wanted me to do sexually, he'd leave me somewhere and drive away, never to return. I was under constant intimidation and the threat worked. Just the possibility hanging over my head was highly traumatizing; he didn't even need to do it."

"Hmmm."

"The panic attack I had driving to San Francisco years ago was related to this abandonment threat. My big city fears were coming back."

"I'd agree with you on that." Peter smiled a weak smile.

I stared away. "I can't imagine how lonely I was. As a preschooler, I didn't have someone to nurture or help me develop any sense of safety. No wonder I was such a scared child. I had to be my own adult—my own protector."

Big cities can still be difficult for me--I'm frequently anxious, although I'm improved. I can feel slightly panicky if Michael isn't with me, grounding me and helping me feel safe. I worry I will be left without any resources as if I'm still that little girl.

To recover, I learned to identify this strange fear that could overcome me and talk to my scared inner child. *I have food, a car, a house, and money to take care of me. I'm grown-up. I'm not helpless now. The abuse is over and won't happen again. I'm safe.*

Carol C.Boyce

It feels silly, but it's the only way to heal my wounds. It's taken many years.

I brought up another problem with Peter. "So, yesterday, I was sitting in our family room after a long day at the office. I started to feel sick—bad headache, nauseous, and achy. I wanted to shut down and sleep. I told Michael, 'I'm getting the flu or something. I don't feel well.' I took Tylenol and tried to sleep, but my symptoms gradually worsened."

"What was going on?" Peter asked.

"As I thought about it, it finally dawned on me--it's emotional, not physical. I'm shutting down from the damn trauma again. I went out for a drive to identify my thoughts. I realized a small perceived emotional distance I felt talking with Carrie had scared me, triggering my old abandonment fears. My brain thought I'd been abandoned and shut down."

"Tell me more about it."

I shuddered with pain and spoke quietly. "I didn't know my current family. I don't 'know' anyone."

"So, you think that's why you felt physically ill?"

"Yes. Like I'd been left on a street corner...just like...just like Dad threatened. I was all alone and terrified. I sobbed over the loss--it's so bizarre."

"That would be very painful." Peter shifted in his chair.

"Luckily, I figured it out and reassured myself the abuse was all over. I could function again." I sat up in my chair. Awareness and recognizing the source of the extreme pain is my only defense.

These triggering events by PTSD are greatly reduced but will never be gone. I had too much trauma. I accept that my brain does what it's going to do. All I can do is identify the trigger and reassure myself I'm safe.

"What do you say to yourself?" Peter asked.

I looked down. 'It's not true, Carol...you will always 'know' everyone you love. Abandonment can't happen anymore. Your family's love is constant. You are an adult now with resources: money, a car, all the food and water you need, and many good people who would help me. You're safe now. I'll never leave you."

"Good work. Keep talking to little Carol—it will strengthen all these healing connections."

I came to understand this phenomenon better as the years went on. When the dark man stood in my doorway, I didn't "know" it was my father. It worked back then. Unfortunately, I can unconsciously transfer this survival technique to my present world, a very painful "leftover."

Now I realize that not only did I tell myself that I didn't know my father, but *I didn't know anyone.* I didn't know my mother, brothers, sisters, or friends. In my dark bedroom, the world became a place of total abandonment. I wiped out everyone I knew in my young life just to survive living with my assailant. I wiped out everyone I cared about to ensure I wouldn't learn Dad's identity. It was critical to my survival.

This survival method made me not trust love. People magically and routinely changed from a loved family member to one I didn't know or recognize. My constantly flipping world went from safe to not safe, family to no family and valued to no value nightly.

I've learned that my complex trauma will never be completely behind me. Sadly, my Complex PTSD, though greatly diminished, remains. Bessel van der Kolk, a Harvard psychiatrist and leader in trauma research, reported that PTSD never completely disappears because severe, young trauma *permanently* changes brain structure. It rewires the brain, so it's physically always with survivors. This rewiring is why survivors can't let go of the trauma—it is sadly always with us.

The brain wiring doesn't heal with medications or conventional talk therapy because the body retains much of the trauma. According to van der Kolk, reconnecting the brain and body is the most direct healing method. Deep breathing for hyper-arousal, self-awareness, strong interpersonal relationships, yoga, neurofeedback, and dance heal the connection between the brain and body. I'm working with these therapies now.

Chapter 43

Friendly Advice

Four years after I remembered, in 1995, few friends, in-laws, or coworkers knew what I was going through. I had never told them for several reasons. I felt so ashamed and couldn't begin to explain what I was going through. I didn't know anyone that had my experience—it seemed too odd for others to understand. Plus, I didn't want my younger nieces and nephews and other friends' children to hear about it until they had more perspective. I knew some would not respect that boundary.

I didn't need anyone else's opinion or doubts about what I was saying. I needed space to figure it out myself and leaned on my therapists for support. I wasn't ready to tell family and friends how hard it was to be me.

While I dealt with crushing pain in those early years, I tried to present a façade of an unsullied life. I wanted everyone to believe I was fine with a shimmering veneer: the beautiful home, the international trips, the big education, and other grand accomplishments. I wanted others to focus on my façade and not see the shame below the surface. Most of all, *I* needed the sparkling topcoat to be me.

Soon after I remembered, my close friend from Girl Scouts, Patti, now a licensed psychotherapist, and her husband came to our house for dinner. Filling our glasses with a nice pinot noir, we sat catching up in our living room. I was so depressed I could hardly hold a conversation. Taking a sip, she leaned forward. "Something is terribly wrong with you. I can see it. What's going on?" She was very alarmed.

I shut my eyes and said nothing. Patti demanded, "Out with it. What is going on with you? Just spit it out." She wanted to "fix" my pain, but I couldn't begin to tell her what was wrong. My whole life had changed, that my family that she had grown up around was a total sham, and my respected father was now a felon. I didn't know which way was up or how severe my depression was. I hung my head, my mind twisted with pain and confusion. The unrelenting invisible prison of my emotions was unreachable.

Eventually, I started telling a few friends, with mixed results. I hoped they'd listen, offer hugs, and provide compassion. What I didn't need were quick or easy fixes. I needed to fumble through the horrible emotions in my own way, on my own timetable.

Shelly said, 'Put it behind you and move on. Stop dwelling on it! That's your problem. If you don't think about it, it will go away, and you can get on with your life." The phrase "dwelling on it" was particularly offensive and I heard it repeatedly during my recovery.

Seething, I wanted to respond, "Do you think I chose this? I forgot about it for decades and now I must face a huge amount of pain head-on. I can't shove it under the couch and make it go away any longer."

Another friend, Chelsey, who had endured long-term child sexual abuse by her father, couldn't understand my amnesia. "What do you mean you forgot about it?" With clenched eyebrows, she stood with her hands on her hips. "I could never forget what my father did to me. They were the most horrible memories in my life. You don't forget stuff like that."

I just stared back at her. I couldn't explain the amnesia either in those early years. I had no idea why I'd forgotten. She felt that my "forgetting" meant it wasn't significant to me. Nothing could have been further from the truth. We were both frustrated and felt diminished by our interaction. But I felt lonelier when a fellow survivor offered no support and didn't believe me.

Chelsey was like most victims molested as older children. They have what most survivors have--hypermnesia. They 'hyper' remember every excruciating detail without the possibility of developing protective amnesia. I fully understood that because I had hypermnesia with the assault in Watts, the one perpetrated by Susie's brother Bob and others. I will never lose the memory of them. Further on that spectrum is losing all memory, what I did with more profound abuse. These reactions are all part of normal trauma responses.

I sat at Starbucks one day with my friend, Mary, and told her some of my story. Her Christian faith prompted her response. "You know, if you just forgive your father, your pain will end. You could get on with your life." She handed me a paper that listed everything forgiveness was and wasn't. "Forgive and lean on God and you'll be over it."

I looked at the paper. It felt minimizing as if my experience came down to one simple decision. It didn't involve working through the incredible mountain of fears, pain, and grief. "It's not as simple as you might think," I replied.

Though she was trying to help, I knew nothing could make the trauma disappear, and forgiveness was out of the question.

Based on these experiences, I stopped telling others or openly discussing my trauma for a long time. Though well-meaning, no one wanted to hear or understand the horrible truth I was facing, and I couldn't blame them. Instead, they liked, loved, and included me in their lives during these dreadful years, and I'll always be grateful to them.

Chapter 44

No One Noticed

I had just returned from a performance in New York City at Carnegie Hall with our symphony chorus. The standing ovation by the packed audience was a thrill I'll never forget. I came home elated, greeted the kids, and quickly headed to my weekly appointment with Peter, exhausted. It was a bright, sunny day when I sat down. Peter smiled warmly and began. "What's on your mind today?"

I frowned as I tapped my fingertips on the table. "Where were the adults that should have helped me? It seems strange that nobody noticed anything unusual. With so many doctors, teachers, clergy, and neighbors around, why didn't anyone notice something was very wrong with me? Nobody tried to help me, ever." My forehead creased tightly.

Peter crossed his legs as he sat forward in his chair. "So, tell me. What were your signs you were being abused?"

I grimaced as I rubbed my eyes. "I was so self-conscious, crying putting on a bathing suit. I couldn't sleep at anyone's house, and I had many nightmares." I folded my arms. "These people had the power to stop the abuse, have my father thrown in jail, and no one did anything! They could have saved me!"

"Do you think, as an adult, you would notice these signs in children around you?"

I paused for a moment. "Well...okay. Truthfully, what people saw was I rarely misbehaved, was a good student, and was too scared of further 'punishment' from my father. I'd question a kid with these symptoms now after my experience, but I wouldn't have before. There are too many other kids with obvious problems--I wouldn't have stood out at all." Looking at the carpet, I shook my head.

Peter shifted in his chair. "Without outright telling someone about it or walking in on the assault in the middle of the night, no one would have noticed. Your symptoms were too subtle. People need to be slapped in the face before they realize sexual abuse is occurring."

Sadly, I could see his point. "My family had 'curb appeal,' a great façade that no one looked past, including me. We appeared highly functional from the outside and I appeared well cared for. I had no attendance issues at school and completed all my assignments." I sat back on the couch, thinking. "There was so little to notice. Luxurious carpet covered our rotten floorboards."

"Right." Peter exhaled, glad I understood.

"With no memory of the trauma, I couldn't have talked about it to anyone either. I would have denied it if anyone asked."

Peter looked me in the eye. "People also expect sexual predators to look slimy, with strange social skills, as if molesters stand out from a crowd. A personable, kind physician isn't who they would suspect."

My brows knitted together tightly. "It was tragic no one could tell."

"Yes, it was and unfortunately is still applicable today."

"Yep. Plus, where was Mom? She had the greatest chance of helping me or noticing problems. Did she know or not know?" I clenched my jaw.

"Well, she was heavily sedated at night with alcohol, overwhelmed, and focused only on her problems. From what you've said, your assaults were all at night after everyone was asleep. She could easily have not known, but I certainly don't know." He drew in a long breath.

"She could have saved me—gotten Dad out of my life." I rubbed my forehead. "She completely dodged her responsibilities. What kind of mother does that?"

"Not a very good one. Your mom wasn't emotionally available or paying any attention to you and your brothers and sister."

"Of course, I never told her anything because I didn't know myself. I didn't even avoid Dad or act scared of him—I had no idea something was going on." I shook my head in disgust, frustrated at the truth. "It's heartbreaking how difficult it is to spot a sexually abused child."

"Your mother contributed greatly to your tragic childhood," Peter leaned forward. "And this coldness frequently leaves children searching for nurturing outside of themselves, becoming addicted. It can lead to all kinds of problems."

"She died young, never hearing anything about the incest. I'll never know what she did or didn't know…But deep down, I believe she didn't know. I would have heard her ripping Dad apart if she did. You know, she always accused him of an affair, though nothing ever suggested that." Disgust churned my stomach. "Maybe she could sense it was with me."

I added my mother's knowledge to my growing pile of un-knowns. Part of me was thrilled Mom died before all the trauma surfaced. It would have just made it all more painful if she had been alive. With sexual abuse, it's tragically common for mothers to support their spouses over their children.

Knowing how desperately I needed rescuing, I pay much closer attention to the children I encounter today. Abused children need all of us to pay close attention.

Chapter 45

Children to Raise

In 1995, three years after recalling the molestation, Peter referred me to a psychiatrist for an anti-depression prescription. Dr. Smith was highly recommended and practiced for over thirty years. I'd never spoken to a psychiatrist before and was a little leery of this visit, but I needed the help.

Her sunny second-floor office overlooked the crowns of towering oak trees and had a lovely waterfall in the corner. Dr. Smith's friendly smile welcomed me with a warmth and kindness I could sense. I sat on a comfortable flowered chair across from hers as the tiny doctor sat cross-legged in her chair. "Nice to meet you, Carol." We discussed medication to help me with my ongoing depression. She handed me a prescription and I stood up to leave.

She rolled her monogrammed pen between her small, wrinkled fingers. "Before you leave, I want to tell you something."

Surprised, I sat back down. "Okay."

"With your permission, Peter explained your background and the duration and severity of the abuse you suffered." The trees rustled outside in the light wind. She cleared her throat and, with

Carol C.Boyce

a wise countenance, went on. "I've never seen anyone face the severity of trauma you have in all my years of practice that functions at your level. I find it incredible."

"Really?" My eyes widened at this unexpected compliment.

"It's amazing how well you're doing." She looked at me intently with her large blue eyes. "Most patients with your extreme trauma would have had a psychotic break, delusional thoughts, hallucinations, and paranoia." She repositioned herself in her oversized chair. "They would never regain full mental function again, shutting down to escape the pain and trauma. Most would be institutionalized. I don't know how you're surviving this."

I took a deep breath, looking intently back at her. "I don't have a choice. I can't shut down--I have to function. I have children to raise that need me to provide a stable home life. As hard as it can be, I won't let the abuse take away my kid's childhoods. I just won't allow it."

"You've shown real strength of character." She smiled at me.

I shifted in my seat. "You know, I don't know anyone who has gone through amnesia from sexual trauma, so I have no one to compare my experience. All I know is it's been so incredibly difficult." I sighed deeply and paused for a minute. "Thanks so much for the encouragement—I can use all I can get."

Her insights made me realize I was battling something much bigger than I realized. I had survived so much. My vows and determination to have a full life kept me from falling into a permanent and crippling mental collapse. Having a psychiatrist say these words made me take my recovery even more seriously and appreciate how far I had come. The consequences if I failed scared me more. I felt great encouragement from her kind words, but my heart broke for those not as lucky.

On a cloudy, cool autumn day, I settled into Peter's couch for our session after dodging colorful, loud roosters at his door. Pulling on a sweater, I greeted Peter and launched into my latest concern. "You know, some of my projections are beginning to make sense now. Remember those early visions I had---the gnarled gray surface that flipped to a pristine white screen?"

"Yes, sure, I remember. The PTSD-fueled scenario haunted you when you went to sleep for most of your childhood."

"Right. My brain warned me that I was leaving my 'safe' world and entering the 'dangerous' one."

"Tell me more about that." Peter scribbled notes on his yellow pad.

"Well, I lived in flipping realities. During the day, I was a member of a prominent, well-respected family. At night, my life flipped to being a tortured member of an abusive one." I stared into space for a few minutes processing my thoughts. "My mother's personality also flipped from daytime to nighttime with her rages. My world was always flip-flopping from pristine and bright to grey and gnarly. My young brain was trying to warn me in its own strange way."

"I can see what you're saying." Peter's eyes lit up.

"Like my vision, my world changed from an understandable routine to a grey, cruel one. Back and forth, back and forth--these visions were my only bedtime story. They lulled me to sleep." I hung my head, remembering the lonely terror.

"You couldn't understand or process these opposite worlds, so you created a warning system of sorts."

"It's unbelievable that I had to do that so young." I looked down, teary-eyed.

"What are you thinking now about the two men outside your window? What were they there for?"

"I understand that one now, too. Dad was always waiting for me to go to sleep to hurt me. Both men throwing the ball were my father--they looked alike. They represented that someone could endlessly wait for me to fall asleep, and I was helpless to do anything about it. My mind was again trying to warn me sleep wasn't safe." I shuddered at the thought. "It was another PTSD projection of the truth—I'd be assaulted if I slept. I had no idea what would happen or what time of night it would occur, and strangely, I never tried to figure it out."

Peter leaned back in his chair. "After you grew up, you had many signs of traumatic assaults--great fears, compulsive food behaviors, nightmares, and strange visions. You believed a defect in you caused the trauma, not that it resulted from sexual trauma."

"That the adulthood visions were coming from events in my past never entered my mind. It wasn't until my life became completely unmanageable that I had to let the memories in," My toes bounced on the carpet as I processed my thoughts.

"Very interesting."

"I didn't have the slightest idea this had happened—absolutely nothing, or I would have had to look at it. Only with tremendous pain was I forced to heal and face the horrible truth. None of my memories or discoveries changed after my brain released them."

"Pain is always what makes us look inward." Peter nodded.

"It's interesting that as a child, I told my parents about my nightmares, but never about the visions. Subconsciously I knew they were about Dad's sexual abuse and connected to his abandonment threats. I knew to keep the visions to myself and face them alone. It's amazing how I coped, even as a little girl."

Peter leaned forward. "Most kids would have gone crying to their parents with the visions, but you knew not to tell anyone. That's how afraid you were."

I shifted in my seat and squeezed my forehead with both hands. "The man I first saw in the garage followed me for many years. It was the same faceless monster--my father's image. Dad will never know how he haunted me for so much of my life, long after the abuse was over."

"As evil as he was, he still didn't realize all of the ramifications of his assaults." Peter straightened in his chair. "He also doesn't care to know."

I closed my eyes tightly. "How could I have not known the man was my father, that all this trauma was from sexual abuse? How could I have gone through so much pain and fear and never let myself know the truth?"

"Sounds like you're blaming yourself." Peter lifted his eyebrows.

"Maybe, but sometimes it feels obvious—I should have put the pieces together much earlier. It would have been easier to let the assaults into my consciousness than suffer the PTSD." I looked down at my wringing hands.

Peter sipped his water. "You still needed to protect your psyche. Your brain knew you couldn't handle recovery until later in your life. Your subconscious knew you might not survive if you remembered earlier."

I shook my head. "Deep down, my subconscious didn't think I'd survive knowing the truth. I knew I had to live in hell and forgetting was the only way I could do it when I was little."

"I believe that's what was going on," Peter said confidently.

"As an adult, I projected images of the scary man into my daily life so my subconscious could prepare me for the truth. It's like it was yelling, 'you need to get ready now—say the word, and I'll let the dam break. It's going to threaten your very survival, but it's almost time to look at your past.'"

"The healthy part of your subconscious was trying to help you decide to heal." Peter smiled at me.

"So strange and so hard to understand that I had to *decide* to face it. One part of my brain said, 'There's a huge secret you need to address,' and another side said, "Don't look at this. Keep hiding it." My subconscious mind must have had tremendous conflict going on. Learning the truth of the sexual abuse was an immense risk to my life."

Peter nodded. "The risk was huge. What the brain does with trauma is truly remarkable."

Unbeknownst to me, my subconscious was in an all-out battle before realizing what had happened. It was like tectonic plates slamming together, creating a volcano in my mind. One plate wanted me to face the forgotten trauma, and one was afraid I wouldn't survive if I did, leaving me disoriented, terrified, and full of anxiety. Eventually, I had no choice but to face the truth. It was life or death.

I exhaled a big sigh of relief, knowing there was logic in what I'd gone through. There were good reasons for my suffering. I hadn't lost my mind. With this new understanding, I could put my haunting projections and more pieces of my mental puzzle together. It became clear that remembering *and* not remembering both threatened my life, and I was lucky to be alive.

The strands of my family's past had woven together into a rich but severely frayed and ragged weaving. I didn't get to pick the weavers of my tapestry, the shuttle, the loom, or the yarns. No child does. My childhood tapestry required a polished, sharp shuttle as the bobbin writhed and twisted with every throw. It created sections of gloriously lush and strong weavings of gold and silk but also tragically weak, frayed, and broken ones. That crucial loom left great holes of terror, pain, and confusion, where love, safety, and truth needed to be. I let the light shine through the holes and rebuilt the weak areas, one thread at a time.

Chapter 46

In Defense of Pedophiles

In 1995, I sat on our living room couch listening to Andrew playing the piano while Carrie sang. I was happy he was developing into a fantastic musician and songwriter and loved both of their beautiful voices. Michael loved to bake and sugar cookies were his forte. The luscious aroma filled our home as he baked, and I couldn't wait till they came out of the oven.

He had gathered the mail earlier and noticed Dad's familiar cursive on a letter. He rolled his eyes, reading it to himself. After the kids went to bed, Michael said, "You may want to read this one. Your dad has a new tactic." He handed me the letter. "You won't believe it."

I frowned, pulled out the letter, and muttered, "How to ruin a perfectly good day."

Great news! The False Memory Syndrome Foundation--a wonderful organization--has proven that recovered memories are all a hoax, made up by therapists."

Our problem is finally over.

Love, Dad

I crunched the letter up in my fist and threw it across the room, so angry to deal with more crap from him. "An organization to support perpetrators--just what I need! It's unbelievable."

"It sure is," Michael said, cleaning the cookie pans.

In my next session, I showed Peter the uncoiled letter. "Do you know anything about this group?"

"Well, let me go back and start with what losing memory is about. Okay?"

I welcomed his perspective and background information. Since man first existed, Peter said, this mechanism has been around. But it was not until the 1700s that amnesia from severe trauma was documented. Traumatic Amnesias (TA's) were extensively researched with war, extreme accidents, and violence survivors. 'Shell-shock' and 'battle fatigue' were used with the many survivors.

Later in the 1940s, forty-six percent of World War II concentration camp survivors were also documented as having experienced traumatic amnesia. Accounts of appalling medical experiments on identical twins conducted at Auschwitz by Dr. Mengele found pairs where one twin had no memory while the other could never forget the exact same experience. TA was a common coping mechanism and not disputed. (Lagnado, 1991)

In late 1980, research emerged that added a new cause of TA's. After noticing that amnesia symptoms from war and sexual abuse were similar, observant researchers enlarged the scope and linked the survival mechanism to childhood sexual abuse. It was reasonable since sexual assaults were known to be the most severe traumatic event someone can endure, causing the most significant psychological damage. Both war and child abuse victims experienced and participated in atrocious behavior necessitated

Carol C.Boyce

by an outside power, so it's not surprising that their reactions were the same.

With the new cause, traumatic amnesia for the first time became *highly controversial*. As adults remembered and accused family members, it became clear that nobody wanted to know their family member was molesting. People didn't believe sexual assaults could cause as much damage as war violence, and nobody wanted to know perpetrators lived in their families. Questions abounded about how someone could forget and later remember, and the victim was blamed. The therapist's role in memory recovery also came into question.

In patriarchal societies, it was more comfortable to protect men and label victims, primarily women, as hysterical or liars than to face the truth. Further oppression and maltreatment of the victims overruled holding fathers, priests, doctors, lawyers, politicians, and others responsible. Deep family secrets about morally 'upstanding' members unveiled themselves, causing an uproar that continues today.

Peter further explained that "The False Memory Syndrome Foundation" was organized to support and protect the many so-called "falsely accused." With lots of press, its purpose was to deny the new research. The group boasted that its members: "were a good-looking bunch of people, graying hair, well dressed, healthy, smiling. Just about every person who has attended our meetings is someone you would surely find interesting and want to count as a friend." They unknowingly demonstrated how difficult it is to identify pedophiles and how easily they blended into society.

Fury pulsed through me. I wondered how there could be an organization that further hurt survivors. I couldn't comprehend how people didn't understand how difficult it was to speak up about incest.

Knowing Dad now had a whole organization supporting him, he had 'official' support to denounce my accusations. It must have brought him great relief and joy. As he said, 'our problems were over.' It seemed unfathomable that families would put time into protecting perpetrators instead of helping the victims. My stomach turned upside down as I digested this information. It felt revictimizing.

I also yearned to know how my amnesia physically occurred. It wasn't until I researched this book that I found 2018 studies on exactly how the 'forgetting' mechanism worked. Extreme terror causes the brain to produce massive amounts of adrenaline and cortisol to physically flee danger. The brain or heart can stop because of these life-threatening releases if the chemicals are not used to escape. To survive the overload, the brain sends out vast amounts of opioid narcotics to counteract the threat trying to protect the heart and brain from stopping.

This extreme anesthesia causes the brain to isolate the assault from normal memory. It interrupts the normal REM sleep cycle and puts the memories into a non-penetrable holding cell in the amygdala at the base of the brain. This improper storage results in post-traumatic stress disorder and depression and no memory of the events that cause the symptoms. This explanation made sense to me and was the first time I'd seen my experience researched and documented. I was relieved to understand it better. (Diamond, 2007)

My survival mechanism caused the craziness I went through. In the end, I'm thankful my brain knew that option. I wouldn't be alive today if I had to grow up knowing I lived with constant assaults and my attacker.

I thank God I forgot.

Chapter 47

Two Tall Trees

Years passed and I continued to work daily on my recovery. In 1995, Michael and I flew to Cabo San Lucas for a get-away. I couldn't wait to see the white sands and hear the crashing waves. Time alone with him sounded heavenly. Though I still was terrified of flying, I muddled through.

We sat on brown lounge chairs overlooking the ocean, sipping strawberry margaritas. When Michael and I first met, his intelligence and strength, quiet, reserved personality, and tall, muscular physique drew me to him. He never showed anger and yelled, traits I craved after my tumultuous mother. I felt safe with him. Our values meshed with his interest in education, other cultures, strong family, and travel, making me love and respect him.

After being happily married for eighteen years, Michael was now paying a hefty price for my childhood—something he hadn't signed on for. He had seen my fearfulness when we were dating but had no idea what lurked in my background, nor did I.

Intimately, there were other problems between us. I always needed a light on though I had no idea why. I'd jump if Michael

Carol C.Boyce

stood over me while I was lying in bed or if he ever stood in a dark doorway. Though I would frequently dissociate, he wasn't aware of it. I felt grateful for how he always honored my emotional and physical needs. I'd always felt the abuse left me with more terror and physical safety issues than sexual ones. I was in denial, however. The abuse took away my God-given right to my unencumbered sexuality, and I blame Dad for that loss. He had no right to do this to me and cause lifelong consequences.

With my memories returning, Michael was witnessing my total emotional collapse. He agonized over whether I would ever recover and nothing he said or did could fix it. Having heard me screaming in anguish, seeing my severe depression, terror, and significant weight gain, he wondered where we were heading as a couple and family. Whether I would heal, how long recovery would take, and would I be a functioning mom to our children were some of his many questions. Watching me suffer terrified him, but he stayed by my side, completely committed to his family. He was amazing.

I was embarrassed and ashamed that I couldn't figure out my emotional problems. I didn't want to burden Michael--he already had huge responsibilities supporting the family, managing the dental practice, and helping raise the kids. I didn't believe anyone could love me enough to remain through the endless recovery, and it terrified me. I didn't think I was worthy.

Michael's quiet and reserved personality seemed a pillar of strength to my outgoing, talkative, and more emotional countenance. As our stress grew with raising the kids, my trauma, and the constant work pressure, his silence felt more like mood swings. He could be smiling in the morning and withdrawn and hostile in the afternoon.

One Sunday afternoon, Michael sat peacefully on our soft recliner, watching a John Wayne movie for the third time. He'd switch to the Kings basketball game during the commercials. My anger had been building all weekend because he wasn't talking to me and seemed to push me away. I felt abandoned. I stood over him with my hands on my hips. "You've hardly said one word to me all weekend. Am I that unimportant to you that you need to ignore me?" I sniffled into my tissue. "And your moods--you seem angry, like you're in a bad mood but don't say anything to let me know what's wrong—that's not fair to me."

Caught off-guard, he looked up at me, shocked I was angry. "Really? Hmmm." Not knowing how to respond, he went back to his movie.

This fueled my inferno. "Is that all you have to say? I can't take this silent treatment."

Hurt by my words, he never responded to me. Mike retreated further into his protective shell for several days while I grew increasingly furious from the perceived rejection. I had hoped telling him how angry I was would clear the air. Instead, it led to three days of a cold war with no effective communication between us. This was not okay.

Sitting down in Peter's office on a sweltering summer morning, I told him about the unresolved conflict between Michael and me. "It's so frustrating. The more I tell him why I'm angry, the more he withdraws from me. We don't seem to get anywhere. I thought he's supposed to make me feel loved--filled up."

"Tell me more about these conflicts?"

"I guess when I look at it, I'm insecure and clingy. I'm so afraid I'll lose Michael and that he won't love me anymore. He'll get rid of me as my father threatened." My eyes widened, surprised I'd said that. "It's scary for me to give him the space and quiet time he needs."

"An important thing here is that you both must heal childhood wounds to have a healthy marriage. As is normal, damaged kids transfer their negative feelings to their spouses in a subconscious effort to heal. You two need to become more aware of how your old issues affect your relationship."

"His mood swings drive me mad—I can't handle them."

"Do they remind you of anyone?" Peter smiled at me.

I thought about it. "It feels like I'm a child again, watching Mom's moods flip." I turned my head sharply. "Wow, I didn't see that link at all. I never connected his moods with hers. I'm hypervigilant, always watching for tension building in our home--like I'm still a kid." My voice trailed off. I had no idea I was bringing my parent's drunk fighting into our relationship.

"You're trying to heal your damage by unconsciously projecting those old feelings onto Michael." Peter straightened in his chair. "This is typical in marriage. We look for that exact someone we love but who can duplicate our childhood problems." He sipped his tea. "How well were you able to discuss difficult issues in your family?"

"Yeah, not good at all. It was Mom yelling and Dad saying nothing. And I couldn't express anything, particularly when I was mad." I thought of how easy it was to duplicate old family patterns. "Michael runs from conflict at all costs, just like me."

"How did Mike's family handle anger? What did his father do?" Peter asked.

"His mom was loud and talkative, and his father rarely said much. Michael learned to run from conflict and not say anything.

He wanted to reduce his chances of being the focus of conflict in his large family." I clasped my hands together. "I guess he's repeating what he learned to get through his childhood.

"Do you see a connection with how you handle anger now? Danger and anger are very connected in your mind."

"I guess you're right--and I refuse to yell and turn into my mother."

Peter nodded. "Right, we all repeat unhealthy childhood patterns—if there's no intervention and awareness. We repeat coping skills we learned as kids and the roles we took in the family."

"So, as children, we...uh... both learned to avoid anger as much as possible--not to fight. I avoid saying anything until I'm ready to blow my stack, and we have silence between us for days. I'll have to learn to speak up and talk calmly before the conflict grows. I want to avoid Michael withdrawing from me."

"Right, let's work on that," Peter said.

"But, I had so much conflict going on as a kid...it was, hmm, a war zone. I don't want Andrew and Carrie to see any fighting, any arguing from us. It's too painful."

"Does that sound reasonable or healthy—even possible, to have no anger ever between you two?"

"No, but I can't stand the thought of them living in a similar environment, even for one day. I won't have it." I steeled my gaze at Peter.

"Anger is essential and can be safe, not dangerous as it was for you. Anger is part of a healthy emotional environment if it's non-threatening. It's natural and it needs to be under control and productive in resolving an issue. "

"I guess Michael's not doing his mood changes to anger me; it's his childhood baggage. That's so important to remember—it's not about me."

"Right." Peter nodded.

"The harder issue is that I want Michael to fill me up to feel valued and safe. He tells me every day about how much he loves me, but I still get angry when he withdraws into silence." I rubbed my forehead.

"A big pit of emptiness grew where you should have felt safe, nurtured, and loved. Growing up with an emotionally unavailable mother or father left you with an unreliable love. You never learned to trust it."

"I thought I could lose my family and loved ones at any moment. If I showed who I truly was, I wouldn't be safe or loved."

Peter looked intently at me. "Michael has his issues and demons to fight also. You can't fix his childhood problems, either."

"Sometimes I feel like I'm always looking for a "mommy" to nurture me and fill me up—Michael, food, busyness, shopping—you name it. I will have to learn to take responsibility for my emptiness and let Michael be who he is. Otherwise, I'll always be angry because he can't fill me up." I thought a moment. "It's like my beliefs about food. I'm looking for that nurturing I never had, that voice of compassion for my little child."

"Exactly. Especially important to be aware of."

"I never realized my role in marriage was to make sure Michael became his real self. I can't try to change him. We must grow through our childhood wounds to feel loved and valued." I looked down at my shoes. This realization was a painful but critical lesson.

We were over a big hump and my anger decreased over time as I matured and understood how our childhoods affected our marriage. We went to marriage programs at church, read relationship books, and sought counseling whenever we were struggling. Michael changed and grew, and we learned to speak about our conflicts with healthy boundaries and treatment of each other.

We needed to be two tall Sequoias growing from the same root, each strong, independent, and responsible for our own emotions. Realizing it was my responsibility to fill myself up and feel safe was a major obstacle I overcame. Trusting Michael and the kid's love to be unconditional and constant was an even more significant hurdle I jumped over.

As I look back on all the trials and challenging times in our forty-five-year marriage, dogged determination and commitment to our family got us through the tough times. I always reached out for help when we got stuck. I learned to change how I responded. We were determined to make it and stay by each other's side. I'm incredibly happy and forever thankful we survived despite my profound challenges. I consider it miraculous that I chose a kind, gentle and loving partner in Michael when many who have survived sexual abuse fall prey to abusive partners in their adult lives. We remained committed to our marriage and raised our kids in safety and love. I remain so thankful to Michael for standing by my side and loving me through all of it.

Chapter 48

Doctor to Doctor

On a cozy fall evening in 2000, the fire in our hearth sparkled gold and amber. Carrie and I rehearsed a scene she needed to prepare for her high school musical role in *How to Succeed in Business*. I loved nothing more than working on music with her and hearing her lyric soprano voice.

Michael was out of town, so I had picked up the mail earlier in the day. Seeing another letter in Dad's handwriting, I dreaded opening it, but I didn't want to wait for Mike's return. The letters caused me grief every time, but I always had a flicker of hope he'd finally confess and apologize.

October 2000

Carol,

You have caused me great pain. You've hurt me deeply.

Peter is putting these thoughts in your head. His license should be removed. No reputable psychiatrist would allow this kind of nonsense. You should have been cleared up in two sessions.

Dad

"You've hurt me deeply' stung my eyes. I shut them, tightening my forehead, trying to digest the words. As illogical as it was and after all the hurt Dad had put me through, my love for my 'good' Dad remained. Damn it. It would be so much easier not to need to grieve along with so many other difficult emotions. The craziness gave me a headache as I scrunched up the letter.

Dad insisted that two sessions with a psychiatrist would "clear me up" of this "kind of nonsense." In other words, a competent psychiatrist would deny my memories. It was comical, considering I faced decades of treatment. I longed for an acknowledgment and apology, but I knew I would never see one. As usual, I didn't respond to his letter. Until he showed signs of remorse, there was no point.

According to Dad, Peter was now the cause of my problems with a new threat of removing his license. I winced when I saw Peter attacked. He had been a savior to my family and me and had worked tirelessly, skillfully, and with great care and determination to help me recover. Though I told Peter as little as possible, he knew Dad was attacking him. He saw right through my father and didn't let these attacks phase him.

Therapists implanting memories through hypnosis and suggestion has been a major defense to discredit survivors' traumatic memories. The concept protects perpetrators every time, and my family still buys the concept. Though there are bad therapists, there isn't motivation for a professional to suggest sexual abuse to a client. Their reputation and income depend on helping their clients, not offering more problems. The risk of lawsuits for therapists providing care to survivors is already real, and they would not relish more liability by 'inserting' memories. It would be the end of their career to "suggest" incest had occurred. This has rarely happened.

The wars over delayed memories continue today. Research has recently shown memories can be suggested through hypnotism. After being told they've been in a bad car accident, clients may believe it for a while and even feel bad about it. However, no one could 'implant' the incredible emotion, terror, and PTSD reactions that traumatic amnesiacs suffer. No one could ever 'suggest' the pain, loss, and confusion from actual abuse. It makes no sense.

Michael Salter, a professor of criminology in Australia, wrote in 2021 an important social posting about historical inaccuracies repeated about child sexual abuse and therapy. He reminded readers that "'Recovered Memory Therapy' never existed. Rather, it is a derogatory term used to discredit anyone sexually abused who discloses it in therapy. It implies that professional counseling somehow lessens the victims' statements as if seeking help means your memories are false. Nothing could be further from the truth and it's cruel and irresponsible to suggest victims shouldn't seek professional care. Survivors absolutely need professional help to deal with their incredible trauma. (@mike_salter)

The letters kept coming. Ten years after I recovered my memories, Dad started to blame someone new.

November 1, 2001

Dear Michael,

Doctor to doctor, you should have taken her to a qualified psychiatrist at the beginning. The psychiatrist would have straightened out this misunderstanding in two sessions. They would tell her immediately these lies were put into her head. She'd be back to normal by now if you had acted as the head of your family and a doctor.

Dad

Michael sighed, putting the letter down on the kitchen counter. "Well, it looks like I'm the one to blame now. Your dad thinks I didn't act like the head of the family and a professional." He shut his eyes and shook his head.

Dragged through so much of my drama already, and as ridiculous as it was, I winced seeing Michael blamed. Like Peter, he had supported me through every step of my journey and didn't deserve any of Dad's false narrative. Though we both knew his letter was wrong, sadness and anger filled the next days. It was impossible not to feel the attack and the minimization of what we were experiencing.

As I continued to battle the overwhelming trauma, many letters from Dad arrived over the years with similar narratives. I stopped reading them. He blamed Mike for not being clearheaded enough to get his mentally ill wife to a psychiatrist. I was incapable of helping myself in Dad's mind, enveloped by 'nonsense' and a 'misunderstanding' put into my mind by Peter.

These insults and attacks made my head want to explode. Dad had done everything he could to destroy my mental health, and now he called out my issues as a defect in me. It was crazy-making and more mental crap I had to deal with on top of what I already had. Michael ignored the attacks on his character and pushed it out of his mind. Sadness infiltrated my depression at the frustration of the situation, my inability to do anything about it, and my anger at Dad's complete lack of compassion and concern for my family and me. I'd drive and yell every filthy thing I could think of at him to get the pain directed at him. Pound, scream, and cry helped me cope.

Because my father refused to stay home, I had stopped attending my extended family's annual campout, a tradition going back over fifty years. I couldn't be around him or control what he did. It felt revictimizing, and I cried every year I missed, giving up the few times I got to see my siblings, aunts, uncles, and cousins. These get-togethers were also important for my children to experience and get to know my family, as they didn't see them otherwise. The folk singing, discussions of our ancestry and travels, hiking, skits, and support were important to my family and me, but it all came to a screeching halt with the abuse revelations.

With Andrew and Carrie off to college in 2005, I decided to attend the annual campout for one day. I was dying to see everyone and resented staying home for years while Dad attended without any consequences. I prayed I could avoid him in the large campground.

The smell of the pine forest and the rich earth brought back precious memories as Michael, and I got out of the car. "I hope this goes well," I said, losing my confidence.

"You'll be fine—I'm here if you need anything."

I could see the towering pines almost touching the billowing clouds. The campground was gorgeous, grounding me with its beauty. I so missed the vivid mountain colors and the sounds of the crickets and birds. As I greeted my cousins with hugs and kisses, I felt so glad to see them and my growing nieces and nephews.

My Aunt Judy was there and despite our previous contentious conversations, I gave her a hug and smile. My Uncle Allen hugged me, and we caught up on our lives. After not attending for a decade, it was nice to see him and everyone else. The get-together was a time for reconnecting, and I hoped to avoid the sexual abuse issue while I was there.

Mom had been gone for twenty-one years by this time. From what I heard, Dad's new wife, Elaine, was a wonderful woman, a kind, gentle soul, and deeply religious though I barely knew her. She approached me at the first campsite I entered. I was surprised when she said, "How are you feeling, dear? Are you doing okay--mentally?"

I was wide-eyed at the comment. "I'm fine. My mental health is great. How is yours?" I was furious at the implication. Paranoia set in as I wondered who else thought I was mentally ill. *Is this how I'm talked about when I'm not around?* A firestorm of doubt filled my mind. I already regretted coming, and I hadn't been there five minutes.

Finding Michael building a fire, I fought the chaos in my mind. I covered my eyes as I kicked the log resting on the ground. I picked up my guitar and tuned it for the campfire I hoped to lead that evening. "Do you realize that Dad thinks he can deflect the sexual abuse by constantly questioning me, suggesting I'm mentally ill to all who will listen? The only mental instability I have is from him." I had fought so long and hard to feel safe and stable.

"It's ridiculous. Sorry, honey." He looked at me with soft eyes, putting more kindling on the growing flames.

"I guess Elaine will never believe her wonderful new husband could be a sexual predator. I feel sorry for her choice. I'm sure she thinks he's too nice, reputable, and upstanding. He can lie and schmooze anyone, even his own wife." I seethed, stomping the dirt.

Michael stood up and hugged me with his charcoal-covered hands. "Wish you didn't have to go through this, honey. I love you and know you're not crazy." He smiled and shook his head at the thought.

"Elaine doesn't know it, but she's a victim of his, like everyone in the family. Here I am struggling to recover and get my life back, and all people can think is I'm mentally ill. Talk about blaming the victim." My voice trailed off as I walked to the parking area to get my stack of song sheets out of the car.

I eyed Dad out of the corner of my eye. My heart stopped, realizing I hadn't seen or talked to him in a decade. I hoped he'd respect and distance himself from me, but I knew caring about my feelings was impossible for him--respect was not in his wheelhouse. True to form, he started aggressively following me around the large campground. *Oh my God, what was I thinking coming today? I must have been nuts.*

Dad had a quizzical look in his brown eyes. With no hint of anger, he said, "Why don't you want to see me? Is this about my new wife?"

I froze in my tracks and stood in silence for several seconds. *Does Dad think this is about his wife?* I was incredulous. Shaking with a fresh surge of rage, I shrieked, "What are you talking about? It has nothing to do with your new wife! It's about your sexual abuse of me." I started to walk away.

"Whaaat?" He froze in his tracks, wide-eyed with his mouth gaping.

It was as if he was hearing this for the first time. "You know exactly what I'm referring to," I said in a strong voice, glaring at my father. "You lost me over this, remember?" *Where was his mind? Where did he hide our previous interactions?* I wondered what world he was living in.

He stepped back. Then thinking for a moment, he demanded, "Get in the car. I want to talk to you." He started unlocking his nearby car.

"I'm not getting in any car with you!"

"Get in the car, now!" He demanded I follow him in a fatherly voice.

Rage seared through me. "No," I was adamant as Dad's jaw dropped. His little girl wouldn't follow directives anymore. I swiftly headed back to where Michael was.

"You're destroying our family." I heard him shout as I hurried away.

I yelled back, "No, Dad, you destroyed it long ago."

It would be the last time I ever spoke to my father.

When I returned to the campfire, my heart was pounding, and I struggled to breathe from running at the high elevation. I tried to calm myself down and took deep breaths after the crazy interaction. *Why did I come? This is worse than I imagined.* After telling him what had occurred, I told Michael, "Dad exists in his own made-up world, in total denial. It's no wonder people believe his lies—he believes it himself. To think he wants to blame it on Elaine now—just unbelievable!" I covered my face with despair as I thought this gaslighting would go on forever, and I couldn't do anything about it.

Michael smirked as he put another log on the fire. "In his made-up world, he's still the good doctor--a healer. It's the only way he can live with himself...I guess....and everyone believes him."

I stared at the fire, unseeing the shooting flames. "I guess I can't attend these events until Dad stops going." Grief overwhelmed me, and tears streamed down my face.

Chapter 49

Innocence Forgiven

In 2005, at my weekly session, I relaxed on the brown sofa across from Peter. I loved the fresh hydrangeas in the vase in the corner and the sunlight coming from his big picture window. I jumped right into my thoughts when Peter and I sat down.

"I've never been too aware before, but I realize now I feel so much guilt over the abuse. How could I have participated in this? I knew this was wrong." With my anger growing at myself, I rubbed my temples. "I mean, why didn't I yell, 'stop,' scream, or tell everybody around me what was going on? Why didn't I fight back?" Tears burned in my eyes. "There wasn't a gun to my head, and I knew it was wrong. Why didn't I stop it?"

"Assuming the blame is typical of abused children. They get a sense of power over an out-of-control situation," Peter looked directly at me, folding his hands.

"I didn't realize how much guilt I carried."

"By flipping the blame to yourself, you created hope of ending the assaults." Peter looked intently at me. "Was there a weapon you couldn't see?"

Carol C.Boyce

After a few minutes of silence, I sighed deeply. "There were several 'invisible' weapons Dad used. Smothering me with a pillow certainly taught me early to do whatever he said." I shivered, remembering the horror. I spoke slowly as I realized the truth. "When he threatened to drop me on a street corner, I was terrified—it affects me to this day. His threats assured my silence and ongoing participation in the abuse...Dad...I guess...had all the control and power." I felt like the child whose parent forces him to rob a convenience store. I shook my head at the desperate world I had survived.

"You were a child, remember. Any child would be helpless to defend themselves and will believe anything...for hope. You were living in total fear and desperation, with no way out." Peter straightened up in his chair. "Abused children frequently accept terrible, untrue things about their character that can affect their entire lives. You did too by taking responsibility for it and assuming guilt."

"It's like I must forgive myself for being innocent--a child. It's so confusing. It was as if my vulnerability was a crime. But I had a right to be a child, like anyone else. I had a right to be totally dependent and helpless." I needed to process this information. "It's so difficult sometimes to realize I wasn't an adult in a small body. Being innocent and so young kept me a target and victim-- I hated that part of me."

Peter nodded, happy my understanding was improving. "The guilt you're carrying is also a big part of your disordered eating. Blaming your body and yourself for being out of control is driving the 'punishment' of your body with food. Your critical voice is also from your mother's constant criticism. Instead of learning to speak with love and compassion to yourself, you adopted these voices as your own. You have great sympathy for others' suffering but not a lot for your own."

I raised my eyes. "In some ways, excess food does feel like a punishment for how "bad" I was. My appetite was the only thing I could see was wrong with me."

Peter looked at me intently. "You were a little child with a gun to your head. You were pre-verbal for critical times of the molestation, without any language to understand. You must have words even to be able to label and file experiences into memory."

"I guess I need to learn to be nicer to myself." I looked sheepishly at Peter.

Peter looked intently at me as he sat forward on his chair. "Yep--remember, you had absolutely nothing to do with his molesting you. It had nothing to do with your body, sexuality, love, or behavior. It would have occurred no matter who you were, what you did or didn't say, what you looked like, or whether you were good or bad—it was only and always about him."

"He just needed someone to use to feel powerful and in control of his life. He had incest in his core, and nothing would stop him from hurting me." I trembled, closing my eyes. The realization was overwhelming on many levels. "I guess, ultimately, it was just horrible luck to be his first daughter."

"Exactly."

"I was an innocent bystander in his pathway, doomed from the day I was born." With my eyes cast down, I rubbed my hands. "It's going to take a while to accept this--I've blamed myself for so, so long."

Peter also emphasized that sexual abuse is not about sex. It's about power and control over someone helpless. There is no higher power difference than an adult having sex with a child. Dad, at some level, was seeking to regain power, triggered by Mom's severe criticism and control over him, but it would have occurred despite Mom. She didn't cause it--he was a predator, and he used me to restore his sense of strength and control. I felt nauseous hearing this, realizing I had been in the direct path of Dad's pathology. Through no fault of my own, nothing would have saved me from his need to assault children.

I later read more research that showed, like sexual abuse survivors, soldiers with PTSD suffer tremendous guilt frequently, also. It's the biggest obstacle to their recovery because it is complicated and painful to face. For veterans, the people they killed and villages they destroyed in the madness of war are the most difficult, guilt-laden memories to face and can keep them stuck in PTSD for years.

Reducing my guilt remains a work in progress.

Chapter 50

They Get It

With both kids in college in 2007, it was time to inform them about my horrible past. I waited years to tell them so that they could have a childhood free from my horror. I wanted them to be mature enough to handle the information. Despite all, I had taught them to be proud of their family and its illustrious ancestry--to value the critical family connections. One bad apple didn't change their incredible legacy.

They were aware something was very wrong with my father's relationship. Unlike Michael's parents, who were involved in their lives, they had never seen my father after the Thanksgiving of 1990 when they were young. I had given them vague explanations when they asked about the rift, but I didn't feel it was in their best interest to focus on sexual abuse during their childhoods. It was time to release the secret and set it free.

Their grandfather's incest would shock them, and I had many concerns. How do I explain that their grandfather was a pedophile, a felon, and assaulted his own daughter? That their mother was a victim of horrifying sexual abuse, and their grandfather was having sex with their mother? I wondered if it would change their

Carol C.Boyce

view of me. It opened my life's pain to them, my vulnerability, the shame I'd lived. They were great young adults and I had to trust they could maturely handle the news.

Andrew and Carrie were home for winter break, sitting on wrought iron bar stools in our kitchen while Mike was at the office. They ate warm blueberry scones from Karen's, our favorite local bakery, with glasses of milk. Andrew leaned on the dark granite countertop to catch the crumbs.

Clutching my coffee cup, I said, "I have something I need to talk to you both about." I could have timed it better, with Michael home supporting me, but I felt like I needed to spit it out before losing my courage. Filled with the loss and magnitude of what I had to say, I wished I would never need to have this conversation.

"What's wrong, Mom? Are you OK? Are you sick or something?" Carrie looked wide-eyed at me. She could tell by my voice that what I had to say was something big.

"I'm OK but very sad about what I have to tell you." I looked down as tears fell.

Andrew put down his muffin. "What is it, Mom? You're scaring me."

Spit it out. It's not going to get easier. "I was molested as a child by your grandfather." *There, I said it.*

"What?" Carrie looked at me incredulously.

I wiped my face with a dishtowel. "It was extremely traumatic and went on a long time."

"Your dad? Really?" Carrie clambered off her chair to hug me.

"I had no idea." Andrew's eyes were huge. "You're kidding." He came over and rubbed my shoulders.

"I never wanted you to have to deal with it growing up. I'm glad you had no idea."

"Yeah, Mom. I had no idea either" Carrie's eyes brimmed with tears. "I'm so sorry."

"Granddad completely denies it, along with the rest of the family. It's been a long and difficult journey." I sighed, relieved the truth was out. I realized they had a right to know, and I could also use more cheerleaders in my corner.

"Healing has been extremely tough." I looked them in the eyes through more tears.

They were shocked and didn't ask many questions. I didn't say much else. The information they received was enough for them to process for now.

The years ahead would tell me how well they were coping with the news.

The next year, Andrew returned to college after his holiday break. Carrie and I were taking down the house lights. My heart sunk as I thought about both kids being back at college soon. I missed them so much but was glad they were doing well.

Grabbing the mail, I cringed, noticing two letters to the kids from Dad. Every Christmas, he sent a check for three hundred dollars to each of them, a lot of money for poor college students. I handed Carrie her envelope.

Putting down the lights, Carrie looked at the letter. "You know, Mom. I'm going to donate it to victims of sexual assault. I'll find a good organization. Andrew will agree with me, I'm sure."

"Wow, Carrie! I know you could really use that money for school. I'm so proud of you for deciding this."

After finishing with the lights, she went into her room and wrote a letter to her Grandad.

January 11, 2009

Dear Whitney,

There are a number of things that I need for you to hear from me. When I first learned what you did to my mother when she was a child, I cried every day for a month, imagining how her own father could abuse her in such a despicable way. Even now, the thought of what you did to the woman I love so much brings tears to my eyes and makes me nauseous. I want you to know that the abhorrent choices you made years ago did not disappear and will not be forgotten as you may have hoped. You have hurt me because you have caused irrevocable pain that haunts my mother's daily life. Before my family formed and I was even born, you placed a devastating burden on us to carry our entire lives. What you did to my mother has had a ripple effect that profoundly affected not just her but my whole family, many members of our extended family, and generations to come.

Although some of our relatives seem to divide you into two people – who you were then and now – I cannot and will not. Although you play the role of a kind grandfather well, I cannot be tempted to believe you have changed or are no longer a person who could do such unspeakable things. A person who has changed acknowledges what they have done wrong and tries to repair the damage they have caused. But you have done no such thing and still deny what you did even in these final years of your life. That you won't even admit, acknowledge, or take any responsibility for the way you have hurt my mother is what simultaneously breaks my heart for her and makes my blood boil in anger at you. How weak of a person are you that you would rather protect your pride than have a relationship with your very own daughter and your granddaughter and grandson? Are you really going to die not ever apologizing to her or admitting to what you did? After all the ways you have damaged my mother, don't you at least owe her that? Where did you ever get the idea that your pride is more important than honesty, relationships, morality, and other people's lives? It disgusts me to think that someone I am related to has lived such a shameful life, completely void of any moral character or value for anyone but himself. You have left your legacy on this family, and as far as I see it, it should be looked upon with nothing but shame and disgust.

Finally, I want you to know that your selfish and weak choices have caused you to miss out on having a relationship with the one thing you have done that you should be most proud of in your life. With no help from you, the daughter you created has become the best mother a person could ask for. Despite what you did to break her and weaken her, she is one of the most knowledgeable, strong, determined, emotionally healthy, and successful women I know. In every way you failed her, she has overcome and been the opposite for us. She and my father have a happy, healthy, loving relationship that my brother and I now will use as a model for our relationships and marriages. As a mother, she has loved us unconditionally, supported and encouraged us in all that we do, and taught us how to communicate respectfully and effectively with one another. She has been the pillar of strength in our family. Her example has enabled my brother and me to develop into emotionally and physically healthy adults who can be and do anything we dream of. Andrew and I will be successful in life because of her and my father. She spared us from the emotional damage of growing up with the alcohol, yelling, selfishness, and sexual abuse you brought into her life. I thank God that your daughter was strong enough to recognize your errors and refuse to let them be repeated in her family. I thank

Carol C.Boyce

God that she was strong enough to stop the cycle of abuse and speak up about what you did to her. It's a shame that you missed out on ever knowing what a strong woman she has become.

The money you sent me for Christmas and my birthday will be donated to two nonprofit organizations that seek to help children, victims of sexual abuse, like my mom. Hopefully, this money will help prevent other children from experiencing the horror you put my mother through.

Sincerely,

Carrie

I hugged her after she read it to me and cried. Carrie had always been wise beyond her years, but this letter still surprised me with her maturity and courage. She said such beautiful things about me that I beamed with pride. I knew then that my kids would ensure their children would enjoy respect, love, and safety. Being a vastly different mother than my own had paid off.

"I must stand up for what is right. I am so angry about what your father did to you and how you suffered." Carrie gave me a look of steely determination. "That's why, in my career, I want to educate women on sexual safety."

"That would be amazing, sweetie. I can't think of a better use of your talents." My smile was endless. "I love you so much." Humming Jingle Bells, I went back to untangling the Christmas lights.

Soon after, Carrie received a letter from her grandfather filled with newspaper clippings about therapists implanting memories. He was trying to discredit me and imply I was lying. My head exploded, and I wondered where to put my rage. I knew any response from either of us would fuel the flames and result in more of the same. It was useless to defend myself. In the end, Carrie had said it all--better than I ever could.

Dad never sent another check.

Another letter arrived from Dad in March of 2008. My Uncle Allen, his older brother, had recently passed away. As his father figure and best friend, Dad suffered a huge loss. In the same envelope were two letters, one with details about Allen's memorial service. I didn't attend because of Dad's presence.

Dear Carol,

We missed you at Allen's service. Queen Elizabeth and Peace roses were planted to signify Allen's long marriage to Aunt Barbara. They placed the roses by the house, and his three sons and grandson dug the holes. Each guest added a handful of dirt. Very emotional.

We have been given another opportunity to reconcile our differences. The timing now has become urgent with my brother's death.

I would love to put my arms around my daughter again. I think about you every day. The other children keep me informed about what you're doing and your music.

I long for the old days when I visited with you and your family.

Love, Dad

It felt like he was reaching out to me for emotional support at the death of his brother, Allen, wanting me to acknowledge his significant loss. Dad longed for the old days as if he had no role in losing our relationship. Once more, he was in total denial and his gaslighting, complete lack of reality and accountability continued to be disturbing. The humanity in this letter was new, though, and was heartbreaking, as I remembered better times, too. The letter was vulnerable, softer with genuine emotion, but it was still all about what he needed. And yet, I also felt the grief for our old relationship. The 'good' dad tugged at my child's heartstrings again.

Chapter 51

New Treatments

I no longer feared flying. In therapy, I connected my total lack of power and control, locked in an airliner, to the same feelings of being locked in my bedroom and sexually assaulted. With therapy, the PTSD reaction completely left me. I healed when I realized the pilot wanted to help me and keep me safe and that I wasn't a helpless little child trapped anymore. I was thrilled to be able to get on a plane happily again.

In 2009, I arrived late at Peter's office after a rehearsal for Madam Butterfly. Having broken my arm in a fall, the costumers struggled to hide the cast in my kimono, and it took time. I needed to look authentic in the Japanese setting.

I propped my cast up on several pillows as I sat on the couch. It was an overcast March day, and the dreariness was depressing. Peter greeted me as usual and sat down, asking about my broken arm. He started right in. "As we've discussed before, to survive the sexual abuse, you encapsulated all the memories and emotions in one area of your brain. Healing will be about accessing that sealed-off area, processing, and assimilating the memories into your existing ones. It's the purpose of REM sleep and will be critical to releasing the trapped emotions."

"I have incorrectly stored memory?" I sat more forward in my chair.

"When thinking of a terrible experience, such as 9/11, we don't want to forget it happened. We need to get the emotion out and merge it with other memories so it's not a daily distraction. Eye Movement Desensitization and Reprocessing (EMDR) is an effective new therapy I'd like you to try. Okay?"

"Sounds good."

Peter handed me headphones and I put them on. "Let's go back to the trauma seen in your childhood bedroom. Close your eyes and tell me what you see, where you're feeling it in your body."

"I feel it in my chest. I can see my bed in the darkness."

"I want you to listen now to the alternating sounds in each ear and follow them with your closed eyes, from one side to the other."

I'd move my closed eyes back and forth as I would do in REM sleep. This procedure seemed strange and too simple. "What do you see now, Carol?"

"I see the man's silhouette in the doorway and blackness.

"Stay with it and follow the beeps with your eyes."

The uncomplicated process continued, allowing me to dig deep into my trauma. I kept going back to my bedroom, where all the assaults occurred. With EMDR, I would relive the trauma to get my rational cortex to access the hidden memories. I had to reprocess the terror and bring it into normal memory to recover. Over time, this method helped me correctly process the assaults, and it was the most effective trauma therapy I used.

I was helped by other types of therapy, also. Although traditional "talk" therapy, or cognitive behavioral therapy, is not considered beneficial with trauma, it did help with growing the parts of me that froze as a child. Peter utilized Transactional Analysis to understand the critical, destructive parent, the defiant child, and the healthy adult aspects of my personality. We also did 'Inner Child' work, visualizing myself as a child and helping develop my adult voice.

I spent hours in counseling, changing the narrative, imagining myself turning the lights on in my dark bedroom, having Michael there, the police, and my close friends with me, too--whatever it took to feel safe. These were slow and difficult processes but crucial to my recovery.

Nothing was ever suggested or implanted by Peter. I was never hypnotized. I'd have changed therapists immediately if anyone had tried to "suggest" anything had happened to me. Implantation of the incredible emotions I endured from the abuse--the PTSD, the terror, the dissociation—would be impossible.

Chapter 52

This Never Happened

By 2010, Andrew and Carrie couldn't dodge the family denial any longer. Relatives, to my great disappointment, involved them in the uproar. They wanted to tell them the 'truth' as they saw it. Carrie and Andrew believed and supported me, to my family's dismay. The kids were easier targets than me, as I'd become infuriated by their continued denial.

My Aunt Judy, Dad's younger sister, called Carrie. "You must get help for your mother. Fix her delusion. How could she do this to your poor grandfather? She should just forgive, forget, and move on."

Another relative called Carrie. "Your mother is ruining the family with her false accusations. How could she *not* have remembered this? It's ridiculous!"

I squeezed my eyes shut when I heard about the conversations, trying to hold in my rage. How could they draw my children into the discussion? Couldn't they realize how much pain and loss our family was already suffering? That they had enough to deal with without their negative opinions? It boggled my mind how insensitive they seemed and how strongly they defended Dad. They were also further persecuting me.

Thankfully, Andrew and Carrie supported me staunchly and didn't tolerate it. They knew my character and had seen my grief and pain. They were my unflinching advocates. Along with Michael, they have been my most incredible, fervent, and endless supporters and, with me, are horrified by the uneducated and unenlightened responses they've experienced. I couldn't have been prouder or more appreciative of their backing.

I was sipping my morning coffee, leisurely reading the newspaper on my laptop, when I opened my email. One had arrived from my Aunt Judy, and I cautiously opened it.

Jan. 7, 2015

Dear Family,

I just got back from Walt's 90th birthday party. It was a great party for my brother and wonderful to see his lovely new home. He was thrilled to have so much of the family there. The family was well represented, and it couldn't have been more fun.

Love, Aunt Judy

Jolted awake, I burned inside with her flaunting of the family's denial. It felt like they were oblivious to Dad's predator status, ignoring and minimizing my devastating sexual assaults. They hadn't experienced what I had and wanted to play happy family again. I couldn't let the comments go, so I responded with my own email.

Jan. 9, 2015

Dear Family,

In response to the fun at my father's birthday celebration, I wanted to say how very painful hearing about this event was for me. Having been molested by him for a large part of my childhood and having to work every day of my life on recovery from the horrific trauma I endured, I find it abhorrent to celebrate anything about him and his life. The sexual abuse has taken a huge toll on Andrew, Carrie, Mike, and me emotionally and financially. I know families never want to know this or face a terrible truth, but we continue the unhealthy patterns and don't hold the perpetrators accountable without it.

Love, Carol

Their silence after my email told me they didn't agree with my thoughts. Andrew sent out his own response to support me.

Dear Family,

I support and stand wholeheartedly with what my mother voiced this week. I am so proud of my mother for speaking up against celebrating such a dark figure in our family's history. I am upset to hear that many of our closest still have not chosen to accept the sexual abuse caused by my grandfather.

As an educator of young people, I guide my students toward understanding the value and importance of supporting each other with empathy and compassion. If they witness wrongdoing against their peers, they practice speaking up against hurtful situations. Being a "bystander" versus an "upstander" is repeatedly discussed. Every time we choose silence or avoidance, we vote with our actions to support the wrongdoing.

Do not shelter my grandfather. Instead, spend your energy speaking with him about apologizing for the horrific choices with his own daughter. I have no sympathy for a person, no matter how old they are, if they are not willing to face the legacy of damage they are leaving behind. If you choose to see him, decide to pressure Walt to admit his wrongdoings. This discussion may allow him peace within himself. I can't imagine holding on to that guilt for a lifetime.

I encourage our family to continue sharing time with my mom to deeply understand and accept the accurate dark history of a person you call Dad, uncle, cousin, Grandpa, or brother. Together I hope we move forward with this history as a steppingstone toward supporting each other unconditionally through empathy and compassion to ensure that this hurt is not celebrated or sheltered. We may not have had control over our past, but we do control the path we build together now.

People with trauma and resulting PTSD often become addicted to drugs, die, or commit suicide. Mom has shown infinite strength and courage to overcome her demons. Granddad's actions have destroyed her ability to live a life that feels safe and trusting. A life free of fear will never be given back to her. Healing doesn't take away memories and though my mother is fine on the outside, she struggles daily to cope with the damage Whitney caused.

My mother knows how much I love and support her, and we talk regularly about how it affected us kids. I dealt daily with a mother who feared letting me out of her sight, out of the safe bubble she created for us. It was difficult for me, but I respect her trauma and fears.

None of us chose to have a child molester in our family, but the truth is, we do. Love, Andrew 2014

Aunt Judy's response was that I needed an 'intervention.' My therapy was clearly not working. I knew an intervention was used for alcoholics or drug addicts to confront *their* illness. I laughed aloud when I heard about her 'solution,' showing that I was the problem. Dad was again blameless, and I was the designated sick one.

Andrew responded to her soon after.

January 2015

Aunt Judy,

The ball is in all our courts to choose how to interact with the man who has single-handedly caused a wonderful woman to suffer and develop post-traumatic stress disorder.

We are lucky my mom is still alive.

Love,

Andrew

I was so proud of Andrew for keeping the focus on his grandfather. That I was the continual target of the family infuriated me. I couldn't understand how my family didn't understand. I wondered if they thought I was doing this for the fun of it—for decades.

Though it had been twenty-five years since I first confronted my father, I continued to receive letters from him every couple of years. Trying to convince me the abuse never happened, he thought I would eventually agree with him. Taking accountability and apologizing for his actions never crossed his mind.

By the fall of 2015, I received what was to be Dad's last letter.

September 1, 2015

Dear Michael,

I recently learned that Carol is still being treated for Repressed Memory Syndrome. She could be well again in one or two office visits with proper treatment.

Carol has been treated by Peter for 20 years and it is time to get him out of your life. She needs to cut the cord and move forward. I recommend that you speak with the Psychology Committee Chairman at your local hospital for a referral. If Carol does not go with you, you should go by yourself and explain the situation.

Remember, Michael, you are a doctor and the head of your family. You have the knowledge and experience to deal with this situation. It is way past time you acted on this.

Love, Dad

Although accustomed to this narrative, the letter added to the anger and frustration of my situation. Dad was still lying, even as a ninety-year-old, and using the amnesia *that he caused* to negate his abuse. He continued to attack Peter, Michael, and my mental incompetence, placing blame anywhere but on his shoulders. He maintained I was too mentally incompetent to make my own decisions or take care of myself. It was odd because my life was full and exemplary, despite my challenges. I had a long, good marriage, was well-educated, and had wonderful, thriving kids and financial security. It made no sense.

In the fall of 2015, soon after Dad's letter, my sister Debbie, an attorney, and our families were invited to a cousin's wedding in Carmel. Andrew was now teaching elementary school nearby. Carrie was on a Fulbright Scholarship in Nicaragua and couldn't attend. Despite our differences, my sister and I had kept our relationship going. We avoided discussing the abuse issue as much as possible, though it was always simmering in the background. She didn't believe a word I said about Dad.

The beautiful reception room overlooked the ocean where the moonlit ripples shimmered on the shore. A million stars, like crushed diamonds, sparkled in the warm, velvety night. Michael and I had returned to our hotel room in another building when Debbie noticed Andrew sitting on the balcony. Relaxed after drinking all evening, she grabbed her wine glass and joined him. "Hey, I need to speak to you about your mother."

Putting down his beer, Andrew looked up at his aunt. "Look--this isn't a great time to talk. It's late and we've all been drinking too much. If you need to say anything, talk to Mom directly." He knew this conversation wouldn't go well.

Undeterred, Debbie sat down on the damp deck chair next to Andrew. "I've waited a long time--I wanna do it now. I've heard you still believe your mom. The family wants me to set you straight. You need to know the truth."

Andrew closed his eyes, dreading the conversation to come.

"Grandad never molested your mother. He's a great person and would never do something like that." Debbie looked at him confidently. "Plus, I was sleeping in the same room near her—I would know if anything happened."

Andrew's forehead tightened as he stared into the sea. "Tell Mom directly, please."

She sat up straight in her chair and leaned forward. "Your mother has destroyed this family. How could she do this? It's been the hardest thing I've had to deal with in my entire life." Her eyes welled up. "I'm going to sue her therapist. Peter put these memories in her head. He's got to be stopped before he ruins another family. He needs his license removed!"

"Mom is telling the truth." Andrew took a deep breath, trying to stay calm.

Debbie's eyes clouded over. "What would you do if Carrie said this about your father? How would you react?" Tears flowed from her eyes as she acknowledged the intense pain she'd endured with her fractured family. She pensively sipped her glass of wine. "Plus, I'm worried your mother will commit suicide because of it."

"This did happen, whether you believe it or not, and she's not going to commit suicide." Andrew's neck became rigid, and his eyes bulged. "I'm going to bed. Good night. "

Andrew was shocked that his mother's only sister didn't provide any support. The backlash and character assassinations baffled him, along with the incredible family conflict my abuse accusations caused. He found it unbelievable that his family could support his grandfather and not me.

The following morning, Andrew came to our hotel suite and updated me on the exchange. Steam shot out of my ears. It was one thing to confront me but unacceptable to involve my kids. They had nothing to do with my abuse, and I didn't want their lives impacted any more than necessary. Defending me wasn't Andrew's responsibility—he had enough confusion and loss without this.

Debbie came over to my room shortly. Andrew, Michael, and I were eating blueberry muffins in our room. "How ya doing? " she asked meekly. "You weren't at breakfast."

I was ready to pounce, shaking with anger. "How dare you bring my son into this and accuse me of lying. You have no right to question my moral character. Are you trying to drive a wedge between Andrew and me?"

"I wanted him to know my side—the...uh...the family's side of things." She had a sheepish look on her face, surprised by the intensity of my reaction.

She had broken my cardinal rule to keep my children out of the battle. My pent-up rage now had a target. I sobbed loudly from all the pain and loss I'd suffered. My shoulders heaved with a release I hadn't shown her before. "And why would you concern Andrew about his mom committing suicide? I've never said anything about it." I wiped my eyes with a wet tissue

She stared wide-eyed at me, having never seen me this angry. "Your kids need to know the truth. I just don't believe you—I was in the same room!"

"You know you're saying that I'm either gullible, mentally ill, or a liar. Those are the only choices if you question the abuse. Which one is it?"

Debbie looked blankly at me.

With no reply, I demanded again. "Which is it? Pick--what am I? Mentally ill, a liar, or gullible?" My eyes bulged as I glared at her.

"I just don't believe you. I never heard or saw anything—I would have known. This never happened."

"You were under five years old and asleep when we shared a room. You'd have no idea what was going on. Don't be ridiculous." Grief engulfed my heart, thinking about my only sister choosing not to believe or support me.

I narrowed my eyes and scowled. "Ya know…I've never had the luxury of wondering whether my memories were real or not, popular, or not, proven or not. They were dumped in my lap and all but destroyed my life. I don't have the same luxury as you do. I must deal with it every day of my life." I wiped the tears from my face

"Well, this has been the most horrible thing that's happened in my life. It's been terrible." I'd never heard her say this before and it saddened me. She didn't deserve to endure this pain either. The reality of our mutual grief and divided family lay bare in front of us.

"Be glad you weren't the oldest daughter." I shut the door behind me as I went into my bedroom. I sobbed on the bed. My family's decades of rejection and accusations had come to a nasty head. I wondered if the pain would ever end. How could I forgive her and continue our relationship? I didn't deserve this treatment. My integrity, mental health, and long reputation as an honest and reliable person were questioned in full view of my kids. I didn't know how I could get past this interaction and still have respect for myself.

Carol C.Boyce

Several months later, Michael and I rocked in our white wicker chairs on our front porch, enjoying the flock of peacocks that had come up our street. After a beautiful, sunny day, they strutted their glorious colors in the setting sun. I breathed in the fresh cool air. Sipping my iced tea, I stared into space. "I just can't shake the pain from the confrontation with Debbie. Ya know, I've known for a long time that Mark, Tim, and Debbie don't believe me. They've never once supported me, asked for clarity, or been compassionate about what I've gone through. I love them dearly, and I've never wanted Dad's actions to come between us. I've had so much loss already--I couldn't bear any more."

A vein on Michael's forehead pulsed. "Debbie was extremely aggressive with her views and involved Andrew. The family's entire focus has been on dismissing your allegations because of your amnesia. I get your frustration."

I sat in silence for several minutes. "You know, I feel expendable to them---and it really hurts. I'm again thrown away, as my father did." I thought hard, rocking my chair. "Sometimes, I wonder how I would have reacted if I were in their shoes. If Debbie had said this happened to her, I'm sure I wouldn't want to believe her. I'd also support and protect Dad initially. I'd be torn and wouldn't want to give up either relationship."

"It reminds me of that horrible movie scene in *Sophie's Choice*. Remember, a Nazi guard makes her choose which of her two children will live. Though not life or death, your siblings also must make a horrible choice between you and your father."

"Yep, they have a horrible but critical choice. If I were them, I'd research trauma responses much more. I'd ask many more questions and realize this must be true."

"Yeah. Hopefully, we'd support the victim and not deny the whole issue. They don't want to know anything because of the potential loss of their father."

"No one comes out with these allegations for the fun of it. Truthfully, I don't know how I would have reacted. The choice between my father and sibling would be devastating, as it is for them. But you can't support evil. Part of loving someone is holding them accountable."

Michael picked up his drink and headed indoors. "It puts them in a horrible position."

Chapter 53

Reaching Out

With a now empty nest at home and much recovery on board, I felt the need to help other abused children. I couldn't stand by when so many kids were in need. I wanted to make a difference in even one child's life, let them know they were valued and not at fault for their family's chaos.

Michael and I began volunteering one night per week at a large government-run home for abused children. All had been removed from their homes by Child Protective Services. The kids had suffered extreme trauma and abandonment, often orphaned due to parental drug abuse and physical or sexual abuse. Most had failed every foster placement because of acting out their pain inappropriately. The children's PTSD was frequently undiagnosed and triggered by unknown causes: a smell, a tone of voice, an object, a food, or a gesture that reminded them of their abuser. Across the board, they displayed aggressiveness and hostility.

On our weekly visits, Mike and I focused on nurturing, encouraging, and providing enrichment to them. We'd read, take them on field trips, listen to whatever they wanted to talk about, sing, teach guitar, or do crafts--anything to enrich or brighten their day.

I pushed Tyra, an adorable eight-year-old, on a swing outside the "home" one warm summer evening. I knew her background included neglect due to her mother's drug addiction and sexual abuse from her stepfather. Tyra was an intelligent, beautiful eight-year-old who was hostile to everyone, trying to cope with incredible pain and confusion at such an early age. Tina trusted no one to be kind and consistent in her life. Though she had hit me and spit on me in the past, I tried patiently to help her cope in her sterile, cold world. Tina would let me see her anger but not her soft feelings of sorrow, fear, and grief--typical for these traumatized children.

While she swung, I tried to connect with her. "How was school today?"

"Bad," Tina answered, pumping her legs as hard as she could, soaring into the empty sky.

"Why?"

"I threw things at the teacher and got in trouble." Dry-eyed with a scowl, she continued to pump her legs furiously.

"Oh. What made you so angry you needed to throw things?" I probed.

Her nostrils flared and her eyes bulged." Mommy died yesterday."

Wide-eyed, I went to the front of the swing and tried to hug her. It was against the rules to embrace the children, but I couldn't help myself. She pushed me away. I knew I needed to honor her boundary, so I went back around and continued to push her on the swing—she allowed that. Back and forth, I pushed her for several minutes in silence. "I'd be really angry, too. I can see why you wanted to throw things." I tried to mirror her thoughts to help her understand her feelings were normal.

"Mommy took too many drugs," Tyra explained.

"Yep, and you had nothing to do with it. You're a wonderful daughter, and Mommy was sick. You didn't cause her problems." It was all I could think to say. "I bet you're sad and scared. It must hurt so badly." I pushed her until dusk came and we went into the grey facility.

My heart broke for Tyra and the shocking cold and abrupt ending of any maternal nurturing in her life. It resonated with me. I wondered how she would remember and process this early trauma and what devices she'd use to handle the incredible over-load. I realized I was watching live as her traumas were entangled and layered in her mind. Though much of her and the other children's traumatized past will remain unknown and undocumented, it will permanently alter their brain development. I wondered what I could do to help her and prevent a future of heartache, PTSD, and confusion. Would any treatment she received be effective?

Many of the children in the home have been diagnosed with heavy labels: Attention Deficit Disorder (ADD), Attention Deficit Disorder with Hyperactivity (ADHD), Borderline Personality, Obsessive-Compulsive Disorder (OCD), Oppositional Defiant Disorder (ODD), and Conduct Disorder (CD), to name a few. The extensive list of medications they are prescribed is daunting. I've learned that many trauma researchers, including the renowned psychiatrist Bruce D. Perry, now believe the accurate diagnosis for these problematic children is PTSD from Developmental Trauma Disorder. They are frequently and easily misdiagnosed and treated. Despite the staff's best intentions, given difficult children to manage and incorrect diagnoses, their ability to change the course of these children's lives remains limited, and treatments are in their infancy.

The chances that these children will receive corrective therapies for their trauma before their lives self-destruct is low.

They're at significant risk of being incarcerated, drug-addicted, violent, and unhoused. Their fractured lives remind me of myself and it's daunting to see the effects of child abuse in real-time. From what I've seen, effective trauma therapy for adults is in its infancy, and for children, effective treatments remain desperately needed. We must train professionals in the new trauma research and take kids back to their missing nurturing, safety, and consistency needs. Much more needs to be learned and funds allocated to provide early interventions and prevent much more expensive and tragic consequences later in their lives.

Having been an abused child, I have always felt passionate about helping other children. I know that with Girl Scouting, one lone woman, a leader with no children of her own in the troop, profoundly influenced and improved my life. Volunteering time with abused children is one of the best things to spend my time on, though difficult emotionally. While many other causes move me, going forward, nothing deserves my nurturing and caregiving more than helping traumatized children.

Chapter 54

The Whole Story

My shoulders slumped as I plopped down on Peter's sofa. "Ya know, after all my work, my memory still holds many secrets. It's hard to recover when I don't know everything." My forehead scrunched as I looked sideways. "I want the memories in the palms of my hands so I can see, feel, and touch my history. I just don't have clean, linear memories, and it's so frustrating." I can still be haunted, not knowing my whole story. Having a large part of my life history gone is unnerving. I have clear flashbacks, but other memories are vague or completely missing. *Will they suddenly come to me when I least expected them, or are they gone forever?* Either my assaults never entered my memory, or I continue to protect myself from them.

"Unfortunately, it doesn't look like your story will ever be fully known. It's just the nature of severe trauma, I'm afraid." Peter looked at me with softness in his eyes. "The memories frequently don't come fully back. It all happened in a dark room, leaving you no markers. The severity of the abuse and resulting dissociating to the ceiling caused you to block out everything possible, as many children have done."

"I can date the assaults by when I got a double canopy bed. When I was eight, Debbie moved to her own room, and they placed my new bed against an adjacent wall." I tapped my foot. "My memories are clear about where my bed was during the assaults."

Peter sighed deeply. "Moving your sister out also gave your father more exclusive access to you."

"I never thought about that." I rolled my eyes. "How sickening."

"Something to think about."

"Well, I can date the assaults--before I was eight or after. That's about as far as I know. I also have a vague sense of my body size and puberty changes. It's a broad range of time." I twirled my hair into a knot, horrified about the extended period of my childhood involved.

"That's not much information to date the assaults. I can see why it's disappointing." Peter took notes on his pad. "What years do you think the abuse happened?"

"The abuse started when I was about three because of my early memories, but I don't know when it stopped, sometime after puberty. I'll never know." My voice trailed off as I closed my eyes.

Peter shifted in his chair.

My eyes narrowed as I burst out, "I have a damn right to know what happened to me. It's my basic human right to know what occurred in my life. How can I continue to heal without more details?"

"And your father does know, but he refuses to tell you."

I fumed, shaking my head. "It's so frustrating. I want the details but will never know my full story." After the session ended,

I pounded the passenger seat hard when I got in my car. I had to release my anger.

Truthfully, I frequently vacillate between wanting and not wanting to know more details. In 2022, the unknown can still scare me as my childhood protection mechanism stays partially in control. My mind must still think I need protection at some level, or it's released all it retained from the assaults. I must accept the reality.

Chapter 55

Drowning in Self-Doubt

It was a glorious, cold January day in 2016 near Monterey Bay on the northern California coast. It was a day so crisp and clear that I couldn't believe the world could be so glorious. Michael and I were excited that Andrew and Carrie, both excellent swimmers now in their late twenties, could join our adventure.

We unloaded our kayaks carefully and carried them down to the water's edge. "What's taking so long? Jump in your kayaks and let's get going." Andrew pleaded with us to start the expedition up the briny waters of the ocean slough.

Carrie and Andrew got in their single kayaks and Michael, and I got in our double, foot-peddled one, with me in the front seat. Andrew and Carrie headed out ahead of us, dressed in wetsuits. Michael and I were warm against the winter chill with heavy socks, jeans, tennis shoes, warm jackets, and turtleneck sweaters.

We paddled into the icy, cold, and calm waters with the three boats. Over one hundred large sea lions and otters played near us, diving and lounging with their pups near the sandy shores. Their loud barking and the cawing seagulls created a raucous musical accompaniment. I smiled broadly paddling past these fantastic creatures on this brilliant, icy winter day.

We peddled several miles up the briny slough, enjoying the views. Calmly, Michael announced from behind me, "I'm going to get the camera out of the hold—I wanna take some pictures."

"Okay," I said, happy he would capture the moment. My next memory is plunging headfirst into the icy sea, the kayak turning upside down, dumping us and everything onboard. The water swirled around my head with my eyes open, making me dizzy and disoriented. My knees came toward my head as if a giant wave tumbled me. The water swirled around me, and I rolled.

My head was spinning, and I couldn't tell which way was up. My heart raced as my legs became unmovable, frozen from the extreme cold. The wet, heavy clothes I was wearing weighed me down, and I couldn't kick my legs. *I'm drowning--this is it. I'm going to die.*

When I finally surfaced and found fresh air, I was relieved Michael's head was above water. He was a powerful swimmer and I thought he'd be okay. I took a huge gasp of air. "Help, help!" I finally yelled. I gave a big sigh of relief, seeing Andrew paddling toward me.

I'd never seen Andrew so powerful as he went into emergency mode. He had been a lifeguard and waterfront trainer at a summer camp for many seasons and was well-trained in water rescue. Thankfully, he knew to stay calm--I was anything but. "Mom, grab the front of my kayak. Stay calm. Don't try to get in—you're not strong enough and the boat will dump us. I'm going to tow you."

Flailing around, gasping for air, I said, "Andrew, I'm going to drown. I'm drowning. I can't move my legs!"

"Mom, you have a life jacket on! You can't drown. Do as I say, and you'll be okay. I promise you that you won't drown."

His strength amazed me and calmed me down. Carrie was doing the same with her father.

"A life jacket? Oh, my God. I forgot all about the life jacket." In my fear, it never crossed my mind that I was safe and protected all along.

Andrew and Carrie eventually got Michael and me to the shore. We were safe at last, shaken, hypothermic, and bleeding from climbing the shoreline rocks. Our car keys and cell phones remained forever buried in their briny grave, but I was so proud and thankful for our courageous kids.

After we got home, Michael and I sat in our living room, warmed by a roaring fire. It felt so good to be dry and safe. My eyes were red and tired from the long day.

I looked at Michael. "You know, in that split second in the water---I genuinely thought that I would die. I thought it was over. I didn't even know I had on a lifejacket. Isn't that crazy? I was that scared."

Michael finished folding our clean kayaking clothes. "Hey, I was scared too, but I never thought we wouldn't survive. I knew we were okay because of the jackets—it'd be tough to drown with them on." He smoothed his cleaned jeans. "Besides, Carrie and Andrew would get us to shore—we were in good hands."

I thought some more. "I felt all alone--I thought I would sink and drown like there was no one to help me." I raised my eyebrows. "I had given up on me and my strength--like I was still a helpless child on my own." I looked down at my freckled hands.

"I didn't believe in my strength, the lifejacket, or the family who loved me."

"Hmmm." He put the clothes in neat piles.

"I said to myself, 'You're too weak to manage this.' Parts of me still think I'm a child--helpless and weak--despite all I've been through."

"Like you believe whatever you must deal with is more than you can manage on your own?"

"Yes, like I did as a kid. I still want something outside of me to take care of me, a magic substance of some sort, I guess. I don't believe in my strength."

Michael cleared his throat. "The power was in you."

"Sometimes, I think babies are born perfect with unencumbered souls. Growing up, though, some of us have to change. Our souls get molded and squashed like Play-Doh with unhealthy and immature parents ~~box~~ to fit into our family's invisible box. To squeeze into mine, I had to lose ~~be molded to survive my family dysfunction.~~ essential and critical beliefs about myself."

Mike looked at his hands. "I never thought about it." Analysis wasn't his thing.

"I wasn't allowed to be a big, strong, and confidant voice ~~for ourselves~~ to be large. I wasn't allowed the safety of venturing into the world with my own confident beliefs. That's what abuse does. It stuffs you into a tiny space to almost disappear within the family structure. I twisted into what my ~~into~~ parents needed based on what they could tolerate in themselves. Do you ever think of that?"

"Not really." ~~Analysis wasn't his thing. He rolled his eyes. Carol's analyzing again—here we go.~~ He took a swig of his beer, yawning after a long day.

"What I've learned through all of this is that your love and the kid's love are constant and allow me to be who I am. I can be powerful and strong and still know your love will be there."

"Yep, it's always there, and you are strong enough to help yourself."

"I always have my own life-preserver—but it's me and my power. I am an adult, but I have trouble believing in my strength." I looked Michael in the eyes and held his hands, "As silly as it sounds, I must remind myself that I am grown-up now and don't need someone else to save me. I'm strong enough to get me through my most difficult situations and emotions."

"You can trust yourself." He turned out the lights as we headed to bed.

"I'm strong enough on my own. I am my lifejacket now."

Carol C.Boyce

Chapter 56

Just Diet

'And I said to my body softly, 'I want to be your friend.'
She took a long breath and replied, 'I've been waiting
my whole life for this.' Nayyirah Waheed

Michael and I were sitting in our hot tub in 2019, enjoying a beautiful spring bloom of white azaleas and burgundy rhododendrons. As the spring day began, the gray squirrels busied themselves, burying their seeds in our yard. "Our lives are so good now," I said. "We've come through so much. We're happily retired, and the kids and their families are doing great."

"Isn't it the best? Life is finally much easier."

I looked out over the backyard. "I have an appointment with Dr. McMurphy tomorrow for a physical." I rolled my eyes." I'm still so overweight—it's so damn embarrassing." I rubbed my temples. "I've overcome so much. I can't believe I still struggle with eating normally after all these years."

"Well, you are a lot better, but it's disappointing to see you still battling your weight—it scares me." Michael had lived with my eating disorder for three decades. He rarely said much about it, but I knew he worried about my health, as did I. He couldn't understand why food was so difficult for me, nor could I.

"What else can I do? I've been on every diet known to humanity five times—I've failed at all of them. None have worked long term. I always exercise and lift weights...I've seen therapists specializing in eating disorders. What else am I supposed to do?" Sheepishly, I said. "I'm sorry for everything I've put you through. I know it's been hard on you, also." I frowned with shame overwhelming me.

At 6'3", Michael was tall and lean, an athlete at sixty-seven. "Ask Dr. McMurphy again what else you can do."

I drove to my appointment the following day and got on the dreaded scale. "You have to lose more weight. Your BMI is too high," Dr. McMurphy, scratching his beard, stated from the get-go. "Maybe you could try our fasting program."

"I have done that program already. I ate formula for four months, remember?" I swung my feet and looked down at the floor.

"How about Weight Watchers?" He looked bored.

"Been there---done that many, many times. I have a stack of used logbooks at home. I've tried them all. Jenny Craig, medical fasting, Nutrisystem, even Bariatric surgery--none of them have worked long term. None."

"How about a keto diet. Lots of my patients like that one." His jaw clenched with frustration. The assistant opened the door and gave him a paper to sign.

"Hmm...Do you remember me telling you I was severely sexually abused as a child? The connection between childhood trauma and eating disorders is clear. I'm working on recovering."

Carol C.Boyce

"Well, why don't you try exercising more." He ignored my comment. I rolled my eyes and said, "Sure, I'll try it," just to end the conversation.

Despite my doctor's extensive education and experience, he lacked training in the complicated connection between trauma, eating disorders, and other autoimmune, intestinal health conditions. I have found this lack of training particularly frustrating, and it comes across as judgmental and demeaning. There remains the belief that eating-disordered people lack nutrition education, exercise, or self-discipline, deeming us ignorant or uninformed.

Research on compulsive overeating shows a high correlation with childhood sexual abuse. Compassion and information on the cause of the problem, not judgment and simple fixes, are needed. We will never permanently recover without trauma treatment, as is evidenced today by so many. No diet, exercise, or surgery will work long term because the treatments don't address the underlying cause. It will be a huge step forward when professionals become trained in developmental trauma, adverse childhood experiences, and PTSD as a frequent underlying cause of physical and mental damage. (CDC, 2019)

In the spring of 2019, Peter had extensive cancer surgery. My heart broke for him, but he insisted it was time for me to move on anyway. With his excellent guidance, I had healed and grown so much. He had helped guide me through so many difficult personal issues within and outside of the incest and I'd be forever grateful to him. I wasn't sure how I'd function without him in my life--I would miss him dearly.

After a two-year break from therapy, I started seeing someone new. It was great to get Dr. Pam Lower's fresh perspective and knowledge. I had significant recovery on board, but I still felt occasional therapy sessions would help me with my complex issues.

With the Covid epidemic in full swing, I logged in for our regular Zoom meeting and hit Join Meeting. "How are you today?" We both focused our cameras on seeing each other. I adjusted my room lights, trying to look younger. The cameras could be brutal.

"I'm so frustrated with my eating. I thought I had gotten to all the issues, but craving sweets still rears its ugly head. I've worked forever on it, and I don't understand why I still struggle. I feel so stupid." Though I had lost a lot of weight, I was still obese and feared the consequences.

Straightening her hair, she leaned forward in her chair. "There are many layers to food issues. With the abuse, you absorbed many incorrect, negative beliefs. Can you name the ones you're aware of?"

With a long sigh, I sat up, trying to remember as a police siren wailed in the background. "Well, primarily, as a kid, I wanted to end any connection between my brain and evil body-- just to survive and stop the abuse." I looked at my feet with downcast eyes. "It's like my body is three feet to the right of me--even now."

She made a note on her computer, and I straightened my glasses. "What else have you learned?"

"I guess...I took over Mom's critical voice. I beat myself up endlessly if I eat 'bad' foods. Sugar is not allowed at all." I looked at my intertwined fingers. "I guess I'm still looking for that compassion and nurturing, the hug I so desperately needed, the parent telling me I'm safe and everything will be okay. Food is my go-to--the closest thing I can find to nurture me and reduce my anxiety."

Pam looked at the camera and I saw her patient eyes. "Remember, inextricably linked in your brain is addiction and trauma. Addiction is not a character flaw but a normal reaction to what occurred. What you did was find a way to survive at any cost." She had a confident expression. "You should thank yourself for figuring out a way to stay alive and survive. You had no choice but to sedate the pain. Food is frequently the only choice for sedation with young, abused children."

I pursed my lips. It sounded so strange and counterintuitive. "You mean I should thank myself for this horrible disorder? I've been so busy beating myself up that I never thought to connect my survival to it. I just thought it was a defect." My blood boiled, realizing Dad had helped create this problem, too. The consequences will never end, I thought.

"Remember, a harsh inner critic that beats you up is the major cause of compulsive overeating. Without it, you wouldn't be obsessed with sugar." She looked directly at me on her screen. "Abused and abandoned children frequently spend their lives trying to find that nurturing and uncompromising love they never had. They incorrectly look outside themselves when the answer is inside us."

"Hmmm. I didn't know that."

"You must reconnect with your body, learn to speak lovingly to yourself, and allow abundance in your life. You deserve love and physical and emotional fulfillment. All foods are 'good' and allowed."

"Okay, I must think about this. It's hard to identify my critical self-talk. I need to slow way down to become aware of it." I shut my eyes to process it all. I remembered something else.

"Plus, as a teenager, I vowed that no one would ever control or deprive me of food again. Ever. That voice is always in charge."

"So, who controls your food now?"

"Nobody, that's the problem. I won't allow anyone control over it, even myself." There was so much emotional chaos I felt around food growing up. Healthy eating equals Dad's control of me. It's like I'm saying, 'I'll show you, Dad, who controls my eating and my body now. You'll never control me again!'"

"How is that working for you?" Pam raised a brow.

I looked sideways, avoiding the truth. "Okay—it's not. If I restrict my intake and diet, I'm reminded of the emotional and food deprivation I experienced as a child. It feels like I agree with Dad's strict eating regime. Like he's still controlling my eating. But it also means that I agree with him and that my body doesn't deserve care. It's so confusing. There's a significant conflict that I still can't resolve."

"I can understand why you feel that way, given your background." Pam straightened in her chair. "As children, compassion learned from our primary caregivers is critical to learning how to do it for ourselves. You had an 'attachment rupture,' causing you to link fear and emotional abandonment with eating. It makes it difficult to be kind and understanding of yourself."

"Plus, Mom's drinking and being so out of control made me constantly enraged at her. Now, I'm the one out of control with sugar!" I was surprised how complex and mixed up I still was on something so seemingly simple as eating healthy. I was silent for several moments as I tried to absorb the information.

"Trauma makes survivors less capable of regulating their own behavior. Also, you transferred the anger at your mom to yourself." Pam pushed me further. "Tell me what else your father's strict control over food really meant to you?".

I spoke slowly, inaudibly, as tears came to my eyes. "Dad controlled me with food but also sexually. Both were invasive to my body." Disgusted at the new connection, I stared at the floor with downcast eyes.

"So, excessive control of food was bad enough, but your father's control over you sexually was most disturbing. Did I get that right?" Pam frowned. "The two issues are linked tightly in your brain. Some research shows excessive sugar is as physically addictive as opioids, and it can mimic sexual abuse—putting something into your body that hurts you." She smiled at me. "Your self-harming behavior is so difficult to repair because of these incredible complexities, how young you were at the time, and how long it went on. Be patient with yourself."

"Allowing myself to enjoy food--to take pleasure and abundance from it--would mean, in my mind, that I agreed and was complicit with the sexual abuse that occurred. Taking pleasure in anything physical feels wrong because pleasure, guilt, and terror are forever linked. Having a healthy body or looking and feeling sexually attractive meant that I condoned the assaults. It's a lot to keep straight."

The amazing, complex issues with food overwhelm me. It's almost impossible to correct it and that's why I've struggled so long. These were critical insights. I know I will overcome my eating issues one day. I've already significantly improved. I know diets are too simplistic for severe eating disorders, setting up survivors for failure. Keeping these issues in the forefront, treating myself with loving compassion while losing the critical parent voice, and slowing down my life to learn self-care are vital to surviving my disorder.

Chapter 57

Flippers

On a cool fall evening in 2021, the house was painfully quiet after Carrie, Jim, their rambunctious dog, and our adorable grand girls left after a short visit. With Michael playing pickleball, our home seemed calm as I put away the many toys on the floor. I flipped on the TV show, *Dateline* and stretched out on our soft recliner in my pajamas.

Michael arrived home and came into the family room. He noticed me watching Dateline, another true story where the husband had murdered his wife. "I don't get it. Why do you watch these horrible, violent stories? I'd think you'd avoid them."

"Hmm." I glared at him, annoyed he questioned my choice of programs. When I went to bed, I thought more about why these stories did interest me. They're frequently about perpetrators who seem nice and normal but suddenly become murderers: the loving husband who kills his wife because he doesn't want to lose money divorcing her; the wife who hires an assassin to kill her spouse; the neighbor who burns his house down with his family in it for the insurance money—horrible stories.

"You know," I said the next day at breakfast, wiping my hands with a napkin. "I watch those shows because I'm fascinated by people who flip."

"Flip, huh?" Michael looked up, wide-eyed.

"You know, people who change completely from a normal family person into someone completely different. You don't get it--because you haven't been a victim of someone like that."

"Why does it interest you so much?"

As I thought about it, I realized the truth. "These stories are about Jekyll and Hyde personalities—high-functioning socio-paths like Dad—two completely different personalities in one brain. I'm fascinated by regular people with everything in life---families, money, education, good jobs, and friends who destroy themselves and others. They seem compassionate and nor-mal...but turn into dangerous people."

"It's just like the horrible 2002 murder by Scott Peterson and his beautiful pregnant wife, Laci. He had everything--good looks, education, a home, and a loving wife with a new baby on the way. He murdered her and the baby, so he could date again and not pay alimony or child support. Just unbelievable--no one saw his evil side until it was too late."

"So, by watching these horrible stories, you're trying to un-derstand what happened to you, what caused your father to be evil?"

I pushed around my scrambled eggs. "I think because I ex-perienced firsthand the damage from someone like that, the sto-ries become very real. I don't want my family to get hurt by a sociopath again. I want to know what I missed in Dad."

"You mean you're trying to feel safer?"

"Well, yes, I guess so." I thought a moment. "I'm trying to be super cautious. That's why I have cameras and alarms everywhere and was so overprotective of the kids. I couldn't let them out of sight because I knew how fast and easy it was to be a victim."

"Sometimes, your fearfulness drove the kids and me crazy..." Michael poured some orange juice. "So, what have you learned?"

"No matter how many cases I hear about, I'll never be able to identify or predict a high-functioning sociopath. Something is just missing in them, and they're everywhere—an estimated three to five percent of the population. It's frightening when you think about it." I stared off in space for a few minutes. "I know now that I'll never understand bad people, as hard as I've tried. I'll never comprehend evil.

Chapter 58

It Wasn't Your Fault

My good friend, Shannon, recently became a director for a major medical program that intakes sexually abused children. In 2021, knowing my background and that I was authoring this book, she asked if I'd like to tour her facility. I jumped at the opportunity, excited to see what it was like for newly identified victims and what I would have felt like had I been recognized as a child.

I entered the large waiting room, empty of children because of the Covid pandemic. Decorated with bright colors and child-focused activities, many teddy bears and dolls were available for hugging in this warm and friendly environment.

"Let's talk in my office before showing you the clinic." Shannon motioned to a chair. I noticed pictures of her five beautiful grandchildren on the walls. I thought nostalgically about when we had raised our children together--the soccer teams, get-togethers, and playdates were wonderful, warm memories.

Shannon sipped her coffee. "Most sexually abused children physically are doing well. There is usually no bodily injury indicating abuse has occurred. It is exceedingly rare for us to see vaginal or anal damage. "

"That's interesting because I always wondered why no one noticed anything physically wrong with me. Although a good friend of my parents, I've always felt my pediatrician should have noticed something was wrong. I almost wished I had bruises and a black eye." I sighed, deeply frustrated again with another way perpetrators escape punishment.

"It's another tough aspect of identifying sexual abuse. And if we can't see anything, it's easier to assume nothing hurts the child, physically or mentally. Child sexual abuse occurs at all levels of society, socioeconomic groups, and ethnicities. Whereas physical abuse is dependent on drug and alcohol addiction, poverty, and social pressures, sexual assault is not," Shannon explained.

"Interesting--I don't think most people understand that. They still think it occurs with children in low socioeconomic situations." I shifted in my seat.

"Also, these boys and girls have high, established trust with their abuser, typically their father or stepfather. It eliminates the need to groom them. For perpetrators to abuse children outside the family takes more time and effort." Shannon frowned at the disturbing thought.

"I can understand that."

Shannon talked of the damage to the families. "When these children come forward with their abuse, frequently at the hands of their father, stepfather, or mother's boyfriend, older kids are aware their accusations will destroy critical relationships in their family. Younger children are afraid, too, but don't understand why." Shannon looked down, imagining their pain and confusion. "Their accusations can destroy the marriage and source of support, and they know it."

"It must take so much strength and courage for them to speak up." I felt their helplessness and sadness at the position they were put in.

"They wonder, who they'll live with, who'll pay the bills with Dad gone, and what will happen to their siblings and school. It's a heavy load."

"These whistleblowers are amazingly brave and so young."

Shannon stood and led me into the clinical area. I noticed a sign on the wall in the assessment room across from the exam table.

First, I Believe You

I was thrilled and so surprised to see this critical phrase posted for all to see. It was so important these medical professionals got this central concept. I thought back to how affirming those words were when my therapists said them.

As the visit continued, my eyes filled with tears, overwhelmed by the reality of how many children are still enduring sexual assaults. It's heartbreaking and stopping the epidemic is so challenging. My mind wandered to another phrase I thought would help these victims. "You need another sign. Shannon."

"What would that be?" She looked curious.

It wasn't your fault.

"The guilt takes a lifetime to remove. It's important to release the child's responsibility right away and put it back on the offender. Victims get so confused by the gaslighting that frequently comes with abuse, so it's critical they learn this as soon as possible."

"Good idea."

It was time to go, and I thanked Shannon for her tour and outstanding work at the clinic. Compassionate, understanding nurses like her are critical first responders to these frightened and devastated children. There couldn't be anyone better for the difficult job than my empathetic, highly educated friend. I was so proud of her commitment to such challenging work.

She gave me a hand-out with the Bureau of Justice Statistics as I left. The information on child sexual abuse is tragic. Ninety-three percent of child victims know their perpetrators beforehand. It's rarely from strangers, as most think. Family friends, neighbors, coaches, stepparents, significant others, and parents are the primary abusers. Like so many, I spent much more time worrying about strangers hurting my kids than friends and family, even with my background.

I connected so much with what Shannon had said. I realized my circumstances and privilege level only added to not being identified or believed. I was more likely to hide the abuse because it was from my father. With my high trust in him, I was less risky to access and molest than if Dad had gone outside the family. I was an easy victim--no grooming required.

The long-term effects of incest are enormous, with seventy-seven percent of survivors developing a mental illness, regardless of the severity of the abuse. Fifty percent of survivors have attempted suicide. According to recent studies, fifty percent have addiction issues, many of which are eating-related, with a cost just in the US of $9.3 billion per year (Gellman, 2012). Child abuse is preventable and the most expensive and destructive cause of societal problems.

Chapter 59

Death Without Dignity

O n a blustery fall day in 2020, I was in sweats, admiring our flaming-red Chinese Pistache tree out our back window. Michael had sold the dental practice, and we retired a year before. We loved the freedom to do what we wanted every day and helping care for our two new granddaughters was a joy.

I had time to consider relationships in my family. The incest controversy could have easily and logically destroyed the relationships with my siblings and their families, but I wouldn't let it. Despite our conflicts, we all tried to keep our relationships as far from the abuse as possible. I knew they had nothing to do with the sexual assaults. I hated their responses and lack of support, but I realized they were victims of Mom and Dad's drama also and struggled with their own demons. My emphatic insistence on Dad's evilness created uncomfortable situations, but we accepted our differences as best we could. Dad continued to be a big part of their lives and they saw him regularly. I had no contact with him. Despite my disapproval, they kept Dad updated on my life. He didn't deserve any information on my family and me--he had lost the privilege long ago, but I couldn't do anything about it.

One afternoon, Tim called on my cell phone. We were close and talked frequently, so I wasn't alarmed.

In a halting voice, he said, "I wanted to let you know...that Dad...only has days left. He had a small stroke last night and is looking terrible. At ninety-five, he won't last much longer..."

"Hmmm...Thanks for letting me know. I know this is hard for you." I tried to sound sympathetic because I knew Dad's passing would be difficult for Tim. "I love you. Thanks for the heads-up."

As I hung up, my head dropped. As I processed the news, my shoulders heaved, releasing long-suppressed tears. I could have kicked myself. I only wanted to feel my rightful anger, not the old love for "good dad." It hurt too much, and I'd already experienced enough pain, but the tears wouldn't stop.

I wept for the father I once loved, trusted, and admired, the side of him that was good. I cried for the man who made sure I went to college, showed me so many National Parks, laughed and joked with me, played the piano, sang beautifully, and brought music into my life. I wished I could forget the kind parts; they were still painful despite all I'd experienced.

But after fifteen minutes, my blood began to boil in my veins. Thinking of my childhood bedroom, I remembered my father's silhouette in the doorway and how he terrified me, a daughter he should have given his life to protect. I thought about the father I had loved dearly but who never cherished me in return, who couldn't care less about the effects his actions had on my life. He would leave a horrifying traumatic legacy of abuse with our innocent family.

With Michael out of the house, I pounded the sofa and yelled out my rage at my dying father. "How dare you f**king die and leave without any remorse or acknowledgment of what you did. How dare you leave our family without the truth, your four children, in great conflict and turmoil. You're the only one with vital information I needed of all he did to me. You'll go to your grave with it." His cruelty to the end was breathtaking, dying without any remorse or responsibility. The man who told me 'I "wasn't his daughter anymore" and to "get lost" after my mother's death was my real father and I wouldn't grieve for him.

Dad didn't pass away after my brother's call and several months later, in January of 2021, my family and his friends gathered joyously to celebrate his 96th birthday. Hearing about the plans, I couldn't help imagining the balloons, banners, and crepe-paper decorating his luxurious house. With one candle flaming, a large, frosted cake would say, 'Happy Birthday, Walt.' The guests would enthusiastically sing *Happy Birthday* to my smiling father, now confined to a wheelchair. All in the room would cheer for his fantastic longevity and good nature.

I, of course, would never attend. After three decades, I remained an outcast, a whistleblower retaliated against, a pariah in my own family. That they still chose to celebrate and believe his narrative over the truth still amazes me, the rejection palpable. I shook my head in disbelief at how long I'd endured this unbelievable injustice, the sharp dagger of abuse.

Chapter 60

Another Perp

After returning from a voice lesson in 2021, my cousin Maggie left a phone message with an urgency in her voice. "I had an interesting call from Lilly. You need to talk to her." A sweet, kind woman in her early forties, Lilly was one of my Uncle Allen's six grandchildren. He had died twelve years ago.

I called her right way. After some pleasantries, I said, "What's up—Maggie said I should talk with you?"

"Well, I told her my grandfather molested me...for a long time."

"Oh my God..." My temples tightened. *My father's only brother...Please, God, don't let this happen again in our family--not to someone as sweet and kind as Lilly.* "I'm just horrified to hear this! I'm so, so sorry this happened to you." My heart broke for her, and I couldn't have felt more sympathy and compassion. I was happy to give her the support and care that I did not receive. Most importantly, I would believe her without question.

Choking on tears, she said, "I thought it was time I notified the family. I'm planning to email them all soon." She explained that the sexual abuse lasted from age three to fourteen, only stopping when her family moved out of state. It started as a toddler when she was placed in bed with her doting grandfather after her grandmother left to fix breakfast.

I realized she didn't know about my father molesting me as we talked. I was surprised, as I thought everyone in the family knew. I realized she and her immediate family lived across the country when I told everybody, and they hadn't heard. "I am here to support you in any way I can. But do you know...my, uh, father was molesting me also—at similar ages?"

Lilly was silent. "I had no idea—no way...Oh my God, I'm so sorry!" We were both speechless, grasping the shocking and devastating family connection we shared.

"And many in the family have never believed me. They've supported Dad throughout."

"I can't believe this happened to you---or that the family has been so unsupportive—it's just terrible." She was still stunned that my father, her great uncle, was also molesting.

I slowly added, "It's been one of the hardest parts to deal with for three decades. They just refuse to believe it. Maybe that'll change now—how could they keep denying it with your added information?"

"Yep--we have a terrible past linking us together. To think both brothers were pedophiles." Her voice became halting, emotional, choked with tears. "So many children at our family gatherings were around them. They were patriarchs and both brothers were so respected. No one ever suspected them—there were no signs."

I paused, trying to process the devastating latest information, feeling punched in the stomach. It was unbelievable this information was coming out now. I knew sexual abuse runs in families, but I never saw this coming. I shook my head in disbelief, trying to grasp the news. "If you had known about my father, it would have helped you recover sooner. Sorry I didn't get the info to you."

With muffled sobs, she continued. "Yep--it probably would have. When I was about twenty, I did tell my father and he confronted his dad. After significant pressure, my grandfather confessed and wrote me an apology letter."

I was shocked she got an apology from her perpetrator, albeit under duress. I'd have given anything to get a letter like that. "Lilly, I'm so glad you got that letter. Let's keep talking together and help us both heal. I fully support you in your efforts and I'm here anytime you need me. Let's fight this family tragedy together."

"I plan to send an email to the entire family this week. I'm scared because I don't know how they will respond. "

Her courage amazed me, and I was glad she would inform the extended family. "Go for it, Lilly—I'm really proud of you and remember, *it wasn't your fault.*"

"Love you, Carol. Thanks so much."

Later, we learned that this same uncle had also molested another grandchild of his. My rage exploded as I grasped the enormity of the damage to our innocent family. *When would this damn tragedy end?*

That evening, Michael and I talked on our front porch. "How do you think your cousins and Aunt Judy will take it—when Lilly sends them the email? Do ya think they'll finally believe you? It's obvious now—incest is in the family."

I rocked faster, thinking about it. "I want to scream--this is what I've been telling you for thirty years! There is sexual abuse in this family!" My eyes widened. "They should apologize profusely for not believing me."

"Yep--It makes me wonder how far back this went in the family." Michael looked away. "Well, it's obvious now that something happened to your dad--and his brother."

I had wondered about this for years—but it was an even more disturbing thought now. "Someone was probably molesting the brothers--someone close to them." I rubbed my forehead. "But no matter what--there was no excuse. They could have chosen to heal, like Lilly and I have. They could have had no kids, stayed away from their children, or left their families. Anything." I was shooting daggers from my eyes. "There is no excuse for what they did. None whatsoever."

"Yep." Getting chilled, we went in for the night.

In the end, Lilly got a few emails of support from the family, which she appreciated. I heard little and nothing from my immediate family.

Chapter 61

Raising My Voice

My tight-waisted long-laced bodice with its large, petticoated satin skirt swept the black stage floor. My elbow-length white gloves held a matching lace fan and a loop for my skirt. With period detail, the hairdresser adjusted my tightly curled hair. My makeup artist applied heavy cosmetics to "play" to the seats in the back of the 2000-seat theater. The colossal set was in place and the lighting augmented the festive mood of the scene. I could smell the excitement in the air.

After nine months of music rehearsals, voice coaching, dance instruction, costuming, and language experts, it was time to put the Italian opera *La Boheme* together and perform the challenging yet gorgeous historical piece. The stage manager announced, "Places for Act I. Places for Act I." The curtain soon rose as the maestro lifted his baton. I proudly sang the famous Italian music while waltzing, remembering my father's lessons so long ago.

Somewhere in my heart, I had a dream of singing, a destiny I climbed over many hurdles of discouragement and disbelief to achieve. The beauty of my father's voice, the one I loved as a young child, still echoed in my mind. The irony of the gift still struck me as bittersweet.

I continue to have amazing opportunities from singing. The several times I've performed at Carnegie Hall and recently behind Andre Bocelli to a crowd of seventeen thousand thrilled me. Many personal recitals and singing with our regional ballet company and symphony helped me realize priceless moments in my life. With perseverance and a steadfast belief in myself, I finally realized my own voice was hiding somewhere inside me.

My voice—strong and resilient—had emerged along with the truth of my life.

Chapter 62

Safe Now

In 2021, I fearlessly flew to the Burbank airport, near where I'd grown up. It was a crisp January afternoon, and I was heading to a 90th birthday celebration for Shirley, my mother's best friend from long ago. As I entered her home, I was so happy to see her. She'd always been warm and caring growing up, despite having nine children of her own. Reminiscing with her about good times and memories of Mom warmed my heart. It felt good to play the happy childhood fantasy for a few minutes. When I left at eight-thirty, I drove away in the dark, glad I'd made the trip.

I decided to visit my nearby childhood home before heading to the hotel. My parents had moved from this neighborhood after I got married, and I hadn't seen it in five decades. Something inside of me drew me to the house, like the vortex of a riptide. I knew I needed to see it one more time. I wondered if the house was still standing and what I would feel.

As the wind whipped through my light coat on this dark, wintery evening, I smelled the crisp air. The leaves trembled on the now enormous trees of my youth, their limbs intertwined above the earthquake-gnarled sidewalks, making shadows dance across the street. The once young, thin trees that had weathered many storms and intense winds were now grown, battered, and scarred like me. We all had survived our struggles.

I smiled, thinking back on the many good times. I thought of the childhood friends who had grown up here, and I wondered where their lives had taken them. The endless roller skating, hopscotch, and rope jumping with Susie flashed back. My thoughts returned to watching my brother play basketball and Debbie running through the neighborhood, adorable in her full cowboy gear. I remembered taking family photos with my grandparents, Dad singing funny songs, and running around in his plaid shorts, warming me from the inside. The giant oak tree in our front yard that Susie and I had joyously climbed was gone.

These flickers of innocence and happy times melded with the sharp, painful ones. It was like I was looking at myself through a stained-glass window, each of the many panes an unusual color, a distinct texture, a different mood, at once separate, yet forever soldered together.

Though I hadn't physically visited the house, I'd been here a thousand times in my mind since I left, raging and screaming out the horror I'd lived. Oh yes, I had been here. I wanted the house and my room removed from the face of the planet so that they couldn't hurt me anymore. I'd physically burned the house down and destroyed every inch of it. If I could get rid of it and my bedroom, the endless terror of the assaults would leave my mind. Now, I was standing in front of the darkened house, facing all that had happened within its walls.

I thought, imagine if I could see my bedroom one more time. It would be amazing to connect my daylight memories with the nighttime world of hurt, the flipping realities of my young life. I had never physically stood in my bedroom knowing about the abuse. I'd left long before I remembered. I wondered if it would help me heal.

Unexpectedly, a young man came out the front door and started packing up his car. He glanced at me, a single older woman, staring at his home in the dark. He must have thought it very odd that I was standing there. I blushed, getting caught snooping outside his home.

I desperately wanted to see inside—it might be my only opportunity. I gathered my courage and yelled, "Excuse me, but I grew up in this house." I waved to him, attempting to explain myself. His reaction, I knew, would make or break my dream.

This young, dark-haired man yelled back, "Oh really, how wonderful!" Surprisingly, he acted like an old friend and waved me up the driveway.

Incredulously, I walked up our old steep driveway I had stubbed my toe on so many times as a kid. We introduced ourselves. "I'm Kahlil. My family has redone much of the house." He beamed with pride about their substantial efforts. "Do you want to see inside? I'd be happy to show it to you." he offered casually. "Let me check quickly with my parents to see if it's okay." He ran through the front door.

I held my breath. The young man had no idea what he was offering me. I never thought I would ever be inside that house again.

He ran back outside and gave me a thumbs-up, waving me in. "I'd love to see it. Thank you so much," I muttered. Following his lead, I entered. It smelled of the family's wonderful Mideastern cuisine, with allspice and nutmeg permeating the air. His parents sat in recliners in the kitchen. His father said, "I purchased the home from a doctor in the late seventies. I heard he was married with several kids."

"Yes, my father was a doctor, and I grew up here, with my mother, of course." I was stumbling from nerves. "There were four kids--I'm one of them—the second oldest." I smiled faintly, trying not to reveal the real purpose of the visit.

"Oh, wonderful." He proudly described the many renovations he had personally made to update the house. "I'll let Kahlil give you a look around."

"Thank you. I'd love that."

Kahlil began the tour. Everything felt smaller than I remembered. The living room where I'd worried, hated my mother so much, learned the guitar, waltzed, and felt hunger was still there. The once trendy, gold shag carpet was replaced with large white tile throughout, giving the house a much cooler feel. We started down the long hallway, passed the dividing wall between the living room and my bedroom, and looked into my old bathroom. I had been so thrilled when my cat delivered a litter of four kittens in that dated shower. Susie and I had spent hours playing with the adorable, purring furballs. My sister and I took baths in the bathtub for weekly hair washing before Sunday morning church. I remembered being a teenager and playing with my hair endlessly and the beauty parlor I had set up for the neighborhood girls in it.

Going into my parents' large bedroom next brought many mixed memories: dressing up in mom's wedding dress without her knowing, learning to sew, hearing bedtime stories with Nana, and secretly putting on Mom's makeup. It felt unreal to be in their room. For a moment, I wished I didn't know about the abuse, to go back for a second and just think of the fun things that occurred, but my mind clouded over with a sense of loss.

We continued down the hallway and Kahlil pointed to my bedroom door. "You can go in there…but it's a mess," he said with a half-smile. He thought I wouldn't be interested.

"I would like to see it if you don't mind. It was my bedroom."
I smiled back at him. Taking a few shaky steps towards the door,
I closed my eyes and stopped breathing as Kahlil stayed behind.
You can do this—just open your eyes. A chill ran down my back
as I realized I was standing in *the* doorway, *the* doorway where
the silhouetted man had stood, ready to assault and terrorize me.

The room had clothes strewn around the bed and floor. I
could see the big picture window on the far wall, and I pictured
Mark's treehouse and the terrifying men who threw the ball outside. There was no more pink canopy bed with long eyelet lace,
no more beloved doll cabinet, or floral wallpaper. They...were all
gone...forever. It was just a room. Just a normal, typical, no big
damn deal room. I screamed in my head. How could this room
still be standing...after all I'd felt? After all that happened here
and that I was put through? It was like it was taunting me. "See,
nothing's different here. Nothing happened, can't you see?"

I shut my eyes again, trying to process what I was experiencing. A volcano welled up deep in my chest. I wanted to scream
out the pain, loud enough for the walls to shake, crumble down,
and destroy the house. I wanted to watch as my tears rained down
from every ceiling, flooding the house. *How could this innocuous,
innocent room be the same space?* I put my hands on my forehead, feeling disoriented. *Don't these people know what happened in this room? How can everyone be so calm?* My head was
pounding with such intense emotion. I'd lose it if I stayed much
longer. But I had to search the room--I looked repeatedly.

Coming to my senses, I walked back to the living room. I
realized I'd never tell this kind family what had happened within
their walls. They loved and were proud of their home and I
wanted them to continue to make it a loving, happy place. As I

left, I thanked my clueless, sweet hosts and closed the large front door on my past life forever.

As I got in my car in the chilly night air, my shoulders heaved a sigh of relief as tears filled my eyes. I had survived, barely. I was happy so many changes had been made to the house--it was clearly a different era and family now. I wiped my tears on my coat sleeve and smiled.

As I sat in my car, I realized that my bedroom and the living room were separated by one thin four-inch wall made only of wood and wallboard. The four-inch wall marked the difference between my everyday life and hell, just four inches separated my daytime reality and nighttime horror. It seemed so much smaller than when I was little, and I was surprised this stuck out to me.

Without much awareness, I tied everything surrounding the abuse into one big, painful package--my house, bedroom, neighborhood, bed, kitchen, and living room. But now I could see they weren't the problem. They had nothing to do with it. The house was simply an innocent venue for one sociopath, with me in his sightline. He could and would have assaulted me any place and anywhere. It was never the walls or shag carpeting or gold furniture. It was never me. It was Dad and Dad alone.

I'm incredibly grateful these people allowed a stranger into their home, and I had the gift of re-experiencing it. This visit gave me some freedom, closure, and a broader view of my childhood. It helped put a period on my past.

But I realized there was another goal. I had come to confirm the faceless man was gone forever. He could never hurt and haunt me again. Indeed, there was no sign of him, and I had looked carefully. He was gone and done destroying my life. The abuse was over, and I was finally safe.

Epilogue

E ven during my worst despair, the spark of hope in my soul remained. I survived by clinging to that endless flicker, telling me that life was worth living. I got through my bleakest days with an unflinching vow that my children have a better childhood. Compounded by disbelief from those I loved, I faced head-on the terrifying PTSD from my tragic background, with no idea what was wrong. I wouldn't let my father's pathology take away the incredible life I deserved. I developed resiliency and built coping skills because of the adversity. By reconnecting my body and mind, I created a magnificent fabric of strong threads and the large, colorful design that is me.

Though grief has left a ragged, colorless scar on my heart, it's no longer bloody and raw. Though it's a quiet, tender place I must revisit, it doesn't overwhelm me or my life anymore. Recovering memories of incest represented the terrifying end of me as I knew myself and a goodbye to the cherished father I had once deeply loved. The grieving and major depression I experienced resulted from having loved and trusted deeply, something I'll never regret.

Today, my backpack of child-learned fears that once crippled me remains, but I've drained their strength. Though they can still scare me, I know too much about them now, where they come from, what they're capable of, and how to identify each one, a lifetime of work. The intense battle is over, my sanity from an insane childhood restored. I became in control of my betrayal trauma and complex PTSD, not vice versa. I learned I wasn't born fearful—my father taught me to be constantly afraid. The terror I endured caused me to adopt the poorly understood survival mechanism of amnesia, which ultimately saved my life. I will be forever thankful for it.

Incest and amnesia are a significant part of my life's story, but they do not define me. I am not my trauma. I had let my childhood tapestry of my parent's design define the size and shape of who I was. I figured that its faulty fabric and gaping holes were from a defective core in me. My parents had designed it without understanding who I was and who I was destined to become. As I healed, I placed blame where it belonged and strengthened my broken fibers with love, support, and compassion to become the confident, strong fighter I am today. I found my voice and wouldn't be who I am without my past.

I learned my compulsive overeating resulted from my traumatic legacy, not a character flaw. My abuse had nothing to do with me or my body that I blamed for so long. The abuse would have occurred no matter who I was or wasn't, where I lived, or whether I was good or bad. Dad was a pedophile at his core, and nothing would have stopped him from hurting me. It was just horrible luck to be in the pathway of a sociopath, an innocent child caught in her father's pathology.

I am good and good enough. Love for and from the family I created gave me the most compelling reason to fight the decades-long battle. I had to find the courage to face a vast, devastating unknown with no roadmap or guarantee of success. After the starvation and poverty of childhood neglect and abuse, I realized authentic love is life's goldmine, unconditional and unchanging. My amazing family, friends, and therapists provided a constant backdrop of care and inclusion during my most difficult days.

Dad passed away in December 2021, days before his 97th birthday. He knew I was finishing and publishing this book but never said anything about it to me. He lied about what he'd done to his last breath, as I expected, without any acknowledgment or apology to me. I felt sadness and anger about what I had always hoped for in our relationship, but I felt great relief that the story was finally over. He couldn't hurt me anymore.

I never had the gift of seeing my father prosecuted. Our laws did not protect me then, nor would they today, thirty years after recalling the memories. It will remain a challenge to teach the world that traumatic amnesia is a predictable result of young and severe sexual abuse. I authored this book to add legitimacy to changing our antiquated laws. Though only one survivor may come forward with little or no corroborating evidence, it remains a serious crime that demands prosecution. The statute of limitations must end.

PTSD and memories can return in fragments, triggered by a sound, voice, physical feeling, taste, touch, smell, or emotion, making the victim seem mentally challenged. Incest is one of the most terrifying experiences a human can endure, and when the memories return, survivors can be unstable. The perpetrator is to blame. We can help heal the epidemic of trauma disorders by educating the public and professionals and removing statutes of limitations for sexual crimes.

As I write this, Carrie is finishing her Ph.D. in Epidemiology, specializing in women's sexual safety across the globe. She's traveled the world researching and speaking on these critical issues. Andrew is a tremendous teacher and mentor, a great outdoors person, and a musician. I know my kids understand compassion, safety, and respect for all people. I couldn't be prouder to have raised exceptional children and ended the cycle of abuse.

Revealing the tragic truth didn't fix or ensure everyone would believe me. The price was huge, but the cost of silence would have been much higher. For all survivors, I encourage you to speak up, speak out, and speak the truth to anyone who will listen and the devastation it caused in your life. Let others know how prevalent the problem is and identify and prosecute perpetrators for their tragic deeds. It is critical to stop the epidemic and release sexual assault victims from an invisible prison of silence and shame. We must speak openly, unafraid, and proudly, joining the #Metoo movement. We must elect politicians who support abuse survivors and don't mock, lie, and degrade women, regardless of their other policies. Speaking the truth will truly set you free.

Trust the first child or adult identifying a perpetrator, no matter how revered they might be—very few people lie about this. Sexual abuse knows no socioeconomic boundaries, and we must change laws to prosecute all, even 'highly successful' people, not wait for many more to become victims. Have uncomfortable conversations regularly to educate your young children on incest and sexual abuse before hitting vulnerable preteen ages. Practice dialoguing these awkward and unpleasant conversations. Frank, difficult talks will protect them, but our silence will make them easier victims. Be encouraging and empathetic in your relationships with children so they will have someone they can tell. Create caring children and insist on respect for others' feelings and bodies. Clearly state sexual abuse will not be tolerated in your family.

In 2021, when reading this manuscript for the first time, Andrew and Carrie were shocked by what I'd survived. They had no idea I was recovering from horrible trauma while raising them.

One of my greatest joys is to know that their world remained sober, predictable, and supportive, as every child deserves. Michael was also shocked reading the manuscript. Though living with me through my experience, I hid my most agonizing moments, even from him. He never realized just how complex and dark my journey had been.

I couldn't be happier now. I've lived an extraordinary and rich life with my children, husband of forty-five plus years, and granddaughters. I pursued my singing career, enjoyed world travel, and had a fulfilling career. More important than any sadness I have felt, I'm proud and happy I modeled courage, fortitude, and transcendence over a tragic family legacy.

In telling my story, I attempted to shine a beacon of hope on the devastating disorder of Developmental Traumatic Amnesia from incest and sexual abuse. May my experience provide a roadmap for the extraordinary life survivors deserve, free from flashbacks and unknown terror. Despite the high cost of facing my abuser, speaking out remains one of my life's greatest achievements. With love and hope, it is all possible.

And remember--our first words to anyone coming forward about sexual abuse must be:

"First, I Believe You."

References

(2017). CDC Report, CDC, Morbidity and Mortality Weekly Report (MMWR). Retrieved April 2022, from https://www.cdc.gov/vitalsigns/aces/index.html

(2021). Retrieved from National Eating Disorders Association: https://www.nationaleatingdisorders.org

(2022). Retrieved from Out of the Storm: For Those With Complex PTSD Due to Relational Trauma: www.outofthestorm.website

Anda, R. F. (2020;000(000)). Inside the Adverse Childhood Experience Score: Strengths, Limitations, and Misapplications. *Amer. J. of Preventive Medicine*, 1-3.

Bass, E., & Davis, L. (1988). *The Courage to Heal.* New York: Harper & Row.

Celbus, O. e. (Jan. 2020). Evaluation of Incest Cases: 4-Years Retrospective Study. *J of Child Sexual Abuse*, 79-89.

Chiba et al., T. (July 2019). Current Status of Neurofeedback for Post-traumatic Stress Disorder: A Systematic Review and the Possibility of Decoded Neurofeedback. *Frontiers in Human Neuroscience, 13*. Retrieved from https://www.ncbi.nlm.nih.gov/pmc/articles/PMC6650780/

Chu MD, J. A., & Frey, Psych D., L. M. (1999). Memories of Childhood Abuse: Dissociation, Amnesia, and Corroboration. *American Journal of Psychiatry 1999; 156:749–755), 156*, 749-755. Retrieved from https://ajp.psychiatryonline.org/doi/pdf/10.1176/ajp.156.5.749

Crum, K. I. (2021). Oxytocin, PTSD, and sexual abuse are associated with attention network intrinsic functional connectivity. *Psychiatry Research: Neuroimaging, 316.* Retrieved from www.https://www.sciencedaily.com/releases/2021/10/211027121948.htm

D'Andrea, W. F. (2012). Understanding interpersonal trauma in children: Why we need a developmentally appropriate trauma diagnosis. *American Journal of Orthopsychiatry, 82(2)*, 187–200.

Dannlowski, U. (2012, February 15). Limbic Scars: Long-Term Consequences of Childhood Maltreatment Revealed by Functional and Structural Magnetic Resonance Imaging. *Journal of Biological Psychiatry, 71*(4), 286-293.

David Finkelhor, P. (2014). The Lifetime Prevalence of Child Sexual Abuse and Sexual Assault Assessed in Late Adolescence. *Journal of Adolescent Health*, 1-5.

De Bellis, M. M. (2011, September). NEURODEVELOPMENTAL BIOLOGY ASSOCIATED WITH CHILDHOOD SEXUAL ABUSE. *Journal of Childhood Sexual Abuse, 20*(5), 548-587. Retrieved April 2022

Diamond, et al., D. M. (2007). The temporal dynamics model of emotional memory processing: a synthesis on the neurobiological basis of stress-induced amnesia, flashbulb, and traumatic memories, and the Yerkes-Dodson law. *J. of Neural Plasticity*. Retrieved from www.putbed.gov: https://pubmed.ncbi.nlm.nih.gov/17641736/

Dopp, A. R., Borduin, C. M., & White, M. H. (2017). Family-based treatments for serious juvenile offenders: A multilevel meta-analysis. *Journal of Consulting and Clinical Psychology, 85*(4), 335-354. Retrieved from https://doi.org/10.1037/ccp0000183

Dunkley, D. M., Masheb, R. M., & Grilo, C. (2010). Childhood maltreatment, depressive symptoms, and body dissatisfaction in patients with binge eating disorder: The mediating role of self-criticism. *Intl Journal of Eating Disorders*. Retrieved from https://onlinelibrary.wiley.com/doi/abs/10.1002/eat.20796

Erikson, E. H. (1950). *Childhood and Society*. New York: Norton.

Fang, X., Brown, D., Florence, C., & Mercy, J. (2012). The economic burden of child maltreatment in the US and implications for prevention. *Child Abuse and Neglect: The International Journal, 36*(2), 156-165.

Felitti, V. (1998). Relationship of Childhood Abuse and Household Dysfunction-Leading Cause of Death. *American Journal of Preventive Medicine, 14*(4).

Fix, R. e. (July 2021). Changing the paradigm: Using strategic communications to promote recognition of child sexual abuse as a preventable public health problem. *Child Abuse Neglect*.

Frankl, V. E. (1946). *Man's Search For Meaning: The classic tribute to hope from the Holocaust*. New York: Beacon Press (English).

Freyd, J. H. (01 Jun 2017). Perpetrator Responses to Victim Confrontation: DARVO and Victim Self-Blame. *Journal of Aggression, Maltreatment & Trauma, 26,* 644-663.

Gelles, R. J. (2012). Estimated Annual Cost of Child Abuse and Neglect. *Prevent Child Abuse America.* Chicago, IL. Retrieved April 2022, from https://preventchildabuse.org/wp-content/uploads/2020/10/PCA_COM2012-1.pdf

Gerge, A. (2020: 100164). What neuroscience and neurofeedback can teach ...complex trauma. *European Journal of Trauma Dissociation 2020,* Vol 4, Issue 3.

Gladwell, M. (2019). *Talking to Strangers: What We Should Know About People We Don't Know* (1 ed.). Little, Brown & Co.

Griffin, M. (2019). *Tears of the Silenced: An Amish True Crime Memoir of Childhood Sexual Abuse, Brutal Betrayal and Ultimate Survival* (1 ed.). Coral Gables, FL, USA: Mango Publishing.

Harris, C. (2019). *Anti-Diet: Reclaim Your Time, Money, Well-Being, and Happiness Through Intuitive Eating.* New York City, USA: Little, Brown Spark.

Harsey, S. e. (2017). Perpetrator Responses to Victim Confrontation: DARVO and Victim Self-Blame. *Perpetrator Responses to Victim Confrontation: DARVO and Victim Self-Blame, 26*(6), 644-663. Retrieved April 2022

Hendrix, H., & Hunt, H. L. (1993). *Getting the Love You Want: A Guide for Couples.* New York: St. Martin's Griffin.

Holsten, J. (2013). *The Swimsuit Lesson: A Story for Parents and Children to Enjoy Together.* Holsten Books.

Hopper, J. (2014, Dec 9). Why Rape and Trauma Survivors Have Fragmented and Incomplete Memories. *Time Magazine*.

Hopper, J. (2015). Recovered Memories of Sexual Abuse: Scientific Research & Scholarly Resources. Retrieved from www.jimhopper.com

Hopper, J. W. (2020). Values and visions for the field of psychological trauma, from the brain to re-moralization and social transformation. *JOURNAL OF TRAUMA & DISSOCIATION 2020, VOL. 21, NO. 3,, 21*(3), 279-292. Retrieved from https://doi.org/10.1080/15299732.2020.1718968

Hopper, J. W., & Lanius, MD, Ph.D., R. A. (2008). Reexperiencing/Hyperaroused and the Dissociative States in Posttraumatic Stress Disorder. *Psychiatric Times, 25*(13). Retrieved from www.PsychiatricTimes.com: https://www.psychiatrictimes.com/view/reexperiencinghyperaroused-and-dissociative-states-posttraumatic-stress-disorder

Khoury, L., Tang, Y., & Bradley, B. (Dec. 27, 2010). Substance use, childhood traumatic experience, and Posttraumatic Stress Disorder in an urban civilian population. *PubMed-US National Library of Medicine, 12*, 1077-1086. Retrieved from https://www.ncbi.nlm.nih.gov/pmc/articles/PMC3051362/

Kubler-Ross, E. (1997). *On Death and Dying*. New York: Scribner.

Lagnado, L. (1991). *Children of the Flames: Dr. Josef Mengele and the Untold Story of the Twins of Auschwitz*. New York: William Morrow and Co.

Leadership Council. (2022). Retrieved from The Leadership Council on Child Abuse and Interpersonal Violence: www.leadershipcouncil.org

Letourneau, E. J., Brown, D. S., Fang, X., & Hansen, A. (May, 2018). The economic burden of child sexual abuse in the United States. *J. of Child Abuse and Neglect, 79*, 413-422. Retrieved from https://pubmed.ncbi.nlm.nih.gov/29533869/

Levine, P. A., & Frederick, A. (1997). *Waking the Tiger: Healing Trauma* (1st ed.). Berkeley, CA: North Atlantic Books.

Maria M. Wuinones, e. a. (2020). Dysregulation of inflammation, neurobiology and cognitive function in PTSD: an integrative review. *Cognitive Affect in Behavioral Neuroscience*, 455-480.

Mendlesohn et al., M. (2011). *The Trauma Recovery Group: A Guide for Practitioners Paperback.* Gulfport Press.

Miller, C. (2019). *Know My Name, A Memoir.* New York: Viking Press.

Montgomery, E., & Pope, C. (2015, 16 August). *The re-enactment of childhood sexual abuse in maternity care: a qualitative study.* Retrieved from Biomedcentral.com: https://bmcpregnancychildbirth.biomedcentral.com/articles/10.1186/s12884-015-0626-9

Moore-Emmett, A. (2004). *God's Brothel: The Extortion of Sex for Salvation for Contemporary Morman and Christian Fundamentalist Polygamy.* San Francisco, : Pince-Nez Press.

National Sexual Assault Hotline. (2022). *800-656-HOPE.*

Perry, B. a. (2021). *What Happened to You?* Flat Iron Books.

Pinkola Estes, C. (1990). *Warming the Stone Child: Myths and Stories about Abandonment and the Unmothered Child.* Sounds True.

Rainn. (2022). *Rape, Abuse & Incest National Network.* Retrieved from rainn.org: www.rainn.org 800.656.HOPE

Rogers, F. (May 14, 2019). *The World According to Mister Rogers: Important Things to Remember.* New York: Hatchett Books.

Rudolph, J., Zimmer-Gembeck, M. j., & Shanley, D. C. (2017). Child Sexual Abuse Prevention Opportunities: Parenting, Programs, and the Reduction of Risk. *PubMed.gov, 23*(1). Retrieved from https://doi.org/10.1177/1077559517729479

Russell, D. E. (1984). The prevalence and seriousness of incestuous abuse: stepfathers vs. biological fathers. *Journal of Child Abuse and Neglect*, 15-22.

Salmona, M. (2015). *Impact of Sexual Violence from Childhood to Adulthood.*

Salmona, M. (2018, January 19). Traumatic Amnesia a dissociative survival mechanism. Retrieved from Memoire Traumatique: https://www.memoiretraumatique.org/

Salmona, M. (2020, December 12/2/2020). *Muriel Salmona, the psychiatrist who fights for victims of traumatic amnesia.* Retrieved from https://www.lady-first.me/: https://www.lady-first.me/

Sanders, J. (2016). *My Body! What I Say Goes!* Victoria, Australia: Upload Publishing.

Silverman, S. W. (1999, Paperback Edition). *Because I Remember Terror, Father, I Remember You.* Athens, Georgia: University of Georgia Press.

Springer, MPH, et al., K. (2003). The Long-term Health Outcomes of Childhood Abuse An Overview and a Call to Action. *J. of General Internal Medicine, 10*(Oct. 18, 2003), 864–870. Retrieved from https://www.ncbi.nlm.nih.gov/pmc/articles/PMC1494926/

Stout, Ph.D., M. (2005). *The Sociopath Next Door: The Ruthless Versus the Rest of Us.* New York: Random House.

Symonds, L. J. (2020, 3 (3)). Childhood trauma: the cause that needs a cure. *Life Research.*

Terr, L. (1988). What happens to memories of early childhood trauma? *J American Academy Child Adolescent Psychiatry, 27*, 96-104.

Tomeo, et al., M. E. (n.d.). Comparative data of childhood and adolescence molestation in heterosexual and homosexual persons. *Archives of Sexual Behavior, 5*(2001 Oct;30), 535-41.

UNICEF. (2017). *Violence in the Lives of Children.* Retrieved from https://www.unicef.org/publications/files/Violence_in_the_lives_of_children_and_adolescents.pdf.

UNICEF-Traumatic Memory and Victimology. (2015). Retrieved from https://www.unicef.org/publications/files/Violence_in_the_lives_of_children_and_adolescents.pdf.

Van der Kolk, B. (2000). *National Child Traumatic Stress Network.* Retrieved from https://www.nctsn.org/: https://www.nctsn.org/

Van der Kolk, B. (2015). *Body Keeps The Score: Mind, Brain in Transformation of Trauma* (17th ed.). New York: Penguin Books.

Van der Kolk, B. (2018, Oct.). When Nowhere Is Safe: Interpersonal Trauma and Attachment Adversity as Antecedents of Posttraumatic Stress Disorder and Developmental Trauma Disorder. *Journal of Traumatic Stress, 31*(5). Retrieved from https://www.ncbi.nlm.nih.gov/pmc/articles/PMC6221128/

Widom, C. S., & Shepard, R. L. (1994). Accuracy of adult recollections of childhood victimization: Part 1. *Psychological Assessment, 8*(4), 412-421. Retrieved from https://psycnet.apa.org/record/1997-02157-014

Williams, L. M. (1994). Recall of childhood trauma: a prospective study of women's memory of child sexual abuse. *J. of Consulting and Clinical Psychology, 62*(n6), 1167-1176.

Yehuda, R. (2010). The Memory Paradox. *Nature, 11*, 837-9. Retrieved from www.nature.com: https://www.nature.com/articles/nrn2957?proof=t

www.ingramcontent.com/pod-product-compliance
Lightning Source LLC
Chambersburg PA
CBHW030356130626
46549CB00004B/1517